Using
Your Modem

Using
Your Modem

Dave Gibbons
Bruce Hallberg
Lisa Wagner
Faithe Wempen

Using Your Modem

Library of Congress Catalog No.: 95-71439

ISBN: 0-7897-0270-3

97 96 95   6 5 4 3 2 1

Interpretation of the printing code: the rightmost double-digit number is the year of the book's printing; the rightmost single-digit number, the number of the book's printing. For example, a printing code of 95-1 shows that the first printing of the book occurred in 1995.

Screen reproductions in this book were created using Collage Plus from Inner Media, Inc., Hollis, NH.

Composed in *ITC Century*, *ITC Highlander*, and *MCPdigital* by Que Corporation.

Credits

President
Roland Elgey

Vice President and Publisher
Marie Butler-Knight

Associate Publisher
Don Roche, Jr.

Editorial Services Director
Elizabeth Keaffaber

Managing Editor
Michael Cunningham

Director of Marketing
Lynn E. Zingraf

Senior Series Editor
Chris Nelson

Publishing Managers
Don Roche, Jr.
Joe Wikert

Acquisitions Editors
Deborah F. Abshier
Fred Slone

Product Directors
Lisa D. Wagner
Stephen L. Miller

Production Editor
Charles K. Bowles II

Copy Editor
Thomas F. Hayes

Associate Product Marketing Manager
Kim Margolius

Technical Editors
Rick Brown
Rebecca J. Campbell

Technical Specialist
Cari Skaggs
Nadeem Muhammed

Acquisitions Coordinator
Tracy M. Williams

Operations Coordinator
Patty Brooks

Editorial Assistant
Carmen Phelps

Book Designer
Ruth Harvey

Cover Designer
Dan Armstrong

Production Team
John Hulse
Darren Jackson
Kaylene Riemen
Scott Tullis
Karen York

Indexer
Virginia Munroe

CD Compiled By
Tracy Lehman Cramer

To my father, who says "online" is the best place for a fish.

For my mother, Cheryl.

About the Authors

 **Dave Gibbons** is a long-time Que contributor from the wilds of North Dakota, where modems are the cheapest (and warmest) means of travel. A former technical trainer and writer for DATASTORM Technologies in Columbia, Missouri and LaserMaster Technologies in Eden Prairie, MN, Dave has been hip-deep in microchips for several years, but he's not all tech and no play. When not strumming one of his guitars, Dave collects memorabilia from guitar heroes and British comedy (vive le Goons). Like-minded folks are invited to drop him a line at **DaveWriter@AOL.COM**.

 **Bruce Hallberg** has been a computer professional for the past fourteen years, and presently is Director of Corporate Services for a public biotechnology company in California. He has authored or co-authored many other computer books, including *OS/2 Certification Handbook, Byte's OS/2 Programmer's Cookbook*, and *Inside OS/2 Warp*. He particularly enjoys making complex computer topics understandable for beginning and intermediate computer users.

To my dad, Larry, for teaching me to type, and lots of other reasons.

To Margaret.

Lisa D. Wagner is still trying to decide what she wants to be when she grows up. In the meantime, she is a Product Development Specialist specializing in desktop applications and operating systems for Que Corporation in Indianapolis. She has extensive experience (and thus divided loyalties) in both PC and Macintosh environments, and has contributed to several Que books, including *Using Microsoft Office 4* and *Using Paradox 5 for Windows*, Special Edition.

A graduate of Butler University, Lisa is also an award-winning amateur actor, and can occasionally be found crooning at local karaoke hangouts. She lives in Franklin, Indiana, with her friend, Beth, their dog, three cats, and other various critters that come and go as they please. (Actually, she pretty much lives at Que, but that's another story…). You can send e-mail to Lisa at **lwagner@que.mcp.com**.

Faithe Wempen left the corporate world awhile back to become a freelance writer and editor, and has been deliriously happy ever since. She has a M.A. in English from Purdue University, and got interested in computers by accident—through a temp job working on an IBM mainframe back in the 80s. Now a self-described computer geek, her most prized possession is her Gateway P90 computer, and her favorite activities are surfing the Internet and convincing strangers at parties that they need to buy home computers. She lives in Indianapolis with Margaret (an engineer and ex-rugby player) and their two shetland sheepdogs, Sheldon and Ashley.

Acknowledgments

Dave Gibbons

Thanks to my friends, teachers, and students at DATASTORM for helping me understand the online world and the often-painful road from here to there.

Thanks also to the marketing and technical people (far too numerous to mention) at all of the online services, and software and modem companies who helped along the way.

Extra special thanks to Maagret and all my family and friends in Cando and Fargo, North Dakota for putting up with me during the writing of this book.

And, of course, thanks to the Que crew for all their help in making this book possible.

Bruce Hallberg

Books such as the one you are holding require the dedicated efforts of many people. Chief among them include Lisa Wagner, the product development specialist who guided the book into its present form; Charles Bowles, the lead editor who took our mangled English and turned it into smoothly-flowing prose; and I'd be remiss if I forgot to acknowledge Debbie Abshier, my favorite acquisitions editor who nicely kept me on track when my energy started to wane. Rebecca Campbell deserves high praise for her job doing the technical edit on the book, and making many wonderful suggestions that improved the final product.

There are lots of other folks, whom I never talk to, but who also devote their professional talents to the production of this book: the folks in the production department who handle the design and layout of the pages, the marketing folks who ensure that the book is on the shelves of your favorite bookstore waiting for you to buy it, and the proofreaders and indexers that make the book more accurate and easier to use.

Lisa Wagner

Thanks to my co-authors, Dave, Bruce, and Faithe, for a true team effort, and tech editor Becky Campbell, for keeping us all in line; to Charles Bowles, Tom Hayes, and the Que editorial and production teams for their consistently excellent work; to Tim Huddleston for getting me started in this business; to Nancy Sixsmith for keeping me sane; to Don Roche and Deb Abshier for letting me tackle this project even though I didn't have time; and especially to Beth Lucas, for letting me find time.

Faithe Wempen

I'd like to thank Debbie Abshier, Acquisitions Editor, for hiring me, and for her unfailing fairness and good humor. Thanks also to Lisa Wagner, Product Development Specialist, my friend, editor, and fellow author, for telling me I'm doing a good job on days when I need the encouragement and for doing a great job herself! Thanks to Charlie Bowles, Production Editor, for staying on top of things in the face of some crazy deadlines and setbacks.

The authors and the publisher extend a very special thank you to Tracy Cramer for compiling, and recompiling, and again recompiling the great CD that accompanies this book. Your sticktoitiveness is most appreciated.

We'd Like to Hear from You!

As part of our continuing effort to produce books of the highest possible quality, Que would like to hear your comments. To stay competitive, we *really* want you, as a computer book reader and user, to let us know what you like or dislike most about this book or other Que products.

You can mail comments, ideas, or suggestions for improving future editions to the address below, or send us a fax at (317) 581-4663. For the online inclined, Macmillan Computer Publishing has a forum on CompuServe (type **GO MACMILLAN** at any prompt) through which our staff and authors are available for questions and comments. The address of our Internet site, the Macmillan Information SuperLibrary is **http://www.mcp.com** (World Wide Web). Our Web site has received critical acclaim from many reviewers—be sure to check it out.

In addition to exploring our forums, please feel free to contact me personally to discuss your opinions of this book:

CompuServe: **74404,3307**
America Online: **ldw indy**
Internet: **lwagner@que.mcp.com**

Thanks in advance—your comments will help us to continue publishing the best books available on computer topics in today's market.

Lisa D. Wagner
Product Director
Que Corporation
201 W. 103rd Street
Indianapolis, Indiana 46290 USA

Although we cannot provide general technical support, we're happy to help you resolve problems you encounter related to our books, disks, or other products. If you need such assistance, please contact our Tech Support department at 800-545-5914 ext. 3833.

To order other Que or Macmillan Computer Publishing books or products, please call our Customer Service department at 800-858-7674.

Contents at a Glance

Table of Contents

What good is a modem anyway?

see page 9

External Problems
see page 33

What software
do I need?

see page 41

5 Understanding the Online World

*When in
Rome...*

see page 83

My kids are bugging me to go online!

see page 101

Part III: Making the Call

Which service is right for me?

see page 108

Using WinCIM
see page 127

How much does CompuServe cost?

see page 147

WaolExe

Now what was her screen name again?

see page 165

10 Calling Prodigy

Using Prodigy
see page 184

11 Calling the Microsoft Network

*MSN comes
with Windows
95*

see page 213

*The bottom
line*

see page 231

12 Calling the Internet

**All about
the Internet**

see page 234

**What's a
URL?**

see page 253

13 Calling BBSs

**What's the
big deal
about BBSs?**

see page 258

14 Faxing, with or without a Fax Modem

"Just the fax, ma`am."

see page 273

Part III: What Now?

15 Finding Information Online

How did Siskel & Ebert rate that film?

see page 299

16 Finding Software Online

What's a
newsgroup?

see page 320

MUD?MOO?
What's that
all about?

see page 337

4 SAIL, LIKE NU

see page 371

Where can I find movies online?

see page 378

Part IV: Troubleshooting: Should the Modem be Smoking?

Modem woes? Check here for a quick fix!

see page 398

What's on the CD?

see page 411

Part V: Appendix

What's on the CD?

Internet, here I come!

see page 414

Just for fun

see page 420

Introduction

You've probably been hearing about a mysterious place called "online" more and more frequently lately. It's coming at you from all sides: *Time Magazine* had an eight-page article about online romances not too long ago, and your local newspaper just announced that they're going to be publishing an online edition. Your best buddy Al, who didn't even trust computers the last time you checked, is suddenly creating his own Web pages, and your kids want to know when you're going to sign them up for Prodigy. They claim they'll fail History if they can't get online to do research.

Welcome to the Information Age. Computer technology isn't just your desktop anymore—it's all about reaching beyond yourself and plugging into the vast online community. And the tool that can take you there is a **modem**. Welcome to *Using Your Modem*.

What makes this book different?

This book isn't for computer geeks like your brother-in-law, the programmer, or even for advanced users like your friend Al turned out to be. (Who knew? He looks just like the rest of the guys.)

This book is for *you*.

The idea behind *Using Your Modem* is to demystify this online stuff, and make your modem just as easy to use as any household appliance. This book is designed and written to help you get up to speed on this important new technology, and to do it with minimum fuss and as few headaches as possible.

In it, you'll find clear explanations of the buzzwords that you've been hearing so much about, like "Internet" and "cyberspace." There are plenty of pictures that show what you're in for, **Tips** to speed up your work, **Cautions** to help you avoid trouble, and **Q&As** to solve mysteries. Most importantly, you'll find it all in plain English—no technobabble.

If you're new to modems, you'll discover that they're not as frightening as you had feared. More experienced modem users will enjoy reviewing the offerings of all the major online services and learning about new communication technologies like Integrated Services Digital Network (ISDN), which may eventually make conventional modems obsolete.

This book will show you the fastest and easiest ways to buy and install a modem, evaluate the various online services, and find the goodies online that will help your kids pass History, help you find shopping bargains and cool (free!) software, and much more. Who knows, you may even find yourself enjoying those conversations with Al about his Web page.

How do I use this book?

Most of the time you'll probably want quick help with a specific task. The Table of Contents is a good place to start. It's very detailed, and chances are good that you'll see the job you want to do listed there. If not, check the Index in the back of the book. There's also an Action Index, which lists commonly performed tasks, and where to look to do them right. You'll find this at the back of the book, too.

When you have some extra time, try browsing through the book. Each chapter of *Using Your Modem* begins with a list of the topics covered in that chapter. You can scan this list to see what lies ahead in the chapter, or to zero in on a topic that interests you.

Each chapter is divided into several sections. Looking through the headings in each chapter is a good way to discover options you didn't know existed.

Of course, you can also just sit down and read the entire book from beginning to end. It may not be as fascinating as the latest Stephen King novel, but I promise, there will be less blood and gore.

How this book is put together

When you're facing some monumental task (like educating yourself about modems and online services!), it's best to break it down into smaller parts and tackle the job one part at a time. That's exactly how this book is set up:

Part I: Before You Make the Call

This part is the first stop for beginners. If you haven't bought a modem yet, or you don't really understand how they work, you'll find the information in this part of the book is exactly what you need. You'll learn how to select and install a modem, and install communication software. We'll talk about the latest-and-greatest operating system, Windows 95, and its built-in modem helps, and we'll decipher the cryptic and confusing language and customs of the online world.

Part II: Making the Call

Once you're strapped in and ready for launch, Part II will take you boldly into the online world. We'll talk about the options (where ya gonna call?), then take an in-depth look at several major online services: CompuServe, America Online, Prodigy, and the Microsoft Network. We'll discuss e-mail, faxing, and private BBSs (bulletin board services), and tackle that intimidating giant, the Internet.

Part III: What Now?

Once you know where to call, the next step is deciding what to do once you're connected! This part of the book explores the various activities available online. You'll learn how to find information and do research, locate cheap or free software, meet people who share your interests, play games, get the news and weather, spend money (i.e. shopping), and retrieve cool pictures and movie clips.

On the CD, you'll find a bonus chapter that takes a look toward the future by exploring a new technology called ISDN, which will revolutionize the way you connect to your favorite online service within the next ten years.

Part IV: Troubleshooting: Should the Modem Be Smoking?

Everybody runs into problems sometimes, and this part of the book can help. (I've put these troubleshooting chapters off by themselves so they won't depress those of you who don't need them.) You'll learn how to spot and fix common modem problems, as well as other computer problems that keep your modem from working. You'll also learn how to tell when your software is fouling you up, and find out what to do to fix it.

Reference information

There's an abundance of information in this book, and even more on the accompanying CD. At the end of the book, you'll find an appendix describing all the programs and other goodies on the *Using Your Modem CD*, along with instructions on how to use them. On the CD itself, there's four vital files you don't want to miss:

- "Places" is filled with online addresses for interesting places to go online. These are great fun, and can save you hours of searching online for the right address—it's kind of like a "Map to the Stars' Homes."

- The second appendix lists little symbols called **Smileys** that you can use in your e-mail messages to express emotions and look like you're more experienced than you actually are.

- Next, there's a great glossary, filled with all the terms you've always wondered about. From **Acoustic Coupler** to **Zmodem**, you'll find enough terms here to bore people at cocktail parties for years to come. (People might even start avoiding you, like they do your brother-in-law.)

- Finally, we threw in a bonus chapter called "ISDN," which provides you with some important information on this up-and-coming communications technology. If you're curious about the future of the online world, be sure to take a gander.

Special book elements

This book has several special elements and conventions to help you find information quickly—or to let you skip stuff you don't want to read right now.

 TIP **Tips either point out information often overlooked by beginners,** or help you use your equipment more effectively, like a shortcut. Some Tips help you solve or avoid problems.

Cautions alert you to potentially dangerous consequences of a procedure or practice, especially if it could result in serious or even disastrous results, such as harming your computer or modem.

 What are Q&A notes?

Cast in the form of questions and answers, these notes provide you with advice on ways to avoid or solve common problems.

 Plain English, please!

These notes explain the meanings of technical terms or computer jargon.

Throughout this book, when we're talking about selecting a menu command in a particular program, we'll use a comma to separate the parts of the command. For example, if you're supposed to open the File menu and select Exit, it'll be written like this: Select File, Exit.

If you see two keys separated by a plus sign, like Ctrl+X, it means to press and hold the first key, press the second key, then release both keys.

Sidebars contain interesting side information

Sidebars provide interesting but non-essential reading, side trips you can take when you're not at the computer or when you just want some relief from doing stuff. Here you may find more technical details, funny stories and anecdotes, or interesting background information.

Part I: Before You Make the Call

1

What Can You Do with a Modem?

● **In this chapter:**

- What exactly do you mean by "going online"?

- What kinds of research tools are online?

- Getting free and almost free software

- News, weather, sports, and more

- Shop till you drop—without leaving your home

Whether it's education, entertainment, research, or socializing, you'll find it online . . . .

Did you ever have a set of LEGOs? How about Lincoln Logs, Tinker Toys, or an Erector Set? If you did, you probably remember the initial sensation of having an entire world of limitless possibilities at your fingertips—and not having a clue where to start exploring. Your modem is a key to a whole new world too, and it's just as tough to figure out where to start exploring this online world.

This chapter presents a glimpse of some of the things you can do with your modem, letting you decide what you're interested in and what you're not. If a topic sparks your interest, you'll be able to read much more about it later in the book. Of course, if something *doesn't* interest you, you'll know which chapters and sections to skip. Think of this chapter as the beginning of a travelers' guide, giving equal coverage to just about every interest and letting you decide where you want to explore.

TIP **Look for this travelers' guide metaphor throughout this book. It's** hard to resist the parallel, because introducing you to the online world is like showing you a busy new city in an unfamiliar country. Just like any metropolis, the online world offers some places that will interest you, some that won't, and some that are best avoided.

Go online

"You've got to check out all the stuff they've got online. You won't believe it!"

"It's an information economy. If you're not online, you're ten years behind the competition."

"Who needs newspapers (or libraries, or support groups, or singles' bars) when you can get all that online?"

Everybody's talking about online this, online that, and online the other, and everybody's got a different idea of what's out there. The news is full of the latest developments on "The Information Superhighway," "the Internet," "Cyberspace," and dozens of other online buzzwords, and they all have something to do with this mystical concept of "online," right? With your modem, you can do all the things everyone else is talking about—you can go online and see firsthand what all the fuss is about.

Plain English, please!

In its simplest sense, **Online** means "connected to another computer." It's short for "on the telephone line." You can connect to a friend's computer across the street, to your local library, to an online service like Prodigy or America Online, or to any other computer that also has a modem and access to a telephone line.

"Going online" is what you do every time you use a modem—when your modem is connected to another one across the phone lines, you're "online." But the term "online" has grown to have a very broad and ambiguous meaning, like "abroad" or "down south." You may have heard people say, "Check out the program I found *online!*," or "Last night I met a really nice person from Japan *online*." "Online" has become the most visited place around, and you don't even need to leave your desk chair to get there.

Like any new term that floods popular culture through the media, "online" causes a little confusion. In the early days of MTV, for example, there was that slogan, "I want my MTV." It was so successful that people who couldn't tell a Billy Idol music video from a Bing Crosby Christmas Special suddenly were desperate to have MTV. Records and cassettes had always been enough before, but suddenly there was this *new* way to experience music, and millions of people jumped on the bandwagon. "Online" is sort of the same thing—we all got along just fine without it for decades, but now, thanks to mass peer pressure, everyone is lining up, credit cards outstretched, to go online—sometimes without even understanding what they're signing up for.

To compound the problem, the word "online" is part of another important modem term: **online service**. An online service is a company or organization that provides a big computer, jam-packed with interesting stuff, that you can connect to with your modem. Online services (which include CompuServe, America Online, and Prodigy) usually offer software, games, discussions with other users, electronic mail, and many other services (all for a fee, of course).

 CAUTION **Some people mistakenly think "online" refers to America Online** (a fact that probably makes the folks at America Online incoherently happy). But "online" is a generic term that refers to any connection you make with your modem.

There are other computers you can connect to besides online services, though—for instance, local amateur online services called **Bulletin Board**

Systems, or **BBSs**. You'll learn more about these later. Depending on how high-tech your city is, you may also be able to connect to local spots like your city library card catalog. You can also connect to an Internet service provider (**ISP**), who can give you access to the Internet. (More on this later too.)

No matter how you use the term, "online" has become the destination of choice for millions of modem users. So why are we all scrambling to go online? We could have asked a similar question about cable television fifteen years ago—*"What's the big deal about cable television that's got everybody paying for TV all of a sudden?"*—and we'd come up with the same kinds of answers:

- Entertainment

- Information

- Convenience

The online world also provides social interaction (which we can't get through cable—yet).

The rest of this chapter (in fact, the rest of this book) shows you why everyone wants to go online, and how the online world can provide these things and more.

Find just about any kind of information

If it's a fact, it's probably available online somewhere. Here's some of the information I found in one fifteen-minute online information hunt:

- *Reinheitsgebot* is an old German purity law that delineates the ingredients that can be used to make beer. Under this law, a brewer can only use four ingredients: water, barley malt, hops, and yeast.

- There will be no fifth series of *The Black Adder*, according to cowriter Richard Curtis.

- Bonsai is not a specific type of tree. Some trees are more frequently "bonsai-ed" than others, but bonsai can be made from almost any woody stemmed tree or bush species.

- At the time of his death, Dec. 19, 1959, at age 117, Walter Washington Williams was accorded the honors of the last surviving veteran of the United States Civil War. Williams, who was granted the honorary title of "General" late in life, had been an enlisted man in the Confederate army. He claimed to have never fired a shot, but to have heard some.

- To make a good glass of Thai iced coffee, first make very strong coffee (50-100 percent more coffee to water than usual), use something like Cafe Du Monde, which has chicory in it. Pour 6-8 oz into a cup and add about 1 tablespoon sweetened condensed milk. Stir, then pour over ice.

- Walt Disney is not actually in cryogenic suspension—it's just an urban legend. He died at 9:35 am on December 15, 1966, of lung cancer. He was cremated (quite the opposite of being frozen, ironically) and is buried at the Forest Lawn Memorial Park in Glendale, CA.

- The "official" way to wash LEGO bricks is by hand, using warm water— maximum 104 degrees Fahrenheit (40 degrees Celsius)—and a mild liquid dish detergent. Electric parts are not washable.

I also got some great seafood recipes and found out that a vegetarian who also eats seafood is a "pescetarian."

Whether you're writing a business report, planning a party (you can find some interesting home-brewed beer recipes online), trying to settle an argument, or participating in any other information pursuit, you'll get answers a lot quicker online than in most libraries. Many online services offer encyclopedias and newspaper/magazine archives, and you'll be able to find online special interest groups for just about anything you can think of (all of the information above was gleaned from special interest group archives). Figure 1.1 shows the encyclopedia on Prodigy, for instance.

To learn how to search for information online, see Chapter 15, "Finding Information Online." To find special interest groups, read Chapter 17, "Finding Like-Minded Users."

Fig. 1.1
Prodigy, like most online services, offers an encyclopedia.

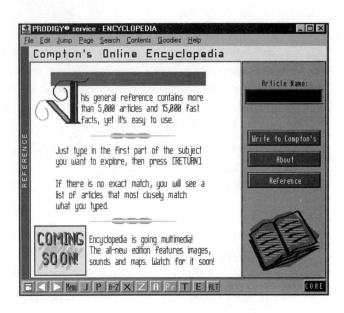

Get software

Online services have always been great places to find software for your computer. You can dig up programs for business, graphics, music, education, entertainment, games, and more. For instance, figure 1.2 shows the file downloading area on America Online.

Fig. 1.2
America Online's downloadable software is conveniently kept in one central location.

Much of the software available online is **shareware**, which means you can use it for a trial period without paying for it. You send payment to the programmer later if you decide to keep using it. Some shareware is as good or better than similar programs you can buy at the software store in the mall, and because shareware programmers don't have to pay for in-store promotions and fancy packaging, the prices are often unbelievably reasonable.

 Plain English, please!

Shareware is software that the author provides to the public freely, encouraging people to "share" it with their friends. If you end up liking and using the program, you are supposed to send its author a registration fee. Believe it or not, this actually works—people are more honest than you might think.

 CAUTION **Whenever you download software from an online location, you** run the risk of transferring a computer virus to your system. (It's a very remote possibility, but it has been known to happen.) You'll learn about viruses—and how to prevent catching one—in Chapter 6, "Online Pitfalls, Real and Imagined."

Some online services have begun distributing commercial software (the stuff you normally find in stores), and charging the retail cost to your credit card. You might not be able to download the Big Guns like WordPerfect and Microsoft Excel right away, but a few commercial games and applications have started to use online distribution as a way to cut back on costs and provide near-immediate delivery.

To find some of the best places to get software with your modem, see Chapter 16, "Finding Software Online."

Send (and sometimes receive) faxes

If you bought your modem in the last two years, it's probably a **fax modem**, which means it knows how to communicate with both fax machines and other modems. Fax modems enable you to use your regular word processor to make a fax document, then send it out to a fax machine, all without the document ever being printed on paper. They also can receive faxes from fax machines and other fax modems, enabling you to read the faxes on your computer monitor and/or print them on your printer. You need special faxing software to use the fax capabilities of your fax modem, but most fax modems come bundled with a simple fax program. Figure 1.3 shows WinFax PRO, one of the most popular fax programs.

Fig. 1.3
WinFax PRO is one of many fax programs available to control your fax modem's faxing operations.

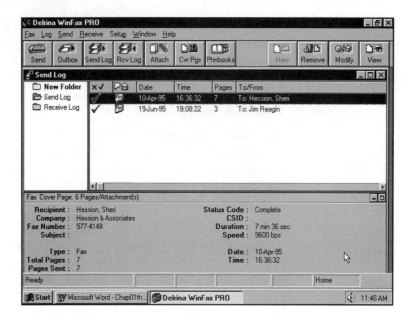

Even if you don't have a fax modem, however, you can still send (but not receive) faxes—provided you subscribe to a major online service. Most online services are able to send faxes for you with their fax modems, charging the phone call to your account.

To learn more about using your modem for faxing, see Chapter 14, "Faxing, with or without a Fax Modem."

Telecommuting: Using your home computer to access your office computer

You've got all the information for the big report on your office computer, but you're working from home today because of the blizzard, mud slides, sick kids, or whatever. With a special type of software called **remote control** software, you can run your office computer with your home computer—as long as they both have modems. Most remote control programs enable you to print on the laser printer at the office, access your network, and (of course) use all the programs and files from your office computer. Some popular remote control programs include PCAnywhere and Reachout Remote. For more information on these and other programs, contact your local software retailer.

Get news, weather, and magazines

Your local paper probably doesn't have correspondents in the Czech Republic (unless you live in a giant metropolis—or, say, Prague). So how does the morning edition know what's going on over there? Newspapers (along with magazines, TV, and radio stations) usually subscribe to news services, which are companies like The Associated Press or Reuters that specialize in knowing what's going on around the world. Some news services have gone online, giving you access to the same kind of news your newspaper uses—and in the same time frame, which means you see it before it comes out in tomorrow's paper. Many online services also enable you to read online editions of major papers like the *New York Times*.

With online weather services (available on every major online service), you can get the current conditions for just about every place on Earth, forecasts from the National Weather Service, and even satellite photos through your modem. Figure 1.4 shows a weather photo from CompuServe.

Fig. 1.4
You can view color
weather maps online.

You want even *more* current information? Try paging through some of the dozens of national magazines that now offer online editions (see fig. 1.5). You'll almost always get all the text from the print editions, and you'll usually be able to view all the pictures as well—sometimes before they even hit the newsstand. Plus, you can search for related articles in past issues, all with a few keystrokes.

To get the latest in news and weather, along with most of your favorite magazines, see Chapter 19, "Getting the News and Weather."

Fig. 1.5
America Online offers
Time Magazine Online.
It may not be quite as
pretty as the newsstand
version, but it offers all
the same information
and pictures—without
advertising.

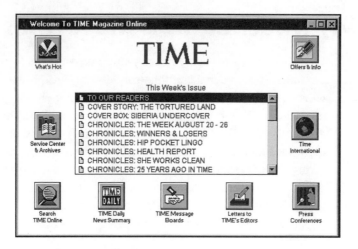

Play games

Not only can you use your modem to get most of the latest computer games
(refer to "Get software," earlier in the chapter), but you also can use it to play
games against other modem users. Some popular games like DOOM, most
chess games, and flight simulators let you call up another modem user
directly and play head-to-head. You also can use online services to play
adventure games, board games, and role-playing games against other users
around the globe. Figure 1.6 shows a trivia game on Prodigy called Guts.

BBSs (which are usually smaller online services run for a local area) usually
have a good selection of games for their callers to play, either by themselves
or against other callers.

To jump into the world of online gaming, see Chapter 18, "Online Gaming."

Fig. 1.6
Guts is a trivia game for Prodigy subscribers, in which you compete against other players for high scores.

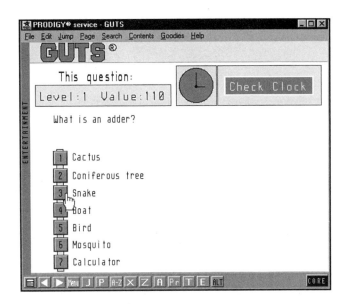

Find a job

Even if you're happy with your job, you still read the want ads on Sunday, right? With your modem, you can look at current want ads from your area and around the world, 24 hours a day. All the major online services have classified ads that list jobs, and there are also several job databases on the Internet (see Chapter 12, "Calling the Internet"). Figure 1.7 shows a job search system I found on the Internet using the World Wide Web. You can also try visiting the Web sites for major corporations; many times they post job openings on the Internet.

TIP **Although it doesn't have anything to do with being online, you** can also find software programs to help you plan your job search and write your résumé.

Fig. 1.7
I found this Online
Career Center on the
Internet at **http://
www.occ.com/occ/**.

Shop

Got a credit card burning a hole in your pocket? You can shop for almost anything with your modem—and no, it's not all computer-related stuff. Clothes, books, jewelry, collectibles, music, and anything else you could buy through mail-order or at the mall is online somewhere. And one nice bonus of shopping online is that the time you spend in the online stores is usually free—that is, the owners of the stores you visit pick up the tab for any hourly online charges you accrue while in the mall area.

Some online services have their own virtual malls, which let you shop at several different retailers on the same phone call. Figure 1.8 shows the Sears store on Prodigy. You also can buy and sell used merchandise through online want ads. And if you want consumer information on anything you're planning to buy, you can get that through your modem as well. All of the online services have shopping available, but Prodigy and CompuServe really shine.

For a free shuttle to the online mall, see Chapter 20, "Shopping!"

Fig. 1.8
You can buy almost anything Sears sells from the online Sears store on Prodigy.

Plan your vacation

If you subscribe to a major online service, you'll be able to get most of the same up-to-the-minute travel and lodging information travel agents use. You can not only book your flight and hotels online, but also read about your destination. You may even be able to talk to some residents who'll be able tell you who makes the best Fettuccine Alfredo in town.

Meet lots of people who share your interests

Are you a collector? A groupie? A hobbyist or scholar? No matter what interests you, you'll find others who share your interests online. The online world is full of **special interest groups**, which are groups that enjoy common pursuits, concerns, or hobbies. They exchange private e-mail, discuss new developments and discoveries in public forums, trade memorabilia, and sometimes even have "real world" conventions where members meet face-to-face at some point on the globe.

The members of these groups literally come from all over the world, so unless your special interest is the history of your hometown, you may find yourself in a group that's headquartered on another continent. Most people join more than one special interest group, because you only have to commit as much time as you want, they work with any schedule (you probably won't have weekly or monthly meetings to worry about), and there's rarely a membership fee.

To find others who march to the beat of your drummer (no matter how different), see Chapter 17, "Finding Like-Minded Users."

Find pictures and movies for your computer

Technology has come to the point that photographers use almost as many computers as cameras. Computers can enhance images, create new ones, and even set them to motion; with online services, the resulting photographs and movies are easy to distribute. Online, you can find photos and drawings of real estate, scenery, people, animals, news events, astronomy, and just about anything else, all of which you can keep on your disk and view on your monitor whenever you feel like it. Some people even send computerized pictures of themselves to people they meet online.

You also can get moving pictures for your computer, from cartoons to real movie clips. Record companies release music videos (usually short clips, but sometimes full-length videos) online, and movie studios have also started releasing short clips of new or upcoming movies on online services. For instance, on CompuServe, I found a great picture of Meg Ryan in *Sleepless in Seattle*. (It's shown in fig. 1.9, opened for viewing in a shareware graphics editing program.)

Fig. 1.9

Look for stills from your favorite movies online, such as this one from *Sleepless in Seattle*, which I found on CompuServe, in the Photo Archives.

2

Installing Your Modem

● **In this chapter:**

- **Tell me about modems!**

- **The ugly technical details of modem installation**

- **External modems are really easy to install**

- **Can I install an internal modem by myself?**

Most parents rue the day they read the words "Some assembly required." Avoid the "do-it-yourself blues" with the tips you read about here . . . . ●

When I was a kid, I remember more than a few Christmases where my dad had to stay up all night putting together those "Some assembly required" toys for me and one of my brothers. Fortunately, my dad is pretty mechanical, so he didn't have too much trouble with those toys. Even in this advanced (ahem) age, buying things and then having to do some kind of mechanical work is alive and well. Modems are no exception.

In some cases, you might get lucky. You buy an external modem, the salesperson sells you the right cable for your computer, you plug it into the back of your machine, connect a phone line, and all of a sudden you're cruising the Infobahn at super-legal speeds. Cool!

 Plain English, please!

Infobahn is slang for the Information Superhighway (a play on the word *autobahn*), and generically refers to all of the online services you can access with your modem.

The key phrase to remember, though, is "in some cases." Chances are, you'll have to get your hands dirty in some way in order to get your spiffy new modem installed and working properly with your computer hardware and software. Here's the good news—it's not really all that tough. In this chapter, you'll learn how to make this process as painless as possible.

So what exactly is a modem?

The term **modem** is short for "modulator/demodulator." This is just a techy way of saying that a modem can take digital information from your computer and convert (modulate) it to sounds that transmit over normal telephone lines. It also can accept that "modulated" data and seamlessly convert (demodulate) it on your end so you can receive digital information from a remote modem.

 Plain English, please!

Digital information is that which is made up of ones and zeros (it's also called binary code). It's the basic language that all computers speak.

You have to use a modem to send and receive computer-based information over phone lines. There's no other way to do it. Furthermore, to connect to another computer over phone lines, both sides need a modem.

Modems vary greatly in speed and capability

Modems are all rated by the amount of data they can transmit and receive in a given second. This measurement is in **bps**, which refers to how many on and off signals your modem can understand in a given second. Some people mistakenly use the term **baud** to refer to this, and use the two interchangeably.

 Plain English, please!

When most people use the word **baud**, they are mistakenly referring to **bits-per-second (bps),** or how many **binary digits** (bits, or ones and zeros) your computer can send or receive in one second. A single letter on a page takes up eight of these bits. Together, eight bits are called a **byte**.

Early modems transmitted the same number of bits per second as their baud rate, but this hasn't been true for a long time. Still, people incorrectly use the terms interchangeably. The correct term is bps. If someone says baud, just translate it to bps for yourself and all will be well. 🙷

Early modems could handle only 300 bps. At this speed, it would take you about 140 seconds to transmit this page of text.

Newer modems can go up to 14,400 bps (also called 14.4 Kbps), and even more recently, 28,800 bps (28.8 Kbps). At these speeds, you could send this page of text in about three seconds at 14,400 bps, and 1.5 seconds at 28,800 bps. In fact, at 28,800 bps, you could send this entire book (without pictures) to another computer in about ten minutes.

These speeds may sound very fast to you. You might even be thinking, "who needs 14,400 bps? I can do just fine at 2400 bps." Well, it's just not true. The reason is this: More and more computers are becoming heavily graphically oriented, and graphical images take up a lot more space than simple text. So, graphical images take a correspondingly larger amount of time to transmit.

Here's a standard of comparison: to send the text of this book at 14,400 bps would take about twenty minutes. But to send just the images from the book at that speed would take about 160 minutes. Graphics take up more room than text, and take a lot more time to transmit. Programs also take up a lot of room, and take a long time to transmit. Retrieving the latest game from your favorite online service can take as long as 30 minutes, *even with the fastest modems.*

Q&A ***If I could use a modem to send a page of this book in only 1.5 to 3 seconds, why does it take almost a full minute to fax a single page?***

Fax machines don't actually send text. Rather, they send a *picture* of the text. So, when you're faxing a page of text to someone, you're actually sending them a full-page picture rather than just a bunch of simple letters and numbers.

Do I gotta know all the techy details of modems?

One of the ideas behind this book is to avoid heaping information on you that you'll never need to know. You've seen all kinds of books at the store that require weight training to get them to the checkout counter, and contain all sorts of arcane information that you'll never need.

But when you're installing a modem, you should know a little bit about how two fairly technical areas in your computer work—serial ports and hardware interrupts. You need to understand these to avoid problems when you install and set up your modem.

OK, tell me about this stuff so I can keep it straight

Your computer connects to **external devices**, like printers and external modems, through two main types of connections—serial ports and parallel ports. The names refer to how they send data to the device—**serial** ports send data one chunk at a time, while **parallel** ports send data in many chunks at a time. Parallel ports are almost always used to connect printers to your computer, while serial ports are used for printers, mice, and modems.

Plain English, please!

A **port** is a connection on the back of your computer to which an external device connects through a cable. Sometimes, a port exists on a device installed inside the computer, like an internal modem, but it's still referring to how the device connects to the computer hardware. Ports are really just like electrical sockets, but they pass data instead of electricity. **99**

 Even though an internal modem isn't an external device, it's treated like one by your computer. It's just as if all the external pieces were put inside your computer, but it's still treated like an external device in important ways.

We're just concerned with serial ports here, since parallel ports are really only used for printers and some other rare devices. Your PC can handle up to four serial ports, and these ports all have names. They are named from COM1 to COM4. (COM stands for COMmunication). Some people just call them **COM ports**, but it's all the same thing we're talking about here.

 Not all computers have four serial ports. Most, in fact, just have two, named COM1 and COM2. You can easily have up to four serial ports, though, if your computer has the necessary hardware installed.

Here's the second big concept I warned you about: Hardware devices in your computer, such as serial ports, communicate with the computer's main processor through **hardware interrupts**. They're called this because when a

How do I know what speed modem to buy?

In the computer world, you're always better off buying the fastest thing you can afford, whether it be an entire computer or just the modem. You don't necessarily get these high-speed components because you need them today, but because you'll definitely need them tomorrow. Software grows in complexity and size over time, and online communications are no exception. Almost every online service is moving to a graphical format that requires a higher-speed modem than the older text-based systems. Because of all this, always buy the fastest modem you can afford. A minimum is 14,400 bps, and if you can afford a 28,800 bps modem, get it. At the time of this writing, good 14,400 bps modems sell for as little as $100-150, and 28,800 bps modems for $250-350. By the way, all these modems include fax capabilities.

device needs the processor's attention, it sends a signal to it called an interrupt. It's as if the device is saying to the processor: "Hey, sorry to interrupt you, but I've got something for you to do." There are sixteen hardware interrupts in your computer, numbered from 0 to 15, and different devices are assigned different interrupts, so that the processor doesn't get confused as to which device is tapping it on the shoulder when it gets an interrupt signal.

Now, let's tie all this together. Each serial port in your computer is assigned a particular interrupt. But—and this is why you really have to know this—they share interrupts in a certain way:

- Serial ports 1 and 3 use interrupt 4
- Serial ports 2 and 4 use interrupt 3

So that you can converse with computer nerds, you should know how they talk about this. Here's the same information expressed in computer-speak:

- COM1 and COM3 use IRQ 4
- COM2 and COM4 use IRQ 3

 Plain English, please!

IRQ stands for **Interrupt Request**. It's just another way of talking about hardware interrupt assignments in your computer.

 Q&A *Why do the different serial ports share interrupts?*

When the PC was first designed by IBM, they expected that people would need to connect modems and printers to their serial ports. But they only allocated two interrupts for this purpose, because they only anticipated that two serial ports would ever be needed.

Progress being what it is, though, it became apparent that some people would need more than two serial ports. So, PC clone manufacturers came up with a way to share the two interrupts for two additional serial ports. This scheme allows you to have more than two serial ports, although there are some limitations because there are only two interrupts available for this purpose. At any rate, that's why the interrupts are shared in this way.

So what's the bottom line here?

The bottom line is this: If you have two devices trying to use a single interrupt simultaneously, they generally won't both work at the same time. Normally, you never have to worry about this because the people who make computer equipment carefully assign standard interrupts to different types of devices, and things are set up so that conflicts won't happen. But because serial ports can share interrupts, and because you might have several things hooked up to different serial ports in your computer, you need to be careful about what devices connect to which serial ports, and you have to take into account the interrupt used to make sure there isn't going to be a conflict. Because modems use serial ports, and because serial ports share these interrupts, there's potential for trouble if you don't set things up right.

How do I decide which serial ports to use?

You really have to look at what devices are used at which times. For example, if you have a mouse connected to a serial port on the back of your computer, you won't want to put a modem on the serial port that uses the same interrupt. So, if your mouse is on serial port 1, you don't want your modem on serial port 3. Similarly, if your mouse is on serial port 2, you don't want your modem assigned to serial port 4.

Most people just have two devices connected to their serial ports, and they're typically a mouse and a modem. No problem here: connect your mouse to serial port 1, and your modem to serial port 2 (or vice versa), and all will work fine. But some people have three devices connected to serial ports, and the third device is usually a printer that uses a serial port. In cases like this, you can do something like this:

- Mouse on serial port 1

- Printer on serial port 2

- Modem on serial port 4

This example, of course, assumes that you have four serial ports installed in your computer. If there are only three, you would have to do something like this:

- Printer on serial port 1
- Mouse on serial port 2
- Modem on serial port 3

In both examples, you just have to remember not to try to print while you're online with your modem, and not to use your modem while you're printing something. What you want to avoid, however, is putting either your printer or modem on a serial port that uses the same interrupt as the serial port your mouse uses. If your mouse uses serial port 1, don't put anything on serial port 3. If your mouse uses serial port 2, don't put anything on serial port 4.

CAUTION **If you *do* try to use a serial port that uses the same interrupt as** your mouse, many things can happen: Your printouts won't work, they might work but be garbled, or your mouse might stop working. What happens depends on your exact computer and the software you're using.

TIP **Many computers have built-in mouse ports, so that your mouse** doesn't have to use one of the serial ports. If your computer has one of these (you can tell because the mouse will have a small, round connector, a little larger than the diameter of a pencil) then you don't have to worry about getting your interrupts and serial ports mixed up.

TIP **Another tip that can avoid all this hassling with interrupts and** assigning devices is, if you're using a printer that connects to your computer through a serial port, look on the printer for a parallel port connection. If there's one there, and your computer's parallel port is free, consider switching the printer over from serial to parallel.

I've got an external modem

External modems, those that exist in boxes that sit outside of your computer, are the easiest to install. Generally, all that's involved is to decide which serial port to use, connect the modem to the port with a cable, plug in a telephone line, plug in the modem's power cord, and you're off and running.

On the back of almost all external modems there's a 25-pin female connector (the exception to this rule are very small portable modems, but they will come with a special adapter cable). On the back of your computer, there will be either 9-pin or 25-pin male connectors. Newer computers almost universally use 9-pin connectors, while some older computers have 25-pin connectors.

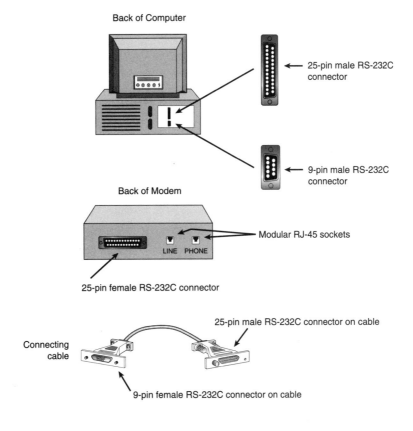

Back of Computer

25-pin male RS-232C connector

9-pin male RS-232C connector

Back of Modem

Modular RJ-45 sockets

LINE   PHONE

25-pin female RS-232C connector

Connecting cable

25-pin male RS-232C connector on cable

9-pin female RS-232C connector on cable

Plain English, please!

Female connectors are those that accept pins, while male connectors are those that have pins. (In fact, they make little plugs that convert male to female and vice-versa. These plugs are called *gender-changers*).

How do I tell which connectors on the back of my computer are serial ports?

Serial ports are the only male connectors on the back of your computer, the others are female. Also, serial ports are always either 9-pin connectors or 25-pin connectors. And, if you're lucky, your computer has labels or symbols next to the connectors that help you identify them. Consult your owner's manual if you're having trouble identifying them.

Plugging it in

To connect your external modem to the back of your computer, you'll need a modem cable. These are common parts that you can get at the same place you got your modem. The biggest thing you'll need to know before getting the cable is what kind of connector you have on the back of your computer—a 9-pin or 25-pin (in some rare cases you might even have both).

Make sure the cable you get is long enough to reach the modem's location on your desk from your computer!

After you have the cable, choose which available serial port to connect the cable to. Consult "How do I decide which serial ports to use?," earlier in this chapter for detailed information on deciding which port to use for your modem. Notice that you might have to move some other device to a different port to make things connect the way you want them to.

Next, connect the phone line to the modem. Most external modems have two modular phone jacks, usually next to the 25-pin connector that hooks up to your computer. These jacks are often labeled Line and Phone. Pop the modular cable from the wall into the jack marked Line, and you can then plug a standard telephone set into the Phone jack.

Plain English, please!
Modular telephone connections are those little clear plastic clips at the end of the phone wire. They should go "click" when you get them inserted all the way.

 If your home isn't wired for modular telephone connections, you'll need to have some wiring done. If you want to do this yourself, any parts you'll need are readily available at your local electronics store. You can also find converters if your home uses the old-style four-prong connectors.

 If your modem doesn't have Line and Phone labels on the jacks on its back, consult the modem's manual. If that sheds no light, then don't worry about it—some modems automatically figure out what each jack is connected to and adjust automatically.

Finally, connect the power line from the modem to an electrical socket. There will usually be a power converter like those that come with portable radios.

I've got an internal modem

Internal modems are more complex to install than external modems. For one thing, you have to open up your computer and wield a screwdriver to install them. For another, you'll probably have to do some reconfiguration of your computer so that the modem (and the computer!) will work correctly. Still, there are two advantages to internal modems:

 If you've bought a computer that already has an internal modem installed, then you have the simplest possible job to get it hooked up. Simply plug the phone line into the back of the modem, into its Line plug, and you're ready to go!

- They don't take up space on your desk
- In many cases, they communicate with the computer faster than external modems
- There are fewer cables cluttering up the back of your computer

The drawback to internal modems is that there aren't neat lights to watch as you use your modem. This isn't really a significant disadvantage, but sometimes those lights do help you tell what's going on "inside" the modem, such as when a transmission of information is complete, in much the same way the light next to your floppy disk drive works.

Staying safe while installing internal modems

The most important rule to safely installing boards into your computer is this: If you're not comfortable messing with the innards of your computer, *don't do it!* Get someone who has experience to help you out. It's not really all that tricky, but why stress over it when you avoid problems by simply asking someone with experience for some help?

Anytime you have the cover off your computer, follow these guidelines so that nothing unpleasant happens:

- Make sure the computer is turned off and completely unplugged from the wall outlet before removing the computer's cover.

- Remove the cover to the computer.

- When the telephone line is connected to your modem, don't handle the internal modem circuit board. Telephone lines carry a little electricity all the time. I've shocked myself more times than I can count by forgetting this rule, and now my hair permanently looks like Don King's. Don't let this happen to you. A good rule is this: Don't connect the telephone line to your internal modem until you've put the cover back on the computer.

Exercise care when working with the insides of your computer, and you'll probably find that it's fun!

Setting your modem up *before* you install it

Before installing an internal modem, there are several things you need to know:

- What serial ports already exist as far as your computer's concerned? Usually, this will just be external ports on the back of the computer.

- What serial port number do you want to install the modem as?

- How do you configure the internal modem and your computer so that you can get your serial ports set up correctly?

What serial ports?

To determine what ports already exist in your computer, you can use a couple of different methods. First, you can run software designed to tell you this information. Norton Utilities and Microsoft System Diagnostics (MSD) are two programs that tell you these things. Your computer also may have come with setup software that tells you what is already installed.

If you're using Windows 95, there's a simple way to find out what serial ports you have. Open the Control Panels, and then open the System icon. This displays a notebook. Go to the notebook page marked Device Manager, and click the small plus symbol next to the Ports entry. You'll see a display in which you can see what ports your computer has installed.

Next, you have to decide which serial port your modem will use. Usually, it's best to use COM1 or COM2, because some older software programs will only work with one of these two settings.

This begs the question: What if there's already a port assigned to one of those COM numbers? How you deal with this depends on what is using the port you want to use. If it's just a serial port built into the computer, with nothing connected to it, you can usually disable that serial port and then the internal modem can be set to use that COM port. Some computers also automatically reassign their internal serial ports if you install a device that uses the same setting, but this is a fairly rare feature. Usually, you have to mess with switches or jumpers inside your computer to disable a port.

 TIP Don't be afraid to call the people who sold you your computer in order to get advice on disabling serial ports. Most reputable dealers and manufacturers maintain help lines to help you out with things like this.

You also can set the modem to use the next highest serial port number. For instance, if your computer has a COM1 and a COM2, you can set the modem to use COM3 and all will be well (assuming you have software that will work with COM3—most do). Remember, though, that you cannot have any "holes" in the series of serial ports. If your computer has a COM1 and COM2, you cannot use COM4 unless there's something using COM3, even if it's just a port in the computer that nothing's connected to.

TIP **Consult the manual that came with your modem for help on** setting its serial port number. Usually, it's accomplished with small switches on the back of the modem (next to the phone jacks) or with jumpers on the surface of the circuit board.

&& *Plain English, please!*

A **jumper** is a small plastic device that makes a connection between two pins. They're usually black, and they're really small—about the size of a push button on a wrist watch. You can slide them on and off pins in order to close connections. (Don't mess with them unless you're sure you need to.) **,,**

Install that modem!

Once you've configured the modem and your computer, and fussed with your existing serial ports so that everything will work right, you can install the modem. This involves sliding it into one of the slots inside the computer until the card edge is slightly inside the slot. Then, firmly press it in until it seats. You'll know when it's all the way in when the mounting bracket is flush with the surface into which you screw down the board.

TIP **Some boards are a tight fit. Don't be afraid to push them firmly** into their slot. If you're worried about breaking something, get someone who has done this before to help you out.

Once your modem is installed, and you've screwed it in, go ahead and replace the cover of your computer, plug it in, and turn it on. In the next chapter, you'll learn about installing your communications software. That's where you'll find out if your modem is working properly.

Installing Your Software

● **In this chapter:**

● **I'd like to install my software onto my computer**

● **What steps are involved?**

● **Tell me about setting up my software**

Your car is worthless without a steering wheel, and your modem is worthless without software. In this chapter, learn how to drive your modem on the information superhighway using special software . . . . ◗

Without a steering wheel and other controls, your car is just a worthless hunk of metal. Those controls let you interact with the car in ways that make it work for you. If your car didn't have them, you'd be like Fred Flintstone, pushing your car everywhere, and picking it up to turn it around.

Your modem is the same without software that drives it and lets you take advantage of its capabilities. You use your **communications software** to initialize the modem, activate the phone line, and dial your destination. Your software also takes care of you once you get connected, by displaying information from the remote system, helping you to transfer files back and forth, and so on.

In this chapter you'll learn how to install and set up your communications software. For example's sake, we'll install PROCOMM PLUS for Windows, one of the top Windows-based communications programs. And we'll do so with a computer running Windows 95. If you're using a different program to work with your modem, or a different operating system, you can take these examples along with your software manual and duplicate the steps on your own. Along the way, I'll point out special places where your software will probably be different from PROCOMM PLUS, and what sorts of things you'll need to watch out for.

What does the software do?

Your communications software fulfills many, many functions for you. Depending on what programs you're using, it will:

- Take control of your modem and make it connect to remote systems using telephone numbers and communication parameters you provide

66 *Plain English, please!*

When you tell your software about a remote system, you have to enter in the remote system's **communication parameters** so that your software knows how to connect. These include the modem speed, the number of data bits, stop bits, and the parity settings. You learn about all of these settings in the section "Communication parameters," later in this chapter. 99

- Display information and menus from the remote system

- Accept things that you type and pass them along to the remote system, such as menu choices or e-mail messages you write

- Upload and download files from the remote system

 Plain English, please!

Upload means to send a copy of a file from your computer to a remote system. **Download** means you're copying a file from a remote system to your own computer.

- Send and receive faxes, assuming you have a modem with fax capabilities and your software supports faxing

- Optionally capture what you do online into a file that you can review later

Plain English, please!

When you use **capturing**, also called **logging**, your software takes all that the remote system displays, plus whatever you type, and saves it to a file on your computer for later reference. You can usually control when capturing starts and stops, and what file name your software uses for the file. It's like making a video tape of what you do with your modem.

What software do I need?

There are several different types of communications programs available. Depending on your needs, you may need all of these, or only some of them:

- **Terminal software** lets you dial into a text-based remote system, use its menus and commands, and exchange files with it. Examples include Windows 3.1's Terminal or Windows 95's HyperTerminal.

- **Fax software** is what you use for sending and receiving faxes. Fax software also usually gives you ways to print received faxes, and to manage your fax files. You can buy programs such as WinFax PRO. Windows 95 includes Microsoft Fax ,which also gives you these capabilities.

- **Online service software** is custom communications software that works only with a specific online service. For instance, if you use CompuServe or Prodigy, you'll typically use those company's custom programs to access the service.

- **Remote control software** lets you take control of a remote computer, as if you were sitting in front of it. For instance, you could run remote control software on your computer at work, and then use your modem at home to dial in and take control of your work computer using the remote control software. You run remote control software on both computers, the one calling and the one answering. Examples of this type of program include PCAnywhere, Reachout Remote, and Carbon Copy.

Installing your software

No matter what type of software you're using, installation follows the same process:

1 Use the software's installation program to put it into your computer.

 Plain English, please!

Installation programs are provided with most software programs. Usually, they make the job of taking the program off of floppy diskettes and installing it onto your computer much easier. They do a lot of the background work for you, like making changes to those scary Windows system files and copying all the needed files into the right places.

2 Tell the software about your modem and computer settings.

3 Set up the software with information about where you want to connect with your modem.

First things first: Run the installation program

The first step to installing the software is to use the software's installation program. Depending on whether you're using DOS or Windows, there are different ways you go about this.

If you're installing DOS-based software, you insert the first diskette of the program into your diskette drive and follow these steps:

1 Change to the floppy drive that holds the diskette by typing the drive letter followed by a colon, and press return. So, **A:** or **B:** (depending on which drive you are using) followed by Enter would change the floppy drive.

2 Run the installation program. This program is usually called something like INSTALL or SETUP. Type the name of the program (check the software's manual for the exact name) and press Enter.

3 Follow the instructions of the program to get the software onto your computer.

If you're installing Windows-based software, the steps are the same, as shown in figures 3.1 through 3.3.

First, open up the My Computer icon and then double-click the A: drive icon. This displays all the files in the folder on the diskette. Now you want to find the installation program—it's usually called SETUP.EXE or INSTALL.EXE. Once you've found it (check your software manual for the exact name; in this case it's called SETUP.EXE), double-click the icon to start the installation program.

Fig. 3.1
You start installation programs using the My Computer icon, opening the icon that represents the diskette drive that contains the program.

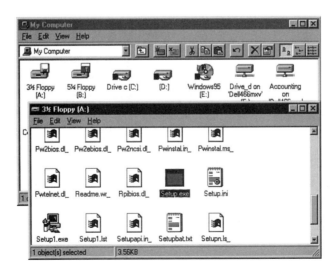

Fig. 3.2
Aha! The installation program begins with—what else?—a legal notice! Click the Continue button to install the software.

With PROCOMM PLUS for Windows, I was asked to enter my name and the software serial number (it was somewhere on the box or the software disks) and then prompted for each diskette. When the installation was finished, a new group was added to my Start Menu displaying all of the icons shown in figure 3.3. The program is now installed, but it's not set up yet.

Fig. 3.3
Once the installation program is complete, your software should appear in your Start Programs menu, as shown here.

Questions you'll probably have to answer

A key part of installing new communications software lies in telling the software about your computer and your preferences. You generally have to be able to answer the following questions:

- What type and speed of modem do you have?

- What COM port is your modem connected to (see Chapter 2 for more information on this)?

- What folder should the software use for storing different types of files, such as files you download while using the software?

You might also be asked less-essential questions, such as what default download protocol you prefer, and what terminal type you prefer. While this is important information, it's not critical during installation, because you can usually define all of this for each connection you set up in the software after it's installed onto your computer.

 Plain English, please!

A **download protocol**, also called a **file transfer protocol**, is a method that your communications software uses to ensure that any file transfers happen without errors in the transmitted information. (If it's available, choose Zmodem.) This is like making sure you and the person on the other end both speak the same language—if you ask a question in French and they respond in Russian, one or both of you is going to get confused before too long (unless one or both of you are multilingual, of course).

Different systems you call into will use different **terminal types**. This defines a method that your computer uses to understand how to layout the screens sent from the remote system, and how to match up your keyboard keys to the remote system's keys. You learn about different terminal types later in the chapter.

The software should be installed at this point, so you can run it. Find it in your Start menu and click it to open it.

Q&A *Is it always this easy to install communications software?*

Generally, yes. While you have to use the instructions that come with your software, getting it installed onto your computer is the easy part. As you'll learn later in the chapter, getting it actually working after you've installed it is where the tricky stuff comes in.

Once you've started the software, you can define the remote systems you want to connect with. This is usually done with some sort of "dialing directory" function that holds all of the phone numbers and definitions for systems you want to call. It's like your "electronic black book." For example, figure 3.4 shows the dialing directory setup screen for PROCOMM PLUS for Windows.

Fig. 3.4
PROCOMM PLUS for Windows lets you define new connections with this screen.

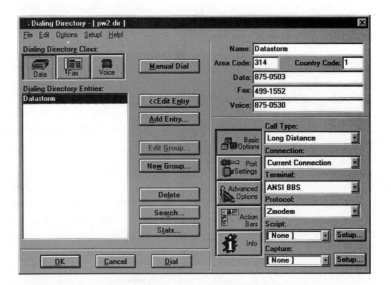

Communication parameters

When you create a new dialing entry in your software, you have to tell it how the remote system needs to communicate with you. You need to know this information for each remote system:

- The remote system's modem speed, often expressed as its **bps rate** or **baud rate.**

- How many **data bits** to use for the remote connection. This will be either seven or eight. Most systems work with eight data bits.

- What **parity** the remote system uses. This is a rudimentary modem transmission error prevention feature. If you are using eight data bits, this is usually set to None, or simply N. If the remote system uses seven data bits, this will either be Even (E) or Odd (O).

- How many **stop bits** to use. If you're using eight data bits, this is usually set to one stop bit. Some systems use two stop bits, but this is very rare. A stop bit defines the end of a chunk of data.

TIP   **Baud rate, data bits, parity, stop bits, it all sounds like a bunch of** gibberish, right? While these things are important to set correctly, understanding exactly how they work and what they mean will not help you to use your modem. Keep your brain clear for important information!

- What download protocol the remote system uses. You don't really need to know this in advance, because most of the time you choose it whenever you download a file.

- What **terminal type** to use. This is critical information. If it's not set right, you'll probably see gibberish on your screen when you connect to the remote system. For most systems, choose ANSI-BBS. If that doesn't work, using either VT100 or VT220 (two common terminal types) will usually do the trick.

Go online!

Once you've set up the system to dial, you use your communications software's command (whatever it is for your software) to connect to it. When you do this, you should see and hear the following things happen:

1 A status message should appear telling you that the software is trying to connect.

2 The modem will be initialized. If you have an external modem, you will see its lights flash as this happens.

3 The modem will go "off-hook" meaning that it will pick up the telephone line. You should hear a brief dial tone as it does this.

4 Your modem will dial the remote system. You'll hear the dialing tones as it does this.

5 The remote system will ring. After several rings, it will answer the call.

6 The modems on both sides will start to connect to one another, and to coordinate between themselves. You'll hear a squealing noise from your modem briefly as this happens, and then the sound should stop. If you have an external modem, you'll see the CD light go on right when the squealing stops.

❝ ❝ Plain English, please!

The **CD** light on your external modem stands for **carrier detect**. It means that your modem has successfully connected to the remote modem at the most basic level. In other words, the two modems have successfully negotiated a speed with each other, and each one "sees" the other one. **❞ ❞**

7 The remote system will display its opening screen, and you can proceed.

TIP **Many communications programs have a setting that lets you turn** off the modem's speaker so you don't have to listen to the ringing and squealing and such. If your software doesn't have a setting like that, you can add the letters **M0** to the modem initialization string, which is defined somewhere in the software.

It didn't work

With so many things going on as you connect to a remote system, there are many things that can go wrong. In this section, each numbered step that you just read will be shown, along with information about what can go wrong at that point, how you know there's a problem, and suggestions for fixing the problem.

Status message

Your communications software should indicate when it starts to try to connect to a remote system. If it doesn't, there are two possibilities: either your software is just not programmed to do this—but it's working just fine— or your computer has frozen and the status message either isn't displayed or stays onscreen no matter how long you wait.

If it appears that your computer becomes frozen whenever you try to use your modem, the culprit is almost certainly an incorrect serial port setting in your communications software. Ensure that:

- The software is configured to use the same serial port number as the modem is set to

- There are no hardware interrupt conflicts in your system, particularly surrounding hardware interrupts 3 and 4

See Chapter 2, "Installing Your Modem" for more information on serial ports and hardware interrupt conflicts.

If the previous steps don't yield any more positive results, you should contact the maker of the communication software you're using for further help.

The modem is initialized

Here, you will see two things happen. First, the communications software will probably display a message telling you that it's initializing the modem, or it will simply send the modem a "setup string" of modem commands that initializes it. Most programs display these commands as they are sent; they look like this (your software may use different commands, so don't worry about specific differences):

```
AT&F&C1&D2&K3&Q5W2S95=44^M
```

If you have an external modem, you'll see the second thing that happens: your modem lights flash on and off as the initialization command is processed.

If you see none of this, and the modem does not give you a dial tone after a short while, then it's almost certainly due to an incorrect serial port setting (once again!). Double-check those settings as in the previous section.

The modem goes "off-hook"

The third step in initiating a call involves the modem going "off-hook." This means that it does exactly what you do when you pick up a handset off of a telephone's switch-hook. When it does this, you should hear a dial tone. (Some communications programs disable the modem's speaker, therefore, you won't hear anything even though all is working well. Generally, though, they leave the speaker on until a connection is established, so that you can hear any problems that occur.)

If you don't hear a dial tone before the modem starts dialing, there are several things to check:

- Is the wire from the modem to the wall jack properly connected?

- Did you plug the telephone wire into the jack on the modem marked "Line?" You *don't* want to use the jack marked "Phone" for the wire that leads to the wall jack.

- Does your modem have a volume setting and is it turned down so far that you can't hear the dial tone?

If you've checked all of this, and you still don't hear a dial tone, try one more thing. Remove the cable going into the Modem's Line jack and connect it to a normal telephone. If you can get a dial tone with the telephone, then you should call the place where you bought the modem—it's probably broken or not working properly. If you don't hear a dial tone with the telephone, then it's time to call your phone company!

Your modem dials the remote system

Once the modem dials, you'll hear a rapid series of telephone dialing tones. If you hear just a series of clicks, then your software is set to use pulse dialing, which simulates the old rotary telephone sets. If your phone company allows tone dialing, it's more efficient to set up your software to use that dialing method.

Another pitfall here is when your modem uses tone dialing, but no connection is established. Some areas don't allow tone dialing, and so you should try pulse dialing in your software. The key here is to listen to your normal telephones when you dial: If your phone uses tones, then it's safe to have your modem use tone dialing. If your phone is a rotary set, or you hear clicks when you press the phone buttons, then you'll need pulse dialing.

The remote system rings

There are lots of things that can go wrong when the remote system rings!

- A **Busy Signal** just means that the remote system is being used by someone else. Try to connect again later. Most programs can do this for you automatically, retrying every 30 seconds or so until the remote system is available.

- **Ringing that doesn't stop** can mean two things. Either you're using the wrong phone number, or the remote system's modem is having some trouble. Recheck the phone number or try again later.

- **A recorded voice** means that the phone number is no longer in service, or the phone number you used is wrong in some way. For instance, if it's a long distance telephone number, did you remember to tell your software to dial a 1 before the area code?

- **A person's voice** means the phone number you're using is definitely wrong! Use whatever command your software needs to tell it to hang up, and then check the phone number your software is using.

The modems start to synchronize

Once the remote system answers the phone, you should hear squealing from your modem's speaker as the two modems synchronize. Sometimes, you'll hear this squealing for a while, and then your modem abruptly hangs up. This can be due to one of several possibilities:

- You've selected the wrong modem speed for the remote system.

- Your communications software is set up for a different modem than the one you're actually using. Double-check this setting in your software. If your modem isn't listed in the software, try telling your software that you're using a **Hayes-Compatible** modem, or possibly a **Generic** modem if that setting is available. This works most of the time. And if that fails, call the company that makes your modem, or the makers of the software you're using. Chances are they'll know what modem setting you should use.

66 *Plain English, please!*

Hayes is a company that was a pioneer in PC modems, and they ruled the marketplace for many years. Nobody could sell competing modems unless they were Hayes-compatible. However, nobody ever *really* made perfectly Hayes-compatible modems; there were always subtle differences that cropped up. Still, if your modem isn't listed in the communications software setting, listing your modem as Hayes-compatible is a good idea. 99

The remote system displays its first screen

Finally, the remote system should display its startup screen. If this comes up garbled, check all of these things:

- Make sure you're using the right settings for data bits, parity, and stop bits for the remote system. There are two common combinations that almost all systems use (but they'll only use one or the other):

  Eight data bits, one stop bit, and no parity

  Seven data bits, one stop bit, and even parity

- Check the terminal type your software is set for, also called terminal emulation. ANSI (sometimes called ANSI-BBS) works with most systems, but you might also have to try VT100 or VT220.

- There may be a lot of static on the line. If you think this is the case, try calling the number with a regular phone, and listen carefully to the remote system ring. If the rings sound clear, then static probably isn't the problem.

Nothing I've tried works!

If you've followed all the steps and suggestions in the chapter and you still can't get connected, consider trying these resources:

- Read Chapter 22, "Spotting and Fixing Common Problems," later in this book.

- Call a customer service representative for the remote system you're dialing. If it's a BBS, call the system operator.

- Call the maker of the software you're using. They might be able to offer some helpful suggestions.

- Talk to the store from which you bought your computer or modem. They might even let you bring your system down to their store, so that they can see what's going on and help you. Be warned, though, that they might charge you for this help.

- Consider calling a friend who does a lot of work with modems and communications. Often, a problem you're having might be something that they've seen, and if they can come by your home or office, they might be able to help you.

- If you have any computer nerds in your company, talk to them. Most computer nerds enjoy helping out on this kind of problem.

Going Online with Windows 95

● **In this chapter:**

- I've heard Windows 95 has all kinds of new online goodies. Is this true?

- Configuring your modem in Windows 95

- Dialing out with HyperTerminal

- Setting up Windows' built-in TCP/IP connection

- What's MSN?

Windows 95's direct connection to the outside world puts it leaps and bounds ahead of the competition—and that means more power and less fuss for you! . . . . ▸

What's the big deal about Windows 95? I started asking myself that way back in late 1994, when I loaded the first Windows **beta** (testing version) on my PC. I hated it instantly. This rude operating system took over my whole computer. It created a bunch of folders I didn't understand and it moved my system files god-knows-where. In short, it took away some of the control that us DOS-diehards hold so dear. Not only that, but it looked strange—not at all like my old familiar Windows 3.1.

Well, it's been almost a year since then, and Windows 95 is now available in stores—you may have even received a free copy when you bought your computer. If you've never known anything else, you'll probably love Windows 95 instantly. But if you're a die-hard Windows 3.1 or DOS fan, like I was, you may need a bit of time to adjust. Just give it a chance, and don't panic like I did! (And by the way, I did adjust, and I love Windows 95 now.)

So why am I telling you all this? Well, because what finally sold me on this strange new operating system was not its "friendly interface" or any of that other stuff they advertise. *It was the online capabilities.* Windows 95 made it easier for me to connect to a BBS, to dial into the Internet, and to create and send a fax, all of which I do on a regular basis. Hey, I may be a die-hard DOS user, but I like saving time and effort as much as the next person.

What can I do with Windows 95?

Here's a quick rundown of the Windows 95 tools that make your online life a little easier:

- **Plug-and-play hardware detection**—Just plug in a new modem and tell Windows 95 to look for it—Windows 95 can figure out what kind of modem it is and what settings it requires. No more setup hassles!

- **HyperTerminal**—a surprisingly full-featured terminal program—that is, a program that dials your modem and connects you to another computer. It replaces the Terminal program from Windows 3.1.

- **Dial-up networking**—a feature that lets you connect to a network by calling into it with your modem. Corporate types can use this to connect to their LAN at work, but I use it to connect to the Internet.

- **Microsoft Network**—a new online service by Microsoft, designed especially for Windows 95 users. Chapter 11 is devoted to it—check it out.

- **Microsoft Fax**—a program that enables you to create and send faxes from almost any Windows program, as easily as you send a document to the printer. (More on this in Chapter 14.)

- **Microsoft Exchange**—a mail-handling program that manages all your e-mail and faxes. It works especially well with the Microsoft Network.

How do I set up my new modem to work with Windows 95?

One of the things that really won me over to Windows 95 is the concept of "plug and play." That is, you just plug in a new component, and Windows 95 figures out what it is and is able to "play" it.

Windows checks out your hardware when you install Windows 95, and automatically loads the right software to control it. So if you had the modem at the time you installed Windows 95, you're all set! Nothing further is required.

Want to check and make sure Windows 95 knows about your modem? Follow these steps:

  1 Click the Start button, then move your mouse over <u>S</u>ettings.

  2 Click <u>C</u>ontrol Panel. The Control Panel opens.

  3 Find the Modems icon and double-click it.

  4 You should see your modem on the list (see fig. 4.1). Click OK.

If your modem isn't on the list, you'll need to set it up, as explained in the next set of steps.

Fig. 4.1
All the installed modems are listed here.

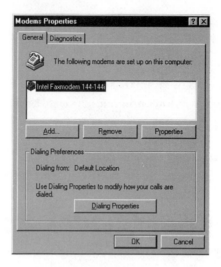

Tell Windows 95 to look for your modem

If you've added a new modem since you installed Windows 95, you'll need to tell Windows it's there. The easiest way to set up a new modem is to have Windows 95 look for it and identify it. About 99 percent of the time, this works successfully. (The other one percent we'll talk about shortly.) To set up your modem just follow these steps:

1 Make sure your modem is plugged in and turned on (if it's an external model), or firmly installed inside your PC (if it's an internal model).

2 Open the Control Panel again if it's not already open from the previous steps. (Click Start, Settings, Control Panel.)

3 Double-click the Add New Hardware icon. A wizard starts, walking you through the process.

4 Click Next to begin. You're asked if you want Windows 95 to detect the new hardware. Click Yes (if Yes isn't already selected), then Next again.

5 Click Next at the warning message, and Windows 95 begins to look for any new hardware that it doesn't already know about (including your modem).

CAUTION   **The warning message in step 5 tells you to close all open applica-**
tions. If you have any open apps, you should close them. (You can tell an application is open if it appears in the taskbar.) Select the application on the taskbar and then close it. Repeat until the only things left on the taskbar are the Control Panel and the Add Hardware Wizard.

6 Wait. It may take several minutes, especially if your computer is slow and old. Eventually, you'll see a screen telling you that Windows is ready to install support for the hardware it found.

7 To find out what hardware it found, click the Details button. (See fig. 4.2.)

Fig. 4.2
As you can see, Windows 95 found my modem, and also an extra mouse port. Lucky me!

8 Click Finish. Windows tells you what kind of modem it found, and gives you the opportunity to change it. (There's about a 99 percent chance that it's correct, though.)

9 Click Change in the unlikely event that you need to change the name of the modem, or click Next to go on.

TIP   **If Windows doesn't detect the modem correctly, you can select** the modem yourself. Just click Change in step 9. The Install New Modem dialog box opens. You select the modem's manufacturer from the list on the left, and the model from the list on the right. Then click OK to return to the regularly scheduled installation procedure.

10 Next, Windows will tell you that it needs to restart the computer to complete the installation. Click Yes to let it.

You're done! Now go back and look in the Modems folder again in the Control Panel, and your modem should definitely be there this time.

Meet HyperTerminal

If you ever struggled with the difficult-to-use communications program in Windows 3.1 (Terminal), you'll really appreciate HyperTerminal. It's another reason why Windows 95 won me over in the end. HyperTerminal is a surprisingly full-featured communications program that enables you to issue commands directly to your modem and connect your computer to other computers with your modem.

There are a lot of powerful settings you can work with in HyperTerminal to customize a connection or troubleshoot problems, but most people won't ever need to use them. Windows 95 passes the information it knows about your modem directly to HyperTerminal, so HyperTerminal already knows what make and model of modem you have, as well as its maximum speed and preferred settings. All you have to do is tell HyperTerminal about the computer you want to connect with.

With HyperTerminal, you set up the information about a destination only once—it remembers that information ever-after. So, as you can imagine, it takes a bit more time the first time you call. From then on, you can reconnect with that same computer with a single mouse action.

Let's start HyperTerminal and create a new connection. Follow these steps:

1 Click the Start button, then choose <u>P</u>rograms, Accessories, HyperTerminal. The HyperTerminal folder opens.

2 Double-click the Hypertrm.exe icon (that's the main HyperTerminal one). HyperTerminal starts up, and starts asking you for information about the new connection.

3 First, HyperTerminal asks for a name and icon for the new connection. Enter a descriptive name that will help you remember the location, and choose an icon to represent it; then click OK.

 TIP **The name and icon you select in step 3 are for future use; once** you create a connection, it'll appear in the HyperTerminal folder you saw in step 1. You can then connect by just double-clicking that icon.

4 Next, you're asked for the phone number to dial. The area code and country are already filled in, and your modem is already chosen (see fig. 4.3). Enter the phone number (with or without the hyphen), and change any of the other information if needed, then click OK.

Fig. 4.3
Enter the phone
number you want to
dial, and check on the
other information to
make sure it's correct.

5 Next, you'll see a Connect box, with the following buttons:

- **Modify.** Click here to change the phone number, if you see that you made a mistake entering it.

 TIP **After you click Modify, you can click Configure to control the** modem speaker volume. After youve clicked Configure, you can click Connection to set the communication parameters you learned about in Chapter 3.

- **Dialing Properties.** Click here if you need to set any special options for dialing, such as dialing a 9 for an outside line or the code in your area for disabling call waiting.

- **Dial.** Click here when you're ready to make the connection.

- **Cancel.** Click here if you've changed your mind about wanting to set up this connection and make this call. (The information you entered will not be saved.)

 TIP **If you accidentally click Cancel in step 5, select Call, Connect to** get the dialog box back.

Now that you're connected, what next? It depends on what kind of computer you connected to. Most online services have their own software, so you won't be using HyperTerminal for them. The major use of HyperTerminal will probably be for BBSs—privately owned and operated local online services. Chapter 13 will give you a full report on the ins and outs of using BBSes.

Finding your way in HyperTerminal

When you're using a terminal program like HyperTerminal, you've got two sets of controls—the ones for your own computer, and the ones for the computer you're connected with. You're in control of your own computer's settings.

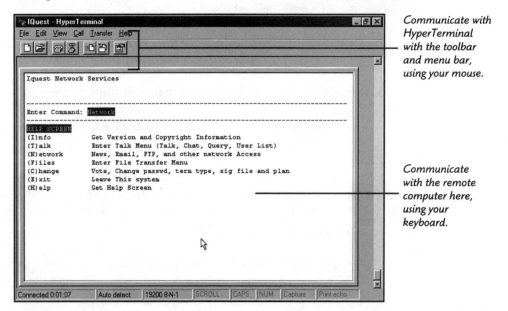

Communicate with HyperTerminal with the toolbar and menu bar, using your mouse.

Communicate with the remote computer here, using your keyboard.

 Creates a new connection

 Opens an existing connection you've saved.

 Opens the Connect dialog box

 Disconnects, if you're connected

 Opens a dialog box where you can select a file to send (upload)

 Opens a dialog box where you can receive (download) a file

 Opens a Properties dialog box for the open connection.

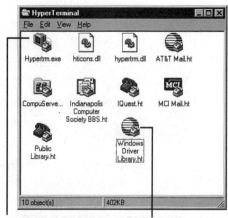

The HyperTerminal icon starts the program and walks you through the creation of a new connection.

Each connection you create has its own icon in the HyperTerminal folder. To connect, just double-click the icon.

I want to hook up to the Internet!

If you're going to connect to the Internet (as you'll learn to do in Chapter 12), you'll need to connect in one of three ways:

- Using a regular terminal program like HyperTerminal. (This is awkward and limited.)

- The best way for most people is through a PPP connection, which allows full graphical access to all the best Internet features.

66 *Plain English, please!*

PPP stands for **Point-to-Point Protocol**. It's a language that two modems can use to transmit Internet data. 99

- Ideally, you can hook up through your company's network, if your company has its own direct connection to the Internet. (Technically, this is the best way, but it's not an option for most people.)

I'll go into more detail in the Internet chapter about PPP and all that technical stuff—for now, let's just see how Windows 95 fits into all that.

Prior to Windows 95, if you wanted a graphical Internet connection with PPP (or **SLIP** or **CSLIP**, two older relatives of PPP), you had to use a special dialer program (Trumpet Winsock was one of the most popular), along with some special driver files. Setting up the dialer program was a nightmare, because every Internet provider required special settings. It was enough to have hardcore computer geeks tearing out their hair.

Windows 95 simplifies things considerably, because it has built-in PPP support. (You may hear it called **TCP/IP support**; PPP is a type of TCP/IP, not that it matters for our purposes.)

There are two steps for setting up Windows 95 to dial and connect to your PPP Internet account. The first is to configure Windows' network settings, and the second is to create a dial-up networking connection.

Before you do anything else, you need to contract with an Internet service provider in your area to get a PPP account. (More on this in Chapter 12.)

Make sure you get the following information from the service provider:

- *Phone number* to have your modem dial

- *Domain Name.* For instance, mine is **iquest.net**, the name of my service provider

- *Domain Name Server address.* Mine is **198.70.36.70**

- *Anything special you might need to add* to your user name when you log on to tell the computer you're using PPP (for instance, I have to add a 1 to the end of mine—**fwempen1**—when I log on)

Once you have that information in hand, you're ready to start setting up Windows.

Setting up Windows 95 to use dial-up networking

The first stop along the way is to tell Windows which network drivers to use for this dial-up connection. Don't let the following procedure scare you! It's a bit more complicated than most Windows activities, but just follow the steps carefully and you'll be fine.

1 Click the Start button, then select Settings, Control Panel. Double-click the Network icon. The Network dialog box appears.

2 If you see Dial-Up Adapter and TCP/IP listed in the dialog box, as shown in figure 4.4, skip to step 7. If you don't, continue to step 3.

3 Click the <u>A</u>dd button. Click Adapter, then click <u>A</u>dd again.

4 Find and select Microsoft from the <u>M</u>anufacturers list. Then click Dial-Up Adapter from the Network Adapters list (see fig 4.5), and click OK.

5 Now you're back at the main Network window. Click <u>A</u>dd, Protocol, then click Add again.

6 Find and select Microsoft from the Manufacturers list. Then click TCP/IP from the Network Protocols list, and click OK.

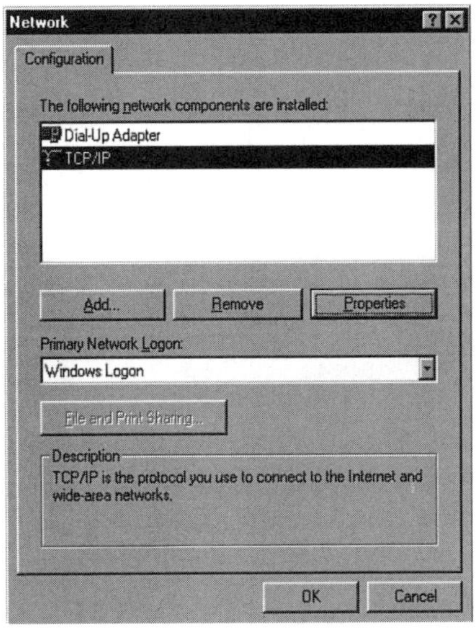

Fig. 4.4
If the Dial-Up Adapter
and TCP/IP are already
installed, as shown
here, you can skip
steps 3 through 6.

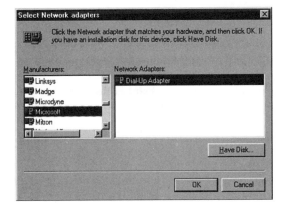

Fig. 4.5
The Microsoft Dial-Up
Adapter is buried
among all the other
network drivers—you
have to dig it out
like so.

7 You're back at the main Network window again. Click Dial-Up Adapter once to select it, then click the Properties button.

8 Click the Bindings tab, and make sure there is a check mark in the box next to TCP/IP. If there's not, click to place a check mark there. Click OK to return to the main Network window.

9 Click TCP/IP to select it, then click the Properties button. Click the DNS Configuration tab (see fig. 4.6).

Fig. 4.6
Here's where you
enter the specific
information about
your PPP connection.

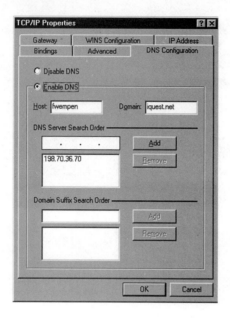

10 Click the Enable DNS button. Then type your user name in the Host box
(for example, mine is **fwempen**), and your service provider's name in
the Domain box (such as **iquest.net**).

CAUTION **If you were given a special code to add to your user ID when you**
log on, like **fwempen1**, don't use it in step 10. That special code is used
later.

11 This is important: In the text box under DNS Server Search Order, type
your service provider's Domain Name Server number (that's what DNS
stands for). Mine is **198.70.36.70**. Then click Add.

12 When you're done, click OK, then click OK again to close the Network
dialog box.

Create your dial-up networking connection

Well, the hard part is behind you! The next step is simpler. We need to create a dial-up networking connection to actually do the dialing. Follow these steps:

1 Double-click the My Computer icon on the Windows 95 desktop, then double-click the Dial-Up Networking folder.

2 Double-click the Make New Connection icon. A wizard starts to help you with the process.

3 Type a name for the connection (it will appear below the connection's icon later), then click Next.

4 Enter the area code (if it's different from what's already entered for you), phone number, and country (if different), then click Next.

5 Click the Finish button. Your new connection appears in the Dial-Up Networking folder.

6 Now double-click the icon for the new connection. You'll see a dialog box, as in figure 4.7.

7 Enter your user name and password in the appropriate blanks, then click Connect.

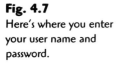

Fig. 4.7
Here's where you enter your user name and password.

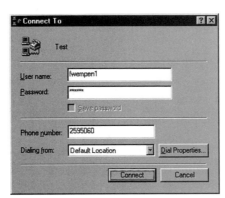

If everything was entered correctly, your modem will dial at this point, then, after it checks your user ID and password, you'll see a box like the one in figure 4.8—your signal that the connection was successful! At that point, you can open up any graphical Internet software you want to work with (such as a Web browser). When you're done, click Disconnect.

In the future, all you have to do to connect with this service is to double-click its icon in the Dial-Up Networking folder—you never have to go through the set up process again (whew!).

Fig. 4.8
Success! If you entered all the right information, you'll be notified that you've connected successfully.

Sending and receiving e-mail with Microsoft Exchange

Microsoft Exchange is a sort of one-stop shopping place for electronic communications. You can use it to manage your e-mail from The Microsoft Network (Chapter 11), your faxes from MS Fax (Chapter 14), and perhaps other mail too, depending on your setup.

No matter what kind of communications you're handling, Microsoft Exchange works basically the same way. Let's look at Exchange now, so you'll be prepared for it when you start working with The Microsoft Network and MS Fax.

 Plain English, please!
MS Fax is short for Microsoft Fax, the fax program that comes with Windows 95. **"**

What's in the inbox?

To start Exchange, just open your inbox. You can do this by double-clicking the Inbox icon on your desktop, or clicking the Start button and selecting Programs, Microsoft Exchange.

The My Exchange inbox is shown in figure 4.9. Since I've already been using the program, I already have some mail waiting for me! You'll have some too when you start working with The Microsoft Network.

This return-to-sender symbol means
the message wasn't delivered.

Unread messages are shown
in bold type.

Fig. 4.9
The Microsoft
Exchange inbox holds
your incoming mail.

*Your inbox is one of
several folders
available. You can
also create your own
folders.*

*This symbol means
the message has a low
priority.*

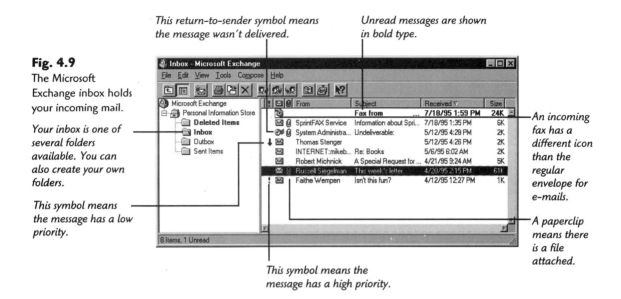

*An incoming
fax has a
different icon
than the
regular
envelope for
e-mails.*

*A paperclip
means there
is a file
attached.*

This symbol means the
message has a high priority.

Let's take a closer look at that toolbar, which has some interesting tools on it:

Moves up a level in Exchange's folder list

Displays or hides the folder list

Starts a new message

Prints the selected message(s)

Saves the selected message(s) to disk

Deletes the selected message(s)

Reply to the selected message

Reply to all recipients of the selected message

Forward the selected message

Display your address book

 Return to the Inbox folder, if you're in a different one

 Get help on a screen element (click the icon, then click the screen element)

Reading an e-mail or viewing an incoming fax

To take a look at a piece of mail, just double-click it. It's as easy as that! Figure 4.10 shows a message I've decided to read (even though it looks like junk mail, now that I'm in it!). Figure 4.11 shows a fax I've double-clicked to read.

Once you've read a message or fax, you can dispose of it using any of the toolbar buttons shown in figures 4.10 and 4.11.

Fig. 4.10
Here's an e-mail I got, with a file attached. I hope the e-mail you get is more exciting.

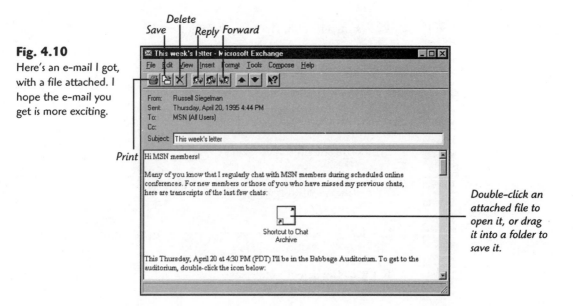

These controls all help
you set how you'll
view the fax.

If the fax is upside down or sideways,
rotate it with these buttons.

Save   Print

Fig. 4.11
Here's a fax from my
editor. Looks like she's
pleased with me!

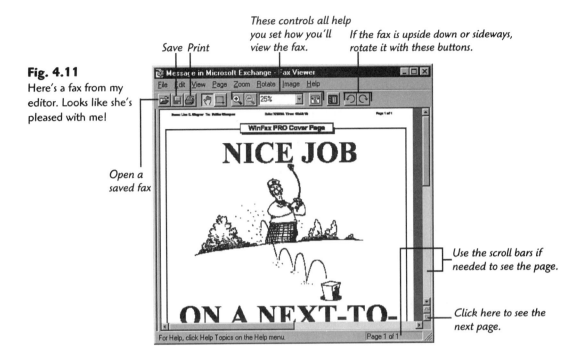

Open a
saved fax

Use the scroll bars if
needed to see the page.

Click here to see the
next page.

How do I send e-mail with Microsoft Exchange?

First, let me state the obvious: To send an e-mail with Exchange, you have to have a means of conveying it. In other words, you have to be hooked up to a local area network in your company that uses Exchange, or you have to be signed up with the Microsoft Network, or you have to be a member of some other service that uses Exchange. Otherwise, your message won't go anywhere.

 To create a new e-mail with Exchange, just click the New Message button on the toolbar. You'll get a fresh new message window, into which you can type all the particulars (see fig. 4.12.).

Of course, you'll fill in a recipient in the To box, and maybe one in the Cc box too. Enter as many recipients as you like—there's plenty of room. Just press Enter after each one. Or, if you like, click the To button and select from your address book.

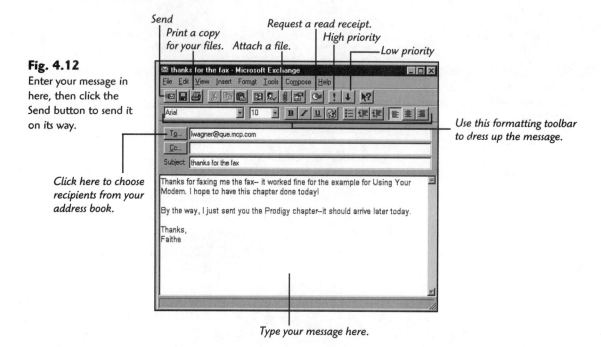

Fig. 4.12
Enter your message in here, then click the Send button to send it on its way.

Click here to choose recipients from your address book.

Type your message here.

TIP

You can add new entries to the address book as you go—just click the To button to bring up the address book, then enter the new name and click the New button. Choose an entry type, then click OK. Enter the person's information, then click To. The address is added to the To line of your message-in-progress, and it's also added to your address book.

Type your message, and do anything else you feel like doing: attaching a file, requesting a receipt, formatting the message with special fonts and colors, and so on. Then when you've finished, click the Send button and the message is on its way.

Q&A

I've heard that you can only send plain text in an e-mail message, but it looks like Microsoft Exchange lets me do all kinds of formatting. What's the deal?

If youre sending e-mail from the Microsoft Network, to someone else on the Microsoft Network, your formatting will come through just fine. However, if you're sending e-mail from one mail system to another (for instance, to the Internet via the Microsoft Network), your message will lose all its pretty formatting in transit. Any attached files may or may not come through on the other end okay—it all depends on the capabilities of the mail system you're sending to.

There's more...

In this chapter, I've explained everything about Windows 95 communications capabilities *except* the two big topics you're probably the most interested in: The Microsoft Network and Microsoft Fax. Well, don't fear. You'll get an entire chapter's worth of information on The Microsoft Network in Chapter 11, "Calling The Microsoft Network," and you'll see how to send and receive faxes with Microsoft Fax in Chapter 14, "Faxing, with or without a Fax Modem."

5

Understanding the Online World

● **In this chapter:**

● **Learn the language and practices of the Online world**

● **Online hype from the media**

● **What are smileys, abbreviations, and my signature?**

● **Some of the online customs**

● **Online things you don't want to do!**

Landing in the online world is a lot like landing on Mars. This chapter is your friendly local guide to the weird customs, sights, and language . . . . **❯**

The online world is like a whole other country (actually more like a whole other planet), and as a new arrival, you're going to see and hear lots of unfamiliar things. This chapter is something of a Berlitz course for this new place (you know, Berlitz that does the language and customs classes for our diplomats). If you read this before you charge headlong into the online world, you'll avoid a lot of the mistakes unwary travelers usually make.

It's a whole new language!

Presumably, you'll be using your modem to connect with people and services that speak the same language you do, right? Well, sort of. Saying that folks online speak the same language as folks in your home or office is like saying folks in England speak English just like Americans. Much of what you'll see online will look familiar, but you'll probably run into enough of the "online dialect" to get a little confused.

Most of the new phrases and customs we talk about in this chapter come into play when you're interacting with other people online, either through electronic messages, in a live conference, or in a realtime game. If your sole activity online will be looking for programs, stock quotes, weather, or anything else that is a solo activity, then online dialect won't get in your way. If you'll be doing research online, you'll want to read this chapter as well, as you'll probably find some information written in the cryptic online dialect.

> ❝ *Plain English, please!*
>
> **Realtime** is just another word for "live." It's like the difference between talking to someone's answering machine and talking to them in person. E-mail is like an answering machine—you leave a message for someone, then they leave a message back to you. But in realtime communication, both parties are on the line at the same time, and the conversation flows. ❞

The online dialect has its own phrases, symbols, abbreviations, and other things that set it apart from spoken language. In this section, we'll try to decode some of the things you'll see online.

Fig. 5.1
Make any sense?
Maybe not now, but
read it again when you
finish the chapter.

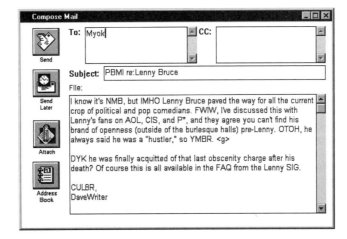

Translating OnlineSpeak to English

Like any slang, the online dialect includes terminology that don't mean anything to "the uninitiated" (that's you). It's like in the old Lenny Bruce routine where a 60s hipster tries to get some "bread" from his new boss. "Bread?" says the puzzled band leader. "You want a sandwich?" In some cases, words that mean one thing in spoken language mean something completely different online. Other times, the online community has come up with brand new words to describe things that just don't happen when you're not "inside" a computer.

Some of the online language comes from a desire to creatively avoid clichés. For example, instead of "looking for information online," or "spending time with friends online," you **surf** or **cruise** or just **hang out**. I used to say I spent time "rock climbing on the Internet," because it was just as plausible as surfing.

As of now, you are a **newbie**. That's someone who is just finding their feet in the online world—like a "greenhorn" or "tenderfoot" in all those old Western cattle-driving movies. "Newbie" is not an insult (usually), so don't take offense when somebody addresses you that way. But by the end of this chapter, you'll be a **cyber-surfer** extraordinare!

The lingo of electronic messages

❝ *Plain English, please!*

When you send a private message, it's called **e-mail**. You can also send public messages to lists or bulletin boards where everyone can read them; these are referred to as **posts**. Both e-mail and posts fall under the broad category of **electronic messages**. **❞**

Electronic mail isn't quite as tight as online chatting. With e-mail, you can spend some time writing complete sentences and using punctuation, and your messages can be of virtually any length. But e-mail isn't just an electronic version of handwriting a letter and mailing it off to Grandma—it's an online phenomenon, so it uses things you wouldn't see in regular letters.

What we'd normally think of as letters are called **messages**, and the good old U. S. Postal Service is called **snailmail**. When someone asks for an **address**, they're usually talking about an e-mail address (your user ID on your online service)—if they want your postal address, they'll ask for your **snailmail address**.

There are special discussion groups called **mailing lists** that operate by e-mail. These are groups of people who share a common interest, like Shetland Sheep dogs or UNIX. When you send an e-mail to one of these mailing lists, the message goes to a computer, which sends a copy of it out to everyone who's subscribed to the list. And, of course, a copy of every message that other people send to the list is mailed to your e-mail box, too.

❝ *Plain English, please!*

Mailing lists go by a lot of other names. You may hear them called **special interest groups** or **SIGs**, **LISTSERVs** (short for List Servers), or just **lists**. **❞**

Smileys and other codes—showing your face around here

Both realtime chatting and e-mail use special ways of indicating facial expressions and other visuals. For example, if you give someone a compliment, they'll likely respond with "<blush>," meaning they're blushing. When you see a word or phrase between asterisks (like <grin> or just <g> for short,

<rolling eyes>, or <puzzled look>), it means the person is trying to show you what they're doing or feeling (these phrases are generically called "actions"). You might also see asterisks instead of the < and > signs.

The online community is traditionally very affectionate, so it's not uncommon for a new acquaintance to give you a *hug* online. Some people use variations on the *hug* theme, like America Online's common practice of

Realtime chat is no place for the grammatically picky

Realtime chatting is a kind of message where the other party is connected and participating at the same moment as you. You type messages back and forth in "real time," hence the name. In realtime chats, people try to get their points across with as little typing as possible (see "Abbreviations," later in this section). This may seem a bit terse, but it's really done in the spirit of keeping the conversation as fluid as possible (and honestly, we're not all lightning-fast typists). Instead of saying, "Hello there, Dave. Glad to see you!," other parties would probably say "Hi, Dave" or "Re Dave" (which means "Regards to Dave").

Messages are also kept brief because most realtime chatting takes place one line-of-text at a time (as opposed to e-mail, which allows longer messages). If you're an English major, prepare to grit your teeth a lot—there's very little proper English (and almost no punctuation) in online chatting (see the figure). Reading an online chat is almost like reading newspaper headlines, in that only the most important words are used. Instead of "Did you happen to see the new version of Word for Windows?", you'd probably say "Seen new WinWord?"

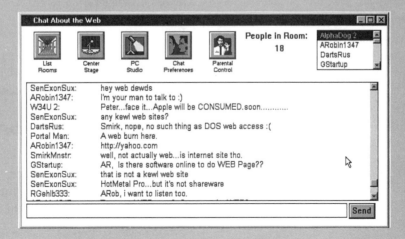

using your name between curly brackets to indicate a hug: {DAVE}. If some-one on America Online really likes you, you might get multiple hugs, like this: {{{{{{DAVE}}}}}}.

Besides the asterisks and descriptions, there's another way people express themselves online: **smileys** (sometimes called **emoticons**). Smileys are like tiny sideways cartoon characters drawn with regular text characters, like this:

:-)

If you tilt your head to the left, you should see a little face smiling at you.

Some people consider smileys to be a concise and charming way of express-ing themselves. Other people despise them, the same way they despise Smurfs and Care Bears. My advice is to start liking (or at least tolerating) smileys now, because they're always going to be a part of online life. People who get annoyed at smileys should throw away their modems now.

Smileys come in all forms, including:

:-(a frowning smiley

:-{0   a mustachioed smiley

8-)   a smiley with glasses (or staring at the screen too long!)

%-)   a tipsy smiley

People use several other variations on the smiley theme, including these:

0\\\\{==========-   a sword or dagger

@}—'—,—   a rose

You'll see smileys with all kinds of headgear, monster smileys, and smileys to represent every kind of emotion, thought, or object. For more smileys, see the Smileys appendix, which is included on the CD that accompanies this book.

Exotic abbreviations you'll see online

To save time and typing, the online community uses some unique abbrevia-tions, most of which mean absolutely nothing until someone explains them to you. For example, would you suspect that "ROTFL" stands for "rolling on the floor, laughing"? If there's a way to abbreviate a common phrase, that's the way you'll see it online. Here are some common abbreviations you'll run into online (if you see something online that isn't in this list, check the glossary that's included on the CD):

Abbreviation	Meaning
P, *P, or P*	Prodigy
AOL	America Online
ASCII	It means "plain text" but technically it stands for the American Standard Code for Information Interchange
BTW	By the way
CI$	CompuServe (a reference to the online charges)
CIS	CompuServe
CU	"See you"
CUL8R	"See you later"
DYK	Do you know
DYN	Did you notice?
FAQ	Frequently Asked Questions (usually refers to a document available in the area)
FWIW	For what it's worth
FYA	For your amusement
FYE	For your entertainment
GDR	Grinning, ducking, and running
IAC	In any case
IAE	In any event
IMHO	In my humble (or "honest") opinion
IMO	In my opinion
IOW	In other words
IDK	I don't know

continues

Abbreviation	Meaning
JIC	Just in case
LOL	Laughing out loud
NMB	Not my business
NOMB	None of my business
OTOH	On the other hand
PITA	Pain in the *derriere*
PMBI	Pardon my butting in
PMJI	Pardon my jumping in
SIG	a special interest group or a signature file (see "Signatures and taglines" later in the chapter)
TIA	Thanks in advance
TTFN	Ta-ta for now
YMBR	You may be right

The same keystroke-saving philosophy shortens many company and product names, so you'll sometimes see Microsoft referred to as "MSoft" or "MS," and WordPerfect as "WP" (sometimes with a version number, like "WP6").

You'll occasionally find a BBS or online service that has made up its own regional slang. There, your best hope is to find a friendly native and ask what the heck it all means.

The media's favorite words aren't really OnlineSpeak

By now, you've probably seen the term **Information Superhighway** used to describe everything from the Internet to automatic teller machines to magazines to radio talk show hosts. In the online world, the term is used in a sort of tongue-in-cheek way, like, "What do you expect? After all, this is *The Information Superhighway*." The implied attitude is the same one people used to use when they said things like, "Boy, I'm sure glad this is a *kinder, gentler nation.*" You also can expect one or two twists on the term "Information Superhighway," like MTV's "SuperInfoEasyWay," and Al Franken's "Infotainment Superhighway," but not as much lately since the phrase has been so dramatically over-used.

Virtual is still in wide use online, even though it is also over-used in the press. In OnlineSpeak, virtual means "a simulated version created by the computer." For instance, **virtual reality** isn't reality, but a computer generated version of it. You'll see people talking about visiting "virtual environments" or sending each other "virtual cups of coffee." By the way, there's an emoticon for that, and you don't even have to turn your head sideways:

Cl_l

Another favorite coined prefix of those unfortunate newsies who cover the mystical online world is **cyber** (which means "technology" or "computer"). Modem users are **cybernauts** or **cyber-surfers**, people who become romantic with other modem users are in **cyberlove**, and if you buy something online with a credit card, they call it **cybercash**. You may see a little of this cyber- prefixing online, but don't expect much.

Signatures and taglines

At the end of your letters, you sign your name, right? Some people also draw flowers or cartoons or add an interesting quote or phrase to give the letter a more personal touch. People naturally want the same personal touch in their electronic messages, but you can't really add a flourishing pen stroke to the bottom of most electronic communication. To compensate, people use signatures (sigs) and taglines.

❝ *Plain English, please!*

Don't confuse **sigs** (short for "signatures") with SIGs (special interest groups). Context is the only real way to tell which phrase is being abbreviated. ❞

An online signature is a collection of a few lines of text that your mail reader or online service software automatically adds to the bottom of each message you send out. (Not all online services offer this feature.) Signatures are usually stored in small files on the online service, so you'll sometimes see signatures referred to as "sig files" or just "sigs." Most people simply put their name and online address in their sig, but some customize their sigs in any number of ways. The most common thing you'll find in a sig is one or more notable quotes, but you'll also see some with elaborate frames, advertisements, and/or text pictures. Some samples are shown in figure 5.2.

 TIP If you customize your signature file, keep it short (see "Using long signature files or taglines," later in the chapter) and remember it goes out on *every* mail message you send. Avoid using private jokes or off-color humor. Even if you think you'll only send messages to your friends, Murphy's Law of Signature Files says that you'll remember your embarrassing sig just after you've sent a message to your mom, your boss, or your church's volleyball team.

Fig. 5.2
Here are a couple of simple signatures that took only a few minutes to build.

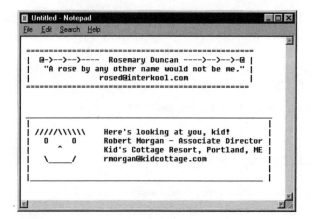

Taglines are like sigs, but they are usually one-line jokes tacked on to the end of a message after the author's signature. Some people have huge collections of taglines, and some e-mail software is able to pick a random tagline from a collection before it sends out a message.

 CAUTION Some online jokesters put mean-spirited tricks in their signature files, like "Press Ctrl+Alt+Delete to view the attached picture" (this one restarts your computer). Always assume computer advice from a sig (no matter how tempting the advice may look) is bad advice, and ignore it.

The strange customs of the common online world

In addition to learning a new language, you'll need to adopt a few local customs when you visit the online community. Don't be too surprised at anything you see—in this virtual world, almost anything is possible.

In this section, you'll get a glimpse at some of what sets the online community apart from your physical neighborhood, and some of the things you can do to ensure smoother sailing for yourself and your online neighbors.

The online community stretches over state and national boundaries, into every kind of belief system on the planet. It is the ultimate melting pot, and people co-exist surprisingly well without a lot of "authorities" to keep the peace. Part of the reason people get along online is that it's so different from the "real" world (whatever real world one happens to live in).

Living incognito: Assumed names and personalities

If you were to envision the online community as a party, it'd definitely be a costume party. You see, online, nobody knows what you look like, where you live, what kind of family you have, or what kind of car you drive. All they know is what you tell them. Many people use this unique feature of the online community to create alternate images of themselves, which they present to people they meet online. (This is easier to pull off on some online services than on others. It's very easy on America Online and Prodigy, for instance, but more difficult on CompuServe or in UseNet newsgroups.)

Before you jump to conclusions, very few of the people who use false names (**handles**) and made-up profiles are insecure or malicious. Most (like my friend "The Batman") make up hugely overblown or comical "selves" just to have fun. Some use alternate personalities to harmlessly pretend they're more like who they want to be—their hero or a more romantic image of themselves.

Like any party, though, the online community has a few folks who might try to make you believe they're something they're not for more sinister reasons. As long as you keep your eyes open, though (by not giving out your phone number, address, credit card numbers, etc.), you shouldn't run into too much trouble with online posers.

TIP **Because you can be anonymous and no one can trace you, people** often become more bold with their propositioning of potential romantic partners than they would face-to-face. If your online name sounds female, expect to get hit on a lot, especially in socially-oriented chat areas. Many women online choose gender-neutral aliases, and decline to indicate a sex on any online profiles they fill out. This cuts down on the unwanted attention.

Falling in love online

You've heard about this, haven't you? If you've followed a magazine, newspaper, or a talk show in the past two years, you've probably run across a feature about online romance. It's not a myth, but it's surrounded by a lot of small myths. As one who is, well, experienced in this field, I'll try to give you the straight dope on online romance.

The online community is filled with places to meet people who share your interests (see Chapter 17, "Finding Like-Minded Users"). You can join special interest group mailing lists where dozens—even hundreds—of people exchange mail about specific topics. There also are a huge number of bulletin board systems and online services that allow realtime chatting between users. You're bound to find interesting people to chat and correspond with. Just like in the real world, you'll develop friendships with the people you associate with online, and you're just as likely to find people with whom you share an attraction. That's where things get a bit tricky.

Since the online community is so huge, you may find yourself attracted to someone on the opposite end of the continent or the other side of the world. Even if you're *only* a few hundred miles apart, you're not going to be able to carry on the "traditional" dating process.

Some couples correspond one or more times a day for months or even years before they meet for the first time. Traditionally (if online romance can be said to have traditions), pictures and phone numbers are exchanged early in the process, so the romance isn't purely "virtual."

The "success rate" for online romances is probably about as good (or bad) as that of any other type of relationship. I know of at least a dozen happily married couples who met over the modem, and almost every online friend I have has been involved in some sort of online relationship.

You'll hear horror stories about online romance (people often overlook the fact that you hear just as many horror stories about every other type of romance), and some are true. To avoid problems, you just have to remember that all is fair in love, and the rules don't change online. Online, people run into the same kinds of pickup lines, little white lies ("I own this bar, y'know"), and other tactics of the conquest game as they do in the real world.

Safe cybersex—how to avoid getting burned

Cybersex is one of those all-inclusive words. It means any kind of romantic encounter online. It can be as sweet and innocent as two people meeting and falling in love through e-mail, or as nasty as an x-rated realtime chat with a stranger. (No, I'm not making this up!) Sometimes it's softened as "cyber-romance" or "cyberlove."

Meeting new people and getting to know them (in whatever way you go for) can be exciting, but it's not without pitfalls. Here are a few things to watch out for:

- Don't assume that *anything* someone tells you about themselves is true. Someone who claims to be an 18-year-old blonde lingerie model could really be a rotund, balding, middle-aged businessman.

- Don't give your real name, address, or phone number to anyone, no matter how safe they sound, until you've established a firm friendship over several weeks (at least). Never give these details out the first time you chat with someone!

- Don't send anyone money, credit card numbers, calling card numbers, etc. Don't *ever* kid yourself into making an exception!

- Don't lead the other person on. If you're not available for a real-life commitment, don't pretend to be.

- If you're trying to be anonymous, and doing things you don't want everyone in your life to know about, don't give clues about your personal life that could be used to identify or find you, such as your last name, workplace, and position.

- Ask questions early, to make sure the person you're talking to is really a legal adult, the right gender, and reasonably sane.

- Ask around in chat rooms about the reputation of someone you are unsure about.

- Get a post office box for a mailing address if you're planning to give out your address on a regular basis.

- Trust your instincts. Don't continue if you have a bad feeling about someone.

And they run into the same kinds of sincere, interesting people online as they do in the real world. There's virtually no difference beyond the fact that in the real world a 98-pound weakling can't convincingly claim to be a 300-pound linebacker.

Things you don't want to do!

Remember that when you first join the online community, you're expected to stumble around a little before you get totally used to the place. Newbie mistakes are usually tolerated by the other online folks as long as you're polite and honest.

> ❝ *Plain English, please!*
>
> You may run into the term "netiquette." It's just what it sounds like: Internet etiquette, another word for online good manners. ❞

Some things are so common, though, that if you try them, you're sure to push somebody over the edge of their tolerance level. Here are ten things that will bring the wrath of the veteran users down on you, but if you're careful to avoid these classic mistakes, you'll do fine.

1: SHOUTING

Typing in all capital letters is called **shouting**, because people use all caps online to emphasize words. For example, someone might write, "I can't believe you FELL for that!" to make it look as if they're shouting the word "FELL." Some new users type their messages in all caps (HI, MY NAME IS DAVE AND I'M NEW. HELP, PLEASE.), which, in context, makes them look as if they're shouting their entire message. If you make this blunder, expect return messages saying, "Please don't shout anymore. It hurts my eyes."

2: Flaming

One of the least-cherished traditions of electronic dialogue is **flaming**. A flame is a message that is rude, angry, or mean, and usually unreasonable. There is a certain anonymity to being online, and people are more willing to be cruel when they don't have to face their victims directly. Flames are often sparked by a message that takes a stand on an emotional issue. Easily excited people see these messages and decide they'll verbally slap some sense into the people with whom they disagree. The other main causes of flames are other flames (which lead to **flame wars**). Don't get caught in this trap.

If you disagree with someone, take some time to think and cool off before you respond. Remember that the other person is a person just like you, and imagine what you'd do if you were face-to-face instead of on the other end of an anonymous keyboard.

3: Playing "little lost child" in public places

Many places online are like libraries—full of information, and constantly in use by people who want to find and share that information. If you've never used a library before, you certainly don't walk to the center of the stacks and start shouting, "I NEED HELP! SOMEBODY HELP ME! HOW DO I FIND A BOOK ON POODLE SHAVING?!" Yet new users often go into public places online and demand that somebody help them figure out how to get or use the information.

If you need help, don't send a message to everybody. If you're using an online service, they have people who can help you. On the Internet, most public places have files called **FAQs** (Frequently Asked Questions) that answer all the questions most new users ask. If you can't figure anything out, just watch for awhile, without posting (this is called **lurking**).lurking

Later, if you're still clueless, you might try writing a private note to someone who's participating in the area where you need help. Ask them if they know who could help you, or if there is a help file available to answer your questions. People in the online community almost always respond to personal mail, so you're bound to, at least, get pointed in the right direction.

4: Bugging the big cheeses

Just as you wouldn't stand in the library shouting for help, you wouldn't go straight to the chairperson of the library's board of directors for help. A common mistake new users make is to demand help from people who are in charge of online services (most notably BBS operators) before trying other options.

Read the online system's policies regarding support. You'll probably find a way to get help without bugging the management.

5: Sending big messages and/or files to everybody

It's only natural to want to share neat discoveries (new programs or games, interesting pictures, etc.) with other people who share your interests, but it's dangerous to expect that a large group of people is interested in your discovery. While you might think those people could just ignore your message, some people have to pay for each message they receive—whether they want it or not—and they usually pay a lot more for larger messages.

If you want to share a large file with a group of people, send a message to the group saying, "Anyone who wants this file, e-mail me and I'll send it to you." Or, if there is a commonly accessible file area or library, you could upload it there and then post a message saying it's available.

6: Using long signature files or taglines

When your recipients are paying by the size of incoming messages, they'll be very upset if they receive a one-line message like "Hi, just wanted to say Hi," with a ten-line signature file listing all the lyrics to your favorite song. Some people go overboard with their signatures, and it's not only visually annoying, it's needlessly expensive for some recipients.

Try to keep your signature to one or two lines, certainly no more than three or four. There's also nothing wrong with just signing your name and foregoing a sig file.

7: Abusing your privileges

Most bulletin board systems (BBSs) are not profitable; they're run by people who just enjoy the online community and want to continue to support it. Some BBS operators are very lax with their policies, trusting that the users won't take advantage of them. For example, some BBS operators don't have a mandatory charge for long distance e-mail, even though they have to pay for the phone calls (in most cases, they expect the people who use long distance e-mail to voluntarily contribute something). Some users only look at the selfish side of these policies ("Wow! Free e-mail to my buddy in Canada!") without considering the consequences. BBSs shut down all the time because the operators' expenses grow too quickly, and phone bills are among the biggest causes.

Be considerate of the system operator. If you're using a service, pay for it, or you could blow it for yourself and all the other users.

8: Advertising without permission

Most of the people who make this mistake use the Internet, but some use other services. It's always a mistake, and on commercial services (like CompuServe or America Online) can lead to expensive consequences.

The Internet is a "free" service (although you may have to pay a nominal fee to your service provider), used by people throughout the world and kept up by companies and governments who have an interest in worldwide communication. As an individual user, you can literally reach millions of people with a few well-placed messages in newsgroups and mailing lists. As stated in its cooperative charter, advertising is not an acceptable use of the Internet.

Some users, however, take advantage of the fact that there is no single "home office" on the Internet to skirt this policy, advertising without fear that they'll be sued or fined. This not only annoys the users (who have a large interest in keeping the Internet from becoming a commercial endeavor) but also needlessly adds to the cost of operating the Internet (some of which comes out of our pockets in the form of tax dollars). If your service provider or online service gets too many complaints about your behavior, they might take your Internet privileges away or cancel your account completely.

If you're going to advertise, advertise in one of the clearly marked advertising areas, such as the "for sale" UseNet groups or the classified ads section of an online service. Or, contact the advertising department of the online service or Internet site and ask about buying advertising space.

9: Straying too far from a topic

Special interest groups (SIGs) on online services are usually dedicated to specific topics, though conversation can range to areas only marginally related to the focus of the group. For example, in a bass fishing special interest group, you might discuss the history of a good bass fishing lake or possibly a marlin fishing trip you took, because they'd probably be of interest to the other folks in the group. If you throw out a message about no-till farming, you'll probably miss the mark with most of the readers. As with some of the other mistakes in this list, this mistake can cost people money (some people have to pay to receive messages), which tends to make folks angry.

TIP **To promote online harmony, make sure all your messages relate** to the topics people want to discuss in each special interest group.

10: Trying to save a group from itself

Newbies often stumble into special interest groups with preconceived notions of what they'll find. Some groups, however, have been around so long that they've become little communities of friends, drifting steadily away from their original charter but maintaining a healthy following.

For example, a group originally founded to talk about stereo speakers may have evolved into a group that discusses classical music. When new users find a "drifted" group, they often send out messages to the group, pointing out the fact that they're not following their charter, or problems with the attitudes people use in their messages. These people fail to consider that the people who loyally follow these groups (the real members) often cherish the dynamics of their groups, even if they don't make sense to the outside world. This mistake usually ends up bruising a lot of egos, causing a lot of flaming, and accomplishing nothing.

If a group doesn't suit your needs, leave quietly. Start your own group if you have to, but don't try to re-shape an existing group that doesn't want to change.

6

Online Pitfalls, Real and Imagined

● In this chapter:

- Should I believe the media's online horror stories?

- How do I avoid viruses?

- Who are the shady characters who hang out online?

- I've got a friend who now spends almost all her time online...it's creepy

- What does all this really cost?

- My kids want to go online

Would you give your credit card to somebody you just met on the street? Hopefully not, but you'd be surprised how many people make that mistake online . . . . **>**

T he online world scares a lot of people, but like most of the things we fear, the reality isn't nearly as spooky as the unknown. In this chapter, you see some of the online world's dark corners and learn how to avoid trouble in this new place.

The online world is similar to a busy metropolis. If you've visited a huge city like New York or Los Angeles, you probably heard some horror stories from friends before you went about the horrible crimes and obscenities you would encounter. When you actually got to the city, however, you found that those gloom-and-doom experiences were the exception, not the rule. You found that the natives weren't all lined up to take advantage of visitors—they were mostly just people like you.

But whether you're talking about the online world or a big city, remember this: There must be some reason millions of people choose to spend a good portion of their lives there, and if you go in with your eyes open, you're likely to find that reason.

Truth and (occasional) lies from the media

It seems like everyone's interested in online communications these days, so it shows up in the media a lot. Until recently, the online world was such a new and unfamiliar beast, the media has scrambled to produce stories about it without necessarily knowing which way to point the cameras. And because they haven't known enough about the technology to offer a real in-depth report, many news sources have resorted to "shock journalism"—preying on people's fears of the unknown. That's why much of what you hear on the news (at least about the online world) is either false or grotesquely over-blown.

Lately, however, the media (especially in the television networks and larger newspapers) has been getting better at fairly covering the online world as they gain more experience with it—and as more and more people on this side of the tube know when they're bluffing.

For example, I saw a television report on a local station a few months ago that said, "Files from computer bulletin boards often contain viruses that can destroy all the data on your disk, so to be safe, make sure you buy all your software in the store instead of getting it from BBSs." To an experienced bulletin board user, that statement is about as true as this one: "Milk is often sour and dangerous, so don't drink it." Is it true that milk gets sour some-times? Well, yes, if you keep it too long or don't store it properly. Is that a good reason to avoid milk? Definitely not—you just need to know what to watch out for and how to stay safe.

So how do you know what to believe in the news? Either ask experienced people you trust or (better yet) see things first-hand. As you gain experience online, you'll be able to tell what's true and what's just a good headline.

The real (but exaggerated) threat of viruses

In the health world, viruses are infections that attack living cells. In the computer world, viruses are tiny programs designed to hide in the system files of disks and programs. When the infected disks or programs are passed from one user to another, the viruses infect the new user's disks and pro-grams, and so on.

 Plain English, please!

A computer **virus** is a tiny and sometimes destructive program that weasels its way into other programs and onto unprotected diskettes. When you run the program that it's attached to, it does its mischief, which can be file destruction, disk corruption, or just filling up all the unused space.

Computer viruses are often dormant for months or years (specifically so they can be passed around without detection), only doing real damage on special occasions like Friday the 13th, anniversaries of famous acts of terrorism, and historic birthdays. One of the biggest computer news stories a few years ago was a virus called Michelangelo, which destroyed all kinds of data on the famous artist's birthday, as a sort of twisted memorial.

When viruses do finally "go off," their effect may be anything from benign taunting (you might see a message on your screen that says, "Your computer is a loser. Buy a different one.") to total destruction of the data on your disk. Some viruses have clever little animations (trains running across the bottom of the screen, letters falling off the screen, etc.) that run while they're de-stroying your data.

Computers get viruses two ways:

- By running programs that are infected

- By starting your computer from a disk that is infected

The first method is where BBSs sometimes come in. If you get an infected program from a BBS and then run it on your computer, it infects your disk and usually any floppy disk you use in the machine after that. If you follow a few simple guidelines, however, you can virtually eliminate the risk of virus infection:

- **Get a virus detection and cleaning program.** These programs are designed to sniff out viruses and "cure" them before they do any damage. Versions 6.0 and above of PC-DOS and MS-DOS include virus cleaners, and companies like Central Point, Symantec, and McAffee Associates all make excellent virus cleaning programs.

- **Keep your virus cleaner updated.** New viruses spring up all the time, so virus cleaning programs are constantly being updated—sometimes as often as every few weeks. Find out from the manufacturer where you can call to get periodic updates (you can usually do this through your modem, and updates are usually free or inexpensive), and check in at least once a quarter if not more frequently.

- **Always use the virus cleaner on new programs before you use them.** If you get a program from a BBS, it can't do any harm until you actually run it. Before you run it even once, have the virus cleaner check it out.

- **Use ASP-approved BBSs whenever possible.** The Association of Shareware Professionals (ASP) is an organization that works to keep the software you get through BBSs reliable and safe. If a BBS meets special, strict criteria (including virus cleaning all programs before they're made available to callers), they can become ASP-approved. If the BBS is ASP-approved, it'll tell you when you first connect—the people who run ASP-approved BBSs are usually happy to advertise the fact, as it makes their users breathe easier.

- **Avoid "New Uploads" and especially "Untested" areas.** BBSs almost always let their users send in files for other users to download. Some BBSs (even ones that normally use virus cleaners on their files) put the incoming files into an area marked "Untested," "Not Scanned," or "Incoming Files," allowing users to download these files before they've been checked out by the BBS's staff. Don't download any of these files. Stick with the areas that have already been cleaned.

If you run a virus checker and find out that you have a virus, the checking program should be able to clean it (remove the virus) for you. If not, contact the company that makes the program for more help.

Avoiding potentially harmful users

The online world has something like 30 million users from the United States alone. If you put that many people in one community, you're bound to find a few unscrupulous folks. Sometime in your time online, you'll probably run into a shady character or two, just as you've probably run into a few at the grocery store or the post office. Thankfully, they're easier to deal with (and avoid) online.

Scams

You have a mailbox in the physical world, right? If it's like mine, it's usually crammed with flyers proclaiming exciting new ways you can become extremely rich without lifting a finger. Sometimes it's pyramid schemes, sometimes chain letters, envelope-stuffing, or "ground floor" investments. This is the true junk of junk mail, and (if you've been around a while) it goes straight into the trash unread.

Some of the same deceitful people who originate these letters in the mail have taken their business high-tech, pestering people online with the same kinds of useless money-making advice. Just because they're sending electronic mail to an online mailbox, that doesn't mean it's not junk mail. All you have to do to avoid this online menace is delete the messages—it's even easier than tossing real junk mail in the trash.

 TIP **If you get unwanted junkmail on an online service, you may be** able to stop it by notifying the management. There are rules against such advertising on most services, and, potentially, the sender can have his or her membership revoked.

Hackers, crackers, and phreaks, oh my!

The people who fall into these categories are also scammers, but their scams are more technical. The terms **hacker**, **cracker**, and **phreak** have specific meanings within the online community:

Hacker   Someone who obsesses. "Computer hackers," for example, write computer programs all the time or (in some cases) try to work around computer security barriers. "Astronomy hackers" are obsessed with the stars. Most people won't identify themselves as a hacker in any sense, and if they do, they're probably just trying to show off. "Hacker" is not necessarily a bad thing.

Cracker   Someone who tries to get around security barriers in computer systems or copy protection in software. There is no good connotation to "cracker," so people almost never identify themselves as such. Sometimes this definition is also applied to "hacker."

Phreak   Someone who tries to get around security barriers in telephone systems, or otherwise steals telephone services.

When you venture into the online world for the first time, you'll probably meet a few of these folks, but you won't know it, just as you don't know how many embezzlers and car thieves you pass on the freeway every day. If you *do* run into someone who makes suspicious claims (like they can get you into prohibited systems, get you free software, or save you a lot of money on telephone service), treat them just like you would treat someone who offered you a $20 Rolex on the street—say "No, thanks" and get on with your business.

Charming rip-off artists

The more dangerous folks to you, of course, are the ones who are out to get the unsuspecting consumer. These folks can be extremely persuasive and charming liars. They use confidence tricks to get you to (unwittingly) give them information they can use to rip you off. For example, someone might say, "I'm from the online service. We're checking out your account and we need your password." They might tell you they need your Social Security number, a credit card number, or your home phone number, for any number of seemingly plausible reasons.

 CAUTION **I can't emphasize this enough:**

Never give your password, credit card number, or telephone number to anyone you meet online! A true representative of an online service will never ask for any of these things—those items are already on file in the online service's computer! The only times you should use your credit card online are to make purchases from bona fide online stores (not individual users claiming to represent stores) and in the initial sign-on for online services (they charge the monthly bill to your card).

You're in control of this information, so if you keep it to yourself, you won't have any worries. If someone approaches you with a suspicious request, contact the online service management immediately.

Pirates

Pirates steal software. People who do this often claim that since it's so easy to copy software onto a floppy disk, it shouldn't be a crime. This argument is like saying, "It's so easy to swipe an orange, it shouldn't be a crime." The people who own the oranges (and the software) rightly think the thieves are incorrect.

One of the problems is that some people become pirates without knowing it. For example, if a pirate puts a copyrighted game on a BBS, you might download the game and use it without knowing it was pirated. If you send the game to another BBS, you're pirating it. In fact, just by using pirated software, you're violating the law. Pirating software is a felony, and software companies are serious about prosecuting pirates.

The software you get legally from BBSs and online services is shareware or public domain software, and is almost always clearly labeled as such. Look for a file called README or one with a DOC or TXT extension (for example, if you get a program called CARDS.ZIP, it will probably include a file called CARDS.TXT or CARDS.DOC), which will be able to tell you if the program is shareware or public domain, and how to register it and pass it on to your favorite BBS legally.

Plain English, please!

Shareware is software you can try for free, then pay for if you decide to keep it, much like test–driving a car. There's also such a thing as **freeware**, which is software that's truly free—you don't have to pay anyone, ever. **Public domain** software, a third kind, is like freeware except you can take more liberties with it—with public domain, you're allowed to use it commercially and make changes to it.

Some big-time software publishers produce special "demo" versions of their software , and distribute them free through BBSs and online services to tempt you to buy the full product. (You might hear these demo versions refereed to as "lite" or "crippled" versions of their full-powered cousins.) It's perfectly legal to download and distribute these. You also can legally get some commercial software from online services, but the software's purchase price is automatically billed to your account or credit card.

If you suspect you've gotten some pirated software, you can check with the Software Publishers Association. They can help you get the software legally and make sure you stay out of trouble. They use tips from people like you to catch the people who really hurt the industry—hard-core pirates who sell and distribute pirated software.

 TIP   **Call the Software Publishers Association (SPA) at (202) 452-1600** for safety tips.

Online abuse and harassment

One of the clearest double-edged swords of the online world is the level of anonymity. You can come and go unnoticed if you want, or you can even pretend to be something you're not. The positive side of this anonymity is that it gives many people the confidence to interact with folks they'd never meet in the real world. The down side is that people sometimes lose track of how their actions affect real people on the other end of the wires.

The most common form of online harassment is **flaming**, which is sending insulting (and usually obnoxious) e-mail messages. The rule with flaming is: Ignore it. If you get caught up in an insulting exchange (a **flame war**), especially in a public forum where other people can read your messages, you'll just look bad and get upset. I've seen (and been involved in) more than my share of flame wars, and I've never known one to end on a friendly note.

If you prefer not to watch a flame war or receive messages from a particular user, you can use an Ignore function on most online services. This feature blocks out all messages from specific users. Check with the management of your online service or BBS to learn how to block out the abusive types.

The step beyond flaming is online harassment (sometimes called online abuse), where the nasty words turn into genuine threats. If you run into this sort of thing, first consider the source. If the antagonist is 2,000 miles away and they've threatened to come toilet paper your trees, you're probably looking at an empty threat that should be ignored. If, however, they are nearby and you have any genuine fear, you should take action right away.

If the problem is manageable, contact the system administrator of the other person's online service. They'll probably warn the harasser that if they don't stop, their access will be taken away. For example, if you use GEnie and you're being harassed by someone from a BBS, contact the BBS's system operator. If the other person uses a major online service, call the service's customer service department and see what action can be taken. If the matter is very serious, call the police. You've probably seen a few of the recent cases of people being jailed for online harassment and threats—in the eyes of the law, electronic harassment is just like phone harassment or any other kind of harassment.

Online addiction

You may have heard the term **online junkie**, referring to a person who spends an inordinate amount of time online. Most people don't consider this danger of the online world when they start out, but it's very real and can become very serious.

Online junkies (also called **online addicts** or **cyberjunkies**) aren't usually people who do research online—that would be like being addicted to a library, which is relatively rare—they're usually the ones who use the social features of their online services—especially realtime chat. As you meet people in this virtual space, you'll develop acquaintances, friendships, and possibly even romances, just like you could at the local tavern. If you find a group of people you enjoy hanging out with online, you might call the BBS or online service for an hour or two after work—again, it's a lot like a bar, where some people go to happy hour with their friends after work.

The problem shows up when socializing online takes up a disproportionate amount of your time, and it happens to more modem users than you'd probably imagine. Like any other addiction, online addiction can lead to problems with your family, finances (especially if you use an online service with an hourly charge), and your ability to cope with the world outside the addiction. It's also a hard habit to kick, because kicking means you have to spend less time with people you've become attached to.

So how do you avoid online addiction? Pace yourself. If you've just dug up fifteen new local BBS numbers, try two or three a day instead of all fifteen at once. If you become a "regular" on an online service, give yourself a specific amount of online time each day (maybe every other day), and don't be embarrassed to set an alarm clock to remind you when the time's up—when you're socializing online, you lose track of time very easily.

You play, you pay—there's always a charge

This is the online pitfall that most people realize too late: the meter's always running while you're online. Online services usually cost from $4 to $10 per hour to use, though most online services allow you a few free hours every month (five to ten, usually). Most people think they'll be able to stay within the free period every month, but it's not as easy as it looks. Once you start using electronic mail every day, downloading a few files now and then, and maybe attending some online conferences, you'll eat up that free time in the first week.

The first month's bill from an online service is usually pretty reasonable, because new members usually get extra free hours so you can get acquainted with the service (or get hooked, some might argue). The second month (when the regular rates kick in) is when you'll start to feel the impact in your checking account.

To get a feel for the online world without having to mortgage your house, try these tactics:

- **Seek out some cheaper alternatives**. Some local BBSs charge once a year (usually from $25 to $100), and you'll probably be able to get shareware, play games, use electronic mail, and chat with other users from your area.

- **Get the fastest modem you can afford**. It'll pay for itself in a few months if you're paying hourly rates to an online service. Most services do not charge any more to connect at a higher rate (although a few do), so a faster connection is nearly always a better value.

- **Use *offline programs* whenever possible**. These programs make your online time as short as possible by grabbing all your incoming e-mail at once, putting it on your disk, then logging off the online service. You can then read your messages and compose replies while you're *offline*, saving you a considerable amount of money, especially if you call long distance.

- **Use your software's logging features** when you use articles, stories, and other text-oriented features. Then, rather than reading them online (while the meter is running), you can read them offline at your leisure.

66 *Plain English, please!*

> **Logging** means keeping a text-file transcript of whatever text shows up on your screen. You can read this disk file (usually called a **log file**) after you log off. 99

- **Shop around for the best deal**. There are lots of online services out there (especially BBSs and Internet services), and you can find some with incredibly reasonable rates.

When your kids want to go online— what's a parent to do?

It's going to happen—I promise. When you start cruising around online, your kids (assuming they aren't the ones who showed you how to do it) will want to try it, too. I'm not about to tell you what you should let your kids do, I can only offer a few suggestions on approaches you might want to take in dealing with this inevitability. Just as you help your kids decide what kind of television, movies, and music to consume, you'll have to decide which parts of the online world are suited for your family.

For young kids (where you'll probably be logging on and doing most of the typing), your best bets are family-oriented online services. America Online, Prodigy, and most of the other major services have "Kids Only" areas, where they can play games, exchange mail with pen pals, and not get into too much trouble. As a general rule, BBSs are not suited to younger kids, though there are a few exceptions.

When they're old enough to log on and type by themselves, local BBSs can give children the opportunity to get software, play games, and chat with other kids in the area. Before you give your child an account on a BBS, though, make sure the service is suitable for her or him. Some BBSs are very technical and some are very intellectual, neither of which would hold the interest of a youngster for long. Though many BBSs contain adult material, this shouldn't be a major concern—all reputable BBSs with adult material keep that material in areas that can only be accessed with special permission from the system operator, and you always have to present proof of age to get that permission.

TIP **Prodigy is one of the best services for families because they cater** specifically to concerned parents. Each child can have his or her own ID, and the parent can block out certain features selectively for each ID. That way you can assign different online privileges to each child, if you like.

If your children are old enough to drive and write research papers for school, your main concern will probably be cost rather than inappropriate material. If they want to use an online service for schoolwork and entertainment, you might want to set them up with their own User ID and password on your online account. This lets you know how much time they spend online each month and enables them to connect to the online service when you're not available to log them on.

Some other commonsense tips:

- Don't let the babysitter log onto your online service

- Remind your kids to always log off before they leave the computer—even if they'll only be gone for a minute.

- Give each child a monthly "budget" for the number of hours he or she can spend online. This is great "real world" training as well as a cost-containment measure!

Part II: Making the Call

Where You Can Call

● **In this chapter:**

- **Which online option fits your needs best?**

- **What separates one online service from another?**

- **Quick overviews of CompuServe, America Online, Prodigy, Delphi, the ImagiNation Network, The Microsoft Network, and the Internet**

- **Where small BBSs score over the Big Guns**

Asking which online option is the best is like asking which color of paint is the best—it depends on what you like and how you're going to use it, not what anybody else thinks . . . . . ➤

You probably know the old joke about opinions being like noses—everybody's got one. If you've asked around about online services, you've probably heard some very strong (and conflicting) opinions as to which one is best. I'll tell you up-front that there isn't a best online service. Though we'd probably have an easier time of it if we could always point to a *best* one (best car, best computer, best cereal), the world doesn't work that way.

This chapter and other chapters in Part II of the book are dedicated to CompuServe, America Online, Prodigy, the Microsoft Network, the Internet, and BBSs. However Chapters 8-14 are for people who know which services they want to use, or people who already use those services. This chapter helps you sort through the opinions and propaganda to find the online options that work best for you.

What makes a good fit for you?

Deciding which online service(s) to use is a major purchasing decision, so you should treat it like one. You'll probably be paying $10 to $50 or more a month to a service, after your initial introductory free period, so make sure you're getting something that meets your needs and wants at a price you can handle.

First off, decide what you need from an online service. Some of the most common answers (in no particular order) are:

- Software

- Electronic mail

- An easy-to-use interface

- Technical support for software or hardware

- Games

- Internet access

- Reference information

- Stock and other financial information

- A place to meet new people

- A place for family activities, including children's education

- Information resources for special interests and hobbies

Now here's the tough part—you can get most of these things on America Online, CompuServe, the Microsoft Network, the Internet, Prodigy, and some BBSs, among others.

As much as these services try to be all things to all modem users, though, each has their own strong suits. Just as you could use a new Mercedes-Benz sedan for just about all of your vehicular needs (fetching groceries, commuting to work, going out for a night on the town, hauling garbage, and maybe rambling along back roads for hunting), you probably wouldn't buy one if your main need was garbage hauling—you could hopefully get something more suited to the job for less money.

The table below lists some common modem uses and shows which online services are stronger in those areas. The rulings here are not statistical, they're more like conventional wisdom in the online community—and I'd be surprised if everyone agreed with them. To beat the car analogy a little further, *conventional wisdom* tells you a Ferrari is faster on the highway than a 3/4 ton pickup, but somebody could probably prove that wrong with a slow Ferrari and a fast pickup.

Conventional wisdom on online services

What you need	Which service(s) to look at first
Software	CompuServe
Electronic mail	Whatever's cheapest
Easy-to-use interface	America Online
Technical support	CompuServe, America Online
Games	The ImagiNation Network
Internet access	The Internet, America Online, Prodigy, The Microsoft Network, CompuServe
Reference information	The Internet, CompuServe
Stock and financial information	Prodigy

continues

What you need	Which service(s) to look at first
Place to meet new people	America Online, Prodigy, The Internet, CompuServe
Family activities	Prodigy, America Online
Special interests and hobbies	The Internet, CompuServe
Windows 95 compatibility	The Microsoft Network

We could just as well have given this table three columns: *What you need*, *Which online service to look at for a tight budget*, and *Which to look at for a really tight budget*. The third column would say the same thing every time, though: local BBS. If you live in or near a metro area, you can find local BBSs to meet all of the needs just listed (with the possible exception of fresh stock quotes—and if you're on a *really* tight budget, you probably won't need them anyway).

Which online service is your best bet?

One of the problems in choosing a major online service is that they're so similar in their offerings—but that doesn't necessarily stop them from advertising features as if they're unique. If you saw a proclamation like "Our service has Internet e-mail!," you'd probably think that was something to crow about. In the online market, however, the big services all have Internet e-mail. When one announces a new feature (as Prodigy did in early '95 with their World Wide Web access), the others introduce the same feature within a few months—sometimes weeks.

The Best Internet Access?

If you want only Internet access (not the other online service features), an Internet service provider is your best bet. For instance, my Internet provider offers me 120 hours of Internet usage for $15 a month. That's a lot more economical than the per-hour charge for using the Internet through an online service.

However, if you're interested in the Internet in a more casual way, you may prefer to try it first through an online service. Most online services offer Internet access for the same hourly rate as their other services, sometimes with a few free hours a month just for Internet use. It may not be complete access to all Internet features, but casual users will probably not mind.

There's an exception to every rule, of course. A notable exception to the "all online services offer pretty much the same thing" rule is the ImagiNation Network. They don't offer much in the way of files, Internet services, or financial information—they specialize in graphical online gaming to a degree not yet reached by other services. By doing this one thing so well rather than trying to be all things to all people, they're managing to carve out a niche in a me-too market.

Here are some things you can count on from all major mainstream online services:

- **Internet e-mail**: that is, the capability to send e-mail to anyone on any online service, or the Internet, anywhere in the world

- **Extensive shareware and freeware libraries** (except for Prodigy, which offers this only through ZiffNet, an extra-charge feature)

- **A large "mall" area** with online stores that sell just about anything you can think of

- **Travel services** that can help you reserve flights and hotels

- **News, weather, and sports** reports

- **Realtime chatting**

- **Technical support** for most major pieces of hardware and software (as well as plenty of the lesser-known products)

- **Special interest** discussion groups

The real differences between the services aren't in the major areas, but rather in the details and the personalities. For example, you may be able to find an electronic edition of your favorite magazine on one service but not on another.

 TIP **Check them out for yourself. All the major online services offer** some sort of free trial, where you go through the full sign-up process (including giving them your checking account or credit card number), then check out the service for ten-fifteen hours without charge. If you decide you don't like a service, cancel it right away—even if you stop using the service, you're responsible for any monthly fees that come up until you formally cancel the account.

Bottom line: How much does it cost to join an online service?

All major services charge a monthly membership fee (usually just under $10), which gives you access to the online service's basic features. Some features, like travel reservations, up-to-the-minute stock reports, and other specialized services, may cost you a few extra dollars an hour.

Between five and ten hours of connect time (each month) are included in your monthly membership fee. Once your monthly allotment is used and/or you wish to access an area not included in your monthly membership fee, most services charge from $2.50 to $5 per hour. Avid users eat up the five free hours very quickly and end up paying an extra $20 to $50 a month.

If your main interest is the Internet, you will probably find an Internet service provider a better deal than an online service. For instance, my Internet service provider, Iquest, offers 120 hours a month for $15, a much better deal than an online service.

Pros and cons of CompuServe

For several years, CompuServe Information Service (CIS) was *the* online service, with no serious competition in the market. CompuServe's early years linked people who used state-of-the-art (for the time) computers like Commodore 64s, Apple IIs, TRS-80s, and IBM XTs, all with modems that are s-l-o-w by today's standards. (A top-of-the-line modem operated at 300 to 1,200 bps back then, while today's best zoom along at 28,800 bps.) But by supporting the burgeoning computer market *before* it was the monstrous profit center it has become, CompuServe gained some important things:

- The somewhat sentimental position as the pioneer in the market

- A huge group of dedicated users, including some of the biggest names in the computer and entertainment fields

- A reputation as the best place to get shareware and freeware

- Huge file libraries

- Most of the online support contracts from major hardware and software companies

Even though CompuServe is no longer the largest online service in America (it is still the largest worldwide, as of this writing), it is still the best place to find support for your equipment and software (see fig. 7.1). It's also the preferred service for businesspeople, and has a decidedly businesslike feel to it. My publisher's parent company, Macmillan Computer Publishing, operates a forum on CompuServe, and some of my editors use CompuServe to exchange files with one another.

Fig. 7.1
WinCIM (CompuServe Information Manager for Windows) makes it easy to navigate CompuServe's twisty passages.

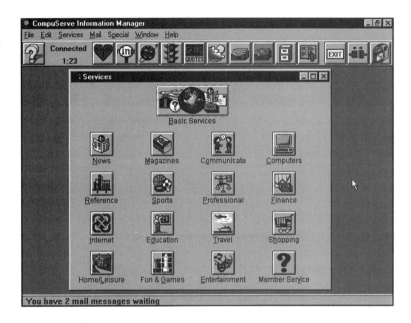

What CompuServe critics will say:

"Sure, CompuServe's great—if you're a millionare."

If you talk to people about joining CompuServe (CIS), you may hear stories about its legendary high prices (which earned it the online nickname "CI$"). CompuServe recently took some giant steps to change this image—they dropped almost all their rates to about half of what they'd been before, making their prices very competitive with the other services.

"CompuServe is fine for business people, but it's not much fun for kids."

There are a lot of features on CompuServe that kids will enjoy, but it's true that CompuServe is probably not the best choice for a family that's looking primarily for an online service that will entertain kids under 18. A better choice would be the all-game ImagiNation Network or the family-friendly Prodigy.

For much more information about CompuServe, see Chapter 8, "Calling CompuServe."

America Online

Viewed by many as the tough, young upstart of the online world, America Online is (as of this writing) the largest online service in America. Their custom interface (available for DOS, Windows, and Macintosh) is the most attractive and easiest to use of any of the major services (see fig. 7.2), though Prodigy's runs a close second. The success of America Online (AOL) is due to a strong three-pronged attack against the other services:

- Innovative marketing, including giving away program disks inside major magazines and through direct mailing, and sponsoring "online events" where celebrities converse with subscribers in real time

- A smart interface that upgrades itself automatically when new features are introduced

- A very affordable pricing structure (which has now caused other services to drop their prices considerably)

What AOL critics will say:

"You'll run into problems on the Internet if you have an America Online address."

This isn't a technical issue—it's an intolerance problem. AOL has given so many new users easy access to the Internet, it has caused quite a backlash from a few grumpy (but vocal) Internet "old timers."

The old timers' wail goes like this: "the Internet is for people *like me* who know their way around a computer, not for newbies who ask dumb questions!" This sour grapes argument is a slightly modified version of the one that goes, "when I was your age, we didn't have fancy school buses—we had to walk ten miles in the snow to school. Kids today have it too easy!"

"America Online has grown too fast for their hardware to keep up with, so the response time is slow during peak hours."

This was very true a few years ago, when America Online was experiencing a phenomenal membership growth. Their hardware was literally maxed out, but they have since invested a lot of money in new hardware and lines, and the problem no longer exists.

"America Online's chat rooms are no place for children."

Agreed.

America Online is known as being less businesslike—and more fun—than CompuServe. America Online's realtime chat areas do a huge business, especially in the evening hours, so it's a great place to meet people. If CompuServe is known as the business service, and Prodigy as the family service, then America Online might be called the "fun for grownups" service. Although America Online offers plenty for businesses and kids, it really excels in keeping adults entertained. For much more information about America Online, see Chapter 9, "Calling America Online."

Fig. 7.2
America Online's slick graphical interface has helped it garner over 2 million members.

Prodigy

As a joint venture between IBM and Sears, Prodigy was probably the best-financed startup in online history, at least until Microsoft stepped into the ring with the Microsoft Network.

Prodigy's marketing has always focused on the family, riding the wave that has brought computers into so many homes in the past few years, but its depth of service suits many small businesses too. The interface is intuitive, with point-and-click access to all the available services, but some people consider the interface a bit chunky and kindergarten-ish, due to the large lettering.

If you are trying to introduce young children to the joys of online computing, you simply can't find a better playground for them than Prodigy. There's plenty to keep kids entertained on Prodigy, and many safeguards are in place to ensure that your kiddies never stumble accidentally into adult situations and language. For much more information about Prodigy, see Chapter 10, "Calling Prodigy."

Fig. 7.3
Prodigy's "market" has always been the family (presumably huddled around the computer), so its interface can be used by kids and adults alike.

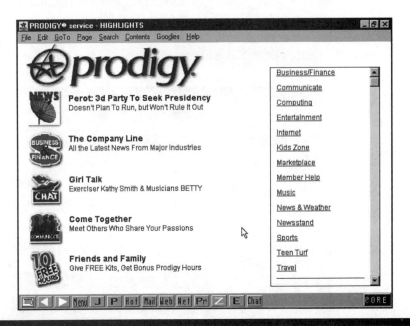

What Prodigy critics will say:

"Prodigy doesn't have files to download, like the other services do."

This used to be absolutely true. Prodigy has never had the extensive software libraries that other online services have provided. However, a few years ago, Prodigy teamed up with ZiffNet, a mini-online-service by Ziff Davis, to offer ZiffNet at an extra charge through Prodigy. And you can download software easily through ZiffNet.

"Why would I pay extra to download files from ZiffNet through Prodigy if I can get downloading for no extra charge on other online services?"

I don't know. Personally, I wouldn't. If software downloading is important to you, choose a different service.

"There's no free speech on Prodigy—their censors dictate what you can say."

It is true that if you post a public message in Prodigy, it's subject to approval by forum monitors. The service is aimed at families, and they don't try to hide the fact that they'll reject messages that are not suitable for that atmosphere. If that goes against your beliefs, use a different service—companies aren't democracies.

Delphi

Formally known as Delphi Internet Services, Delphi is a somewhat smaller player in the battle for your online dollars. At about 400,000 users, though, it's still a major service. Prices for online time are among the best around, and there's no surcharge for prime time (daytime) use.

Delphi scores over its competition by not only offering links to the Internet, but by being totally Internet-focused. Through recent (and typically quiet) agreements with companies who create software for the Internet, Delphi has become the most Internet-oriented online service of the major players. If you're specifically looking for Internet access, but you want a few online service benefits too, Delphi is a good choice. I won't say it's the best choice, because the balance changes every day, as the various online services race to offer better and more Internet access. But there is little on the Internet that you can't do with Delphi.

What Delphi critics will say:

"Who's Delphi?" or *"Are they still around?"* Since its ads are usually a little more subtle than its multitude of competitors' ads, Delphi often goes unnoticed. But that doesn't mean they won't meet your needs. What it does mean, however, is that their user base is smaller, and you won't find the huge software libraries and chat rooms that services like America Online, with larger populations, offer.

"If you want Internet service, it's better to go with a real Internet provider."

This is true, if you're going to be an Internet "power user" and rack up dozens of hours each month on the Internet. But Internet providers tend to cater to experienced users, and do not offer a lot of help in setting up the special software you need to access the Internet through the connection they will sell you. A beginner with any qualms at all about technical configuration might be better off accessing the Internet through an online service, and Delphi excels at that.

The ImagiNation Network

As a specialist in a field of general practitioners, the ImagiNation Network knows the value of doing one thing and doing it right. They do games: online, interactive, graphical, and very addictive games. On INN, you can strike up a game of Backgammon, Chess, Othello (which they call Flip-Flop), or any number of other games with users all over the country. They offer role-playing games, casino games, shoot-em-ups, and classic board and card games (including regional favorites like Euchre).

Two strong suits for INN are its graphical interface (it's an animated aerial view of a town, where you click the building you want to visit) and its toons. **Toons** are cartoony faces that you create yourself with their software. When you're playing against someone else, they see your toon on their screen and you see theirs. You can select all kinds of variations on faces, including face shape, skin tone, eye shape and color, hair style and color (yes, there's a mohawk), facial hair (men only), clothing, eye wear, and hats. You can even create different toons for different moods.

INN costs about the same as other services, but you're more likely to get addicted to its environment, so you might spend more time online.

For more information about the ImagiNation Network, see Chapter 18, "Online Gaming."

What INN critics will say:

"Who?"

The ImagiNation Network is new. Give it time.

"The interface is kind of awkward, and the online help isn't very good."

Okay, you've got a point. But it's bound to get better as the service matures and releases new versions of the software. In the meantime, it's a unique service, and it may be worth struggling through a learning period with the software to get to the fun parts.

"Flirt, flirt, flirt! Doesn't anyone just want to play backgammon?"

True, a lot of folks on ImagiNation Network pretend to be interested in playing board games in order to strike up conversations for romantic purposes. But there are lots of people who *aren't* there for that reason.

The Microsoft Network

The Microsoft Network, Microsoft's entry into the online world, is brand-new. Because it's still in its "growth phase," with new features and benefits being added every week, no one can tell what kind of service it's going to be when it really gets off the ground. But a first look at it shows several good features:

- It's custom-designed to work with Windows 95, the latest version of Microsoft Windows. In time, other online services may come out with Windows 95 tuned versions of their software, but MSN has it now.

- It offers lots of information about and technical help for Microsoft's products, probably better than you can get on any other service.

- The interface is very similar to Windows 95 itself. If you can use the Windows Explorer program in Windows 95, you're well on your way to handling MSN without much of a learning curve.

- The mailbox is tied in with the Windows 95 Inbox, so your MSN e-mail appears right alongside your e-mail that you get from your network (if you're connected to one.)

I could go into a long tirade here about what a feeble service MSN appears to be at the moment—there aren't many files to download; there are few news and information resources; the chat rooms are hard to find; there's no central shopping area. But by the time you read this book, all of this may have changed—it's not fair to judge MSN's offerings based on what it offers during its first few months of business.

Will MSN become a major contender in the online services arena? I, along with the rest of the world, will just have to wait and see.

The Internet

The Internet isn't a company. There isn't really a home office you can sign up with or complain to (except the local service provider that connects you to the Internet). It's a group of thousands of colleges, companies, and other organizations (including online services) worldwide, all linked together and available for anyone who can get access. It *is* the fabled Information Super-highway, where you can find just about anything (software, chatting, e-mail, information, news, and weather, among many other things).

The advantages of going directly to the Internet through a service provider are several:

- **Cost**. Rates vary widely for Internet service providers, but it's usually less per hour than an online service.

- **Flexibility**. Although most providers will offer you free or cheap Internet access software, you are free to find and use better software with your connection if you like. On an online service, because you are accessing the Internet through their proprietary system, you're stuck with the interface software they provide.

What Internet critics will say:

"I've been hearing nasty stories about that Internet. It's all pornography, software piracy, kidnappers, and con-men who lure you in by pretending to fall in love with you."

Where most of the major online services have around 2 million subscribers each, the Internet has something like 30 million users. The law of averages (along with an intense media focus in the past year or so) says you'll hear about more nastiness on the Internet than on the other services, just as you'll hear more bad things about Los Angeles or New York City than Salt Lake City or Honolulu. Some of the stories are true, others are urban legends, but they always diminish as people get wiser and experience things for themselves—not only are experienced people less likely to get caught up in hairy situations, but it's a lot easier to believe the worst about a place when you've never been there.

Incidentally, any negative aspect of the Internet that you encounter using a service provider, you would also have encountered using the Internet through an online service.

"But isn't it dangerous to let my kids play on the Internet, what with all the sexual content?"

You've been listening to C-SPAN again, haven't you? Tsk, tsk. It's true that, unlike the sanitary environment of Prodigy, the Internet is uncensored. (At least it is at this writing. There are some people trying to curb certain activities on the Internet.) That means everything is all lumped together, with no value judgments. Some people call this free speech—others call it an abomination.

Whatever you call it, you should know that the Internet is for adults, or for children with adult supervision. It's not designed to be daycare, and as such is not an appropriate playground for unsupervised youngsters. (Few places are.) If you can't supervise your children's computer usage, get them their own Prodigy account, and keep your Internet password a secret.

- **E-mail address prestige.** Back in the America Online section I talked about the Internet snobs who will be mean to you if you have an online service for your e-mail address. You may get a bit more respect with an address from a "real" Internet service provider.

For more information about the Internet, see Chapter 12, "Calling the Internet."

Q&A *What's the Internet's phone number?*

It doesn't have one. To get access to the Internet, you have to:

- Work for a company that has access

- Go to a school that has access

- Sign up with an online service or BBS that has access

- Sign up with a local Internet service provider

What does Internet access cost for a private individual?

If you use a major online service (Delphi, CompuServe, America Online, or Prodigy), you probably won't have to pay anything above the normal fees. Internet-only services usually cost $20 or so per month, with a $2 to $5 hourly charge after a certain number of free hours (usually 5 or 10). Rates vary widely around the country and even within cities, so shop around.

BBSs

BBSs (**Bulletin Board Services**—often just called **boards**) are the grass roots end of the online world. Anyone can start a BBS, as long as they have:

- An extra phone line to dedicate to the BBS's use; You can share a phone line with your household, but you won't be happy

- At least one modem hooked up to the phone line

- At least one computer hooked up to the modem

- Some sort of BBS software, which answers the phone when people call with their modems, directs them to different files, chats, and so on, and helps turn your computer into a mini online service.

Some BBSs are huge, with hundreds of computers, modems, and phone lines, while others are single-line systems run by hobbyists. Most BBSs run 24 hours a day, but some run only in off hours when their owners don't need the phone lines (the latter type is usually run by a business or its employees).

BBSs can be **commercial boards**, where you pay a membership fee and sometimes an hourly rate, or **hobby boards**, which are usually free, or charge only a small fee.

Most BBSs *do not* make a profit, even if they charge yearly or monthly fees, so it's a pretty safe bet the person who runs the board (the **system operator,** or **sysop**) doesn't regard it as their profession. This means you won't get the same kinds of service, support, and slick software you'd expect from the big online services. On the other hand, BBSs are usually much cheaper than online services and (assuming you call a local BBS) you can meet other people from your local area. BBSs tend to be quite a bit more spicy and colorful than online services, appealing to specific areas and interests rather than the entire spectrum of human interest.

What critics say about BBSs

"Most BBS sysops are amateurs, and some are even kids. You can't expect them to be professional, or even fair."

Well, the first part is true. Most people are amateurs, and a lot of kids do run their own BBSs, sometimes because they like the feeling of power that comes from being a sysop. However, you can't say that just because someone is young or an amateur, they won't treat you well. In fact, I've gotten some of the best and most accommodating online service from BBSs. One sysop even took the time to give me a personal tutorial of how to use his BBS, when I was confused about the interface!

"You have to watch out for viruses on BBSs."

This too is partially true. It depends on the BBS. Some sysops are very vigilant about checking each file for viruses, so downloading a file from them is as safe as (maybe safer than) buying a shrink-wrapped product in a store. Other BBSs are virtual virus dens. It's best to get your own virus-cleaning program (see Chapter 5) and scan all programs you download. (Actually, this is good advice no matter which online service you use!)

8

Calling CompuServe

● **In this chapter:**

- Signing up, signing on, and signing off

- Where can I find help?

- Working with special interest groups, e-mail, and files

- Chatting online with other subscribers

- How CompuServe relates to your wallet

When somebody mentions the term "online service," somebody else will say, "You mean like CompuServe?" This chapter shows you what 3.4 million subscribers already know—why CompuServe is the first name in online services . . . . ➤

Years before entrepreneurs discovered there was gold in modems, CompuServe was already busy defining and shaping the online world. Begun in 1979 ('68 if you count the original, much-different incarnation), CompuServe is the most deeply entrenched combatant in the war for your online dollars. Though it's no longer the largest online service in America (that title belongs to AOL), CompuServe is still the largest commercial network worldwide, and it's not showing any signs of letting the online upstarts roll over it.

CompuServe has the deepest file libraries, the most extensive field of computer support services, and, obviously, the most experience in the business. With all that going for it, CompuServe has been able to absorb attacks from all sides without collapsing. For all its quirks (it's far from the easiest service to use), CompuServe remains a great choice for online research and support. This chapter shows you how to take advantage of CompuServe's strengths and work around its weaknesses.

There are many programs available to access CompuServe, but the most popular is CompuServe Information Manager (CIM). The overwhelming majority of people use CIM, so that's what I'll show you in this chapter. (I'll be using the Windows version.) You'll learn more about CIM later in this chapter, but you can get a quick look at it in figure 8.1.

Fig. 8.1
CompuServe Information Manager is "the only way to fly" when it comes to using CompuServe effectively.

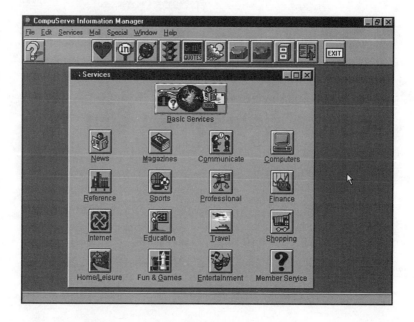

How to speak CompuServe

CompuServe uses a few terms you might not be familiar with:

CB Simulator—CompuServe's version of live chatting, named because it simulates the interaction of people on Citizens' Band radios. (CB radios were big in 1979, when this feature was introduced.)

CIM—The CompuServe Information Manager, an indispensable program (produced by CompuServe) for using the service. CIM is available for Mac, Windows, OS/2, and DOS. The examples in this chapter use WinCIM (CIM for Windows).

CISNav (or **Navigator**) and **TAPCIS**—Other popular programs to help you use CompuServe. These programs focus on downloading as much data to your hard disk as possible, and then letting you read it at your leisure, after you've disconnected (and stopped racking up hourly charges).

CompuServe CD—A CD-ROM published by CompuServe that includes a cross-section of software and information available online.

CompuServe Magazine—A monthly paper magazine included with your CompuServe membership. The magazine highlights forums, software, and other features of CompuServe.

Forum—Most of the areas you can visit on CompuServe are **forums**. Forums usually contain files, messages, and live chat areas related to a specific topic. Many are maintained by companies (the Macmillan forum, for example, is maintained by folks who publish this and other great books), but some (like the Desktop Publishing forums) focus on special interests.

GO or **GO <WORD>**—This is what you do to use different features of CompuServe (you use a GO <WORD> with the GO command). For example, if you want to check out the Macmillan Computer Publishing forum, you click the Go button and type the keyword **Macmillan**. You'll often hear CompuServe users say things like, "**GO BILLING** to check your current charges."

Library—A collection of files, usually within a forum. Libraries have names and numbers, so if the fourth library in a forum is the Graphics library, people refer to it either as the forum's Graphics library or Library 4.

Premium services—Areas on CompuServe that charge an extra fee for use, usually over and above the regular fees. For instance, a search of a magazine article database may be billed at $1 per search, in addition to the hourly charge.

Thread—A group of related messages where one follows another. For example, if you send out an e-mail message called "Good Restaurants in Fargo?," it might lead to several responses listing fine Fargo eateries. These messages (including yours) are all part of the same thread.

How do I join?

Almost every modem, computer, and just about every other piece of software or hardware you buy includes a trial offer from CompuServe. If you haven't already acquired one elsewhere, you can call (800) 523-3388 to get a free copy of CompuServe's CIM software (for Windows, DOS, OS/2, or Mac).

Everyone who joins CompuServe gets a free trial period (usually ten hours of service during a one month period) to try out the service. Even though there are no charges during the trial period (except for premium services or extra hours beyond your allotted time), you'll need one of these to sign up with CompuServe:

- a credit card

  or

- a checking account (for automatic withdrawals)

To start the free trial period, you go through the actual sign-up process.

CAUTION **If you decide you don't want to keep CompuServe, remember to** cancel your membership within a month of your sign-up—monthly fees are automatically charged to you even if you don't use the service anymore.

Installing the software and signing up

Ready to take the plunge and give CompuServe a try? (I'm assuming you've acquired a CompuServe sign-up kit one way or another.) Then follow these steps:

1 Run the SETUP.EXE program on the CompuServe diskette you received. Follow along with the onscreen prompts.

2 When asked if you want to Copy the Sign-up Files, choose Yes.

3 When asked if you want to sign up a new membership, choose Yes.

4 Follow along with the sign-up prompts, entering all the information they ask for.

TIP **If you're one of those people who hates junk mail, make sure you** deselect the Promotional Mail and External Mailings checkboxes. You'll encounter it somewhere along the way in the sign-up process. This will prevent CompuServe from sending you ads (the former) and selling your name to other people (the latter).

CAUTION **When CompuServe presents your local access number, user ID,** and password to you, write them down! Don't rely on your memory.

Now you're ready to start the CompuServe Information Manager program and start exploring the service. A good place to start is to **GO WELCOME**. (You'll learn what this means, and how to "GO" somewhere, shortly.)

Signing on

After you've installed CIM, signing on is as simple as selecting the Connect button in the Connect to CompuServe window that pops up when you start CIM (see fig. 8.2). Assuming you've already set CIM up with your ID and password, it'll log on automatically.

Fig. 8.2
Just click the Connect button to sign on!

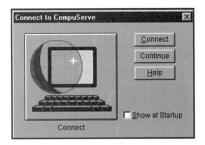

Q&A *I don't see any Connect to CompuServe window!*

It's possible to disable this box so it doesn't appear when you start CompuServe. If someone has done this, just open the File menu and choose Connect to see it. Or, you can just click any of the buttons in the Services window to automatically log onto CompuServe and open that service in a single step.

Q&A *Help! I moved, and now my local access number is no longer local!*

When you sign up, CompuServe looks up a local access number for you. If you ever move, you'll need to get a new number for your new home town. You can do this online (**GO PHONES**), or you can call (800) 848-8199 with a regular phone, not a modem. Press 1, then follow the prompts, which ask you to enter your area code, phone number, and modem speed. Write down the number and the network they give you (for instance, CompuServe, SprintNet, Tymnet).

Then start CIM. If the Connect screen appears, click Continue. Open the Special menu and select Session Settings. Change the Access Phone number to the new phone number, and choose OK.

I travel a lot for business, and it's a real pain to keep changing the phone number depending on the city I'm in.

If you use a laptop, you might call from different cities at different times. If so, you might find it easier to set up different sessions for each city. In that same Session Settings dialog box, click the New button and enter information (including the local phone number) for that location. Then you can choose which location you're calling from using the Current drop-down list.

Signing off

The first thing you should learn about CompuServe (after connecting) is how to disconnect, or "sign off." That's because time is money, and you don't want to be connected when you're not using the service.

There are several ways to disconnect:

- Open the File menu and select Exit. The program closes and you're disconnected.

- Open the File menu and select Disconnect. You're disconnected, but the program remains open. You can exit from the program itself by selecting File, Exit.

- Click the Disconnect button. This is the same as selecting File, Disconnect.

- Click the Exit button. This is the same as selecting File, Exit. (This button is not available when you're in an Extended Services window— it's replaced by a Leave icon, which moves you back to Basic Services.)

WinCIM: up close and personal

Since most people use Windows, let's take a look at WinCIM. The WinCIM window is a lot like the window of any other Windows-based program. It's got a menu bar, a toolbar (called a **ribbon**), and windows you can open, resize, and close. Here's a look at the main window you'll see when you
sign on:

1 There's a menu bar, as with any Windows-based program. Among the menus are: the Services menu, which directs you to various areas of CompuServe; the Mail menu, which controls your e-mail; and the Special menu, which controls your connection settings and preferences.

2 The ribbon is a row of buttons that you can click instead of issuing some of the more common menu commands.

3 The Services window breaks down CompuServe's offerings into sixteen categories. To browse CompuServe, click one of the categories, then wade through a series of menus to find what you're interested in.

WinCIM toolbar

Each button on the ribbon is a shortcut for a menu command. Here's a rundown:

 Click here for help

 Opens a list of your favorite locations you've stored

 Helps find a particular topic

 Reopens the Services menu

 Opens a "GO" window you can use to jump quickly to a particular area

 Quick stock quotes

 Your local weather

 Your inbox—mail you've received ends up here

 Your outbox—mail you're going to send waits here

 Opens a filing cabinet for storing the messages you send and receive

 Opens your address book of user IDs

 Exits the program

 Disconnects from CompuServe

 Opens your mailbox (if you don't have any new mail, this icon does not appear)

Going places

There are three ways to go places on CompuServe:

- Jump there quickly with a menu command, a GO word, or a ribbon button

- Select the location from your list of Favorite Places

- Move through the categories in the Services list, making selections from successive lists until you come to the area you want

Obviously, if you know where you want to go, the first two methods are faster, but if you're just out for exploration, you might discover areas you didn't know existed by using the Services list.

GOing there fast

Each area has a **GO word**—that's a word you can type to go directly to that area. For instance, to go to the Macmillan Computer Publishing area, you'd do the following:

 1 Click the GO button on the ribbon, or open the Services menu and select Go. You'll see the Go box (see fig. 8.3).

Fig. 8.3
Enter your desired destination, and GO whisks you off to it.

2 Type the GO word, **MACMILLAN**, and press Enter.

There are some ribbon buttons that take you directly to certain areas—for instance, the Weather button takes you directly to the Weather area.

 TIP **You can customize the ribbon somewhat—select Special,** Preferences, Ribbon and use the dialog box that appears to change the buttons.

And some menu commands take you to certain areas too—for instance, on the Services menu, you can select CB Simulator to go directly to that area.

 Q&A *How do I know what an area's GO word is?*

Well, until you've been there, you generally don't have any way of knowing. But once you're there, there'll be a GO word listed. You'll see CIS: and then the GO word—for instance, CIS:PETS will take you to the list of resources for pet owners.

Once I know a GO word, is there any way to save it online?

You can add it to your list of Favorite Places, as explained in the next section.

Creating your own custom tour with Favorite Places

No doubt, as you get experienced with CompuServe, you'll find yourself visiting the same areas over and over again—and your fingers will get very tired of typing in all those GO words! The solution is the Favorite Places feature. To check out your Favorite Places list, follow these steps:

1 Click the Favorite Places button in the ribbon, or select Services, Favorite Places. You'll see your Favorite Places list.

2 To add a GO word to your Favorite Places list, click Add. The Add to Favorite Places dialog box appears (see fig. 8.4).

Fig. 8.4
CIM comes with a few favorite places already listed—you can add your own to the list.

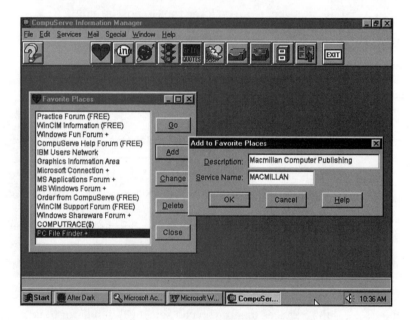

3 Type a description of the area in the Description box, and type the GO word in the Service Name box. Click OK.

4 To remove an area from the Favorite Places list, select it, then click the Delete button, and click Yes to confirm.

5 To change the information for an area, select it, then click Change. Make your changes, then click OK.

6 To go to an area listed in your Favorite Places, double-click it, or select it and click the Go button. The Favorite Places dialog box closes, and you're taken directly to that area.

Strolling through the services

The leisurely, Sunday-afternoon way of finding areas is to wade through the Services menu. When you click one of the sixteen categories, a list of choices within that category appears. Double-click any item on a list, and another list opens. And so it goes, through the lists, until eventually you come to the area you decided upon.

This may seem like a waste of time, but it's a great way to stumble across new areas that you didn't know about, and to expand your knowledge of CompuServe!

TIP **Make sure you write down the GO words of any interesting areas** you find, or save them in your Favorite Places, for later use.

More purposeful strolling with Find

If you don't know the GO word, but you're not interested in browsing menu after menu, check out the Find feature. Find lets you enter the general topic you want, then presents you with a list of GO words that match your criteria. Follow these steps:

1 Select Services, Find, or click the Find button on the ribbon. The Find dialog box appears.

2 Type in a word that represents what you want to find (for example, Publishers), and click OK. After a moment, a Search Results window appears (see fig. 8.5).

3 To add any area you found to your Favorite Places list, select it, then click Add and follow the procedure for adding an entry to that list.

4 To go immediately to any area you found, double-click it. Or, to change your mind and not go to any of them, click Close.

Fig. 8.5
The Search Results window includes your Favorite Places list, so you can quickly add anything you find to it.

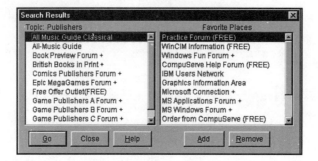

Getting help

If you get stuck on CompuServe, there's plenty of help available. Here are some of the ways you can get help:

- Click the Help button on the ribbon to bring up the Online Help system, then click the topic you're interested in getting help about. This help is available even when you're not logged onto CompuServe, so you can peruse it at your leisure.

- Click the GO button on the ribbon, type **HELPFORUM** and click OK. This takes you to the CompuServe Help forum, which provides help and guidance (see fig. 8.6). You can post questions here, then log in later to see if they've been answered. You'll learn more about forums later in this chapter.

- If you need help right away, and can't wait for your question to be answered in a forum, you might try CompuServe's phone support lines at (800) 848-8199. You might be on hold for a while, but eventually you'll get to talk to a real person.

TIP **If possible, call from a place where you have two phone lines, so** you can talk to the service representative while you try things online. When you only have one phone line, you usually end up in the frustrating cycle of trying to remember details of the problem (which you can't reproduce while you're talking to the rep), writing down a bunch of possible solutions to try after you hang up with the service rep, and playing phone tag if those suggestions don't work.

- To get help with a particular area, go to that feature and look for a section, file, or message for beginners. For example, in CB Simulator (covered in "Chatting with other Users," later in this chapter), Channel 2 in the General Band is the Welcome Newcomers room, where you may be able to find a friendly "face" to help you with your CB questions.

Fig. 8.6
In the CompuServe Help forum, you can post your questions and receive answers, plus read other people's questions.

Here are some categories of questions the other people have asked.

What are forums?

Many of the services on CompuServe are referred to as **forums**, which are similar to special interest groups on other online services. A forum can have:

- Messages about many related topics

- Files for downloading

- Conference rooms for live discussions

- Announcement messages that tell you what's happening in the forum

Some forums are sponsored and staffed by companies, while others are run by individuals—very few forums are actually run by CompuServe. Corporate forums are usually dedicated to supporting one company's products, like the DSTORM forum, which helps users of DATASTORM's software products (PROCOMM PLUS and PROCOMM PLUS for Windows). Some companies, like Microsoft, have several forums or areas. Individually owned and operated forums usually focus on a hobby or profession (like the graphics forums).

You can get to a forum on CompuServe by using any of the ways I talked about in "Going places," earlier in this chapter. You can use a GO word for direct access, or you can stumble upon a forum by browsing the services. To find a forum relating to your interest, use the Find feature I talked about in the section "More purposeful strolling with Find," earlier in this chapter.

When you visit a forum for the first time, you'll be asked to join. Go ahead and join up (click the Join button), but read the introduction first. Most forums won't let you do much without joining, and you don't really have much to lose.

While you're in a forum, you'll have a palette of buttons floating on the right side of the CIM window:

 Message waiting. If you have messages addressed specifically to you in this forum, you can get a list of them by clicking here

 Forum notices. If there are public notices from the sysop, this button will be available; click it to read them

 Browse forum messages. If you want to see a list of all the messages people have left on this forum, click here

 Browse forum libraries (files). Click here to see a complete list of all the files available in this forum

 Search forum messages. If you're looking for a particular message, or want to narrow down the list of messages to a particular date or topic, click here to enter the criteria

 Search forum libraries. The same as the Search forum messages, except you're searching for files instead, according to the criteria you enter

 Compose a forum message. This opens a window where you can enter a message and post it in one of the forum's public areas

 Upload a file to a library. Click here to contribute a file to the forum's libraries

 Enter Conference. This lists all the available conferences in the forum; if there aren't any active ones, this button won't be available

Who's Here. This lists the User IDs of all the people currently using the forum

 Invite. Click here to invite anyone else in the forum to a conference

 Ignore. If someone is sending you unwelcome messages, you can "turn them off" with this button; (you won't see anything they type)

How do I read a forum message?

To read—just click! I'm not being facetious; that's really all there is to it. Follow these steps:

1 Click the Browse Forum Messages button. A list of sections appears.

2 Double-click any section name. A list of the messages within it appears.

3 Double-click any message to read it.

4 When you're done reading, take one or more of the following actions (see fig. 8.8).

- Click the More button to read the rest of the message, or if you're already at the end of the message, to move to the next message in the thread

66 *Plain English, please!*

In the beginning, there's one message. Then someone replies to it, and someone else replies to the reply, and pretty soon you've got a whole chain of messages. As I already mentioned, that's called a **message thread**, and you can see it visually by clicking the Map button. 99

- Click the arrow buttons to move forward or back in the message thread

- Click File It to copy the message to your file cabinet, an area on your hard disk used to store CompuServe data

- Click Reply to open a window where you can compose a public reply; (I won't get into this now, since the procedure is basically the same as for sending e-mail, which I do cover in "Reading e-mail," later in this chapter)

- Click Topic to move to the next message in the section

- Click Cancel to close the message reading screen

How do I download a file?

Downloading a file from a forum is fairly straightforward; follow these steps:

 CAUTION   **You probably won't be able to use the file right way when you** download it—most files are compressed with a program called PKZip. The first file you should download is the "unzipper" program, so you'll be able to uncompress the other files you download. You can find it, among other places, in the Macmillan Computer Publishing forum (**GO MACMILLAN**) in the Utilities section.

 1 Click the Browse Forum Libraries button.

2 Double-click the section you want.

3 Double-click the file you want to examine more closely. A description of it appears.

4 To download the file, click the Retrieve button. A window opens asking you to choose a name for the file.

 TIP   **You can download several files at once by clicking Mark instead of** Retrieve. Once you've marked all the files you want, open the Library menu and select Retrieve Marked.

5 Type a name, then click OK. CompuServe retrieves the file and copies it to your hard disk.

CAUTION   **Don't try to switch to another program and do other work while a** file is downloading. Sometimes this works fine, but sometimes it causes problems with your file transfer, causing it to abort. Then you have to start the transfer completely over again.

How do I search for files and information in a forum?

If you're in a very small forum (or you've got all the time and money in the world), you can browse through all the file libraries and messages. If you've got better things to do, however, you can have CompuServe search for things that relate to your interests.

To search all the current forum messages:

1 Click the Search Forum Messages button. The Search for Messages Matching dialog box appears (see fig. 8.7).

Fig. 8.7
You can search for messages that match your specific criteria.

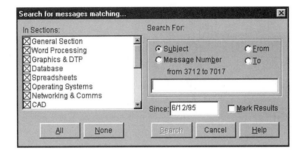

2 To search all the sections, click the All button. To search only a certain section or sections, click None to deselect all the sections, then click the one (or more) you want. In most cases, you can leave all the sections selected. (After all, you never know where some people are going to post messages.)

3 If you want to find information in a message's subject (the most common type of search), choose Subject and type the information you're looking for in the box. Or, select one of the other buttons (Message Number, From, or To) and type the value you're searching for into the text box.

4 To narrow down the search by date, enter a new date in the Since text box.

5 Select the Search button. The subjects of all matching messages will show up in a Search For window.

6 Double-click one to read it.

TIP **Instead of reading a message right away, you can click the** checkbox at the left of the subject(s), then choose the Get button to put those messages on your hard drive for reading later.

Searching for files is almost the same procedure:

1 Select the Library Search button.

2 In the Search for Files window (see fig. 8.8), select the libraries you want to search.

Fig. 8.8
Searching for files
is much the same
as searching for
messages—just enter
the criteria you're
looking for.

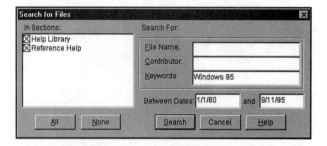

3 Type in the file name, contributor, and/or keywords in the appropriate boxes. Don't worry if you don't know all this information—most people only know the file name or the keywords they want to look for.

 TIP **If you use a file name, keep it to six letters or under. For most of** its online life, CompuServe has limited file names to six letters with a three-letter extension. People looking for something like PKUNZIP.EXE wouldn't be able to find it because CompuServe shortened it to PKUNZI.EXE. CompuServe is experimenting with eight-letter names (like DOS uses), but older files aren't all converted to the new naming format.

4 Select Search. The names and descriptions of the matching files will pop up in a Library Search window.

5 Double-click a file to read its description, or click the box to its left to mark it for later retrieval. When you've marked all the files you want to retrieve in a forum, select Retrieve Marked from the Library menu to download them.

Can I search more than one forum at once?

To search most of the libraries on CompuServe for files, all at the same time:

1 **GO PCFF**. This is CompuServe's PC-compatible file finder.

2 Select Access File Finder. The Select Search Criteria window appears.

3 In the Select Search Criteria window, shown here, double-click Keyword to start a keyword search.

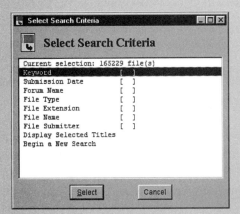

4 Type in one or more keywords in the Keywords window that pops up and select OK.

5 The next thing that happens seems like nothing at all—you're just back to the Select Search Criteria window. But the top line has changed to read `Current Selection:` and the number of files that matched your search. Double-click the Display Selected Titles line to see the files that matched your criteria.

6 Double-click any file in the list if you want to see its description. If you want to download the file, click Retrieve in the description window.

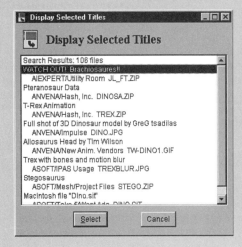

You can practice forum use for free

CompuServe has a special forum complete with files, messages, and chatting, just for new users. It's an easy way to get your feet wet in this giant service, and you don't pay for any time you spend in this practice forum (beyond any hourly network fees and/or long distance charges, over which CompuServe has no control). See "I knew this was too cool to be free" at the end of this chapter for more information. **GO PRACTICE** to check out the Practice forum.

Leaving a forum

To leave a forum, you can exit or disconnect from CompuServe itself, or:

- Leave the forum but remain online by clicking the Leave button on the ribbon (looks like a man going out a door), or selecting File, Leave

- Use a GO word to go to a different area

Sending and receiving e-mail

CompuServe's e-mail system enables you to send messages to just about anyone on the planet who has an e-mail address of some kind. Though several other services make e-mail easier to use, CompuServe's e-mail is one of the most powerful and popular systems on the market.

Sending e-mail

To send an e-mail message, exit from any forums you're in, then follow these steps:

1 Choose Mail, Create Mail. The Recipient List window pops up to let you address the message (see fig. 8.9).

2 To enter a recipient other than someone in your address book, In the Name box, type a recipient's name, then put their user ID in the Address box. Click the Add button to add that person to the list of recipients for the message.

Fig. 8.9

You can choose a recipient from your Address Book, or enter someone new.

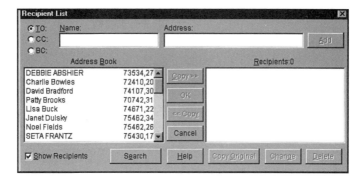

3 To send the message to someone from your address book, just click the person's name, then click Copy>>.

4 If you want to send the message to more than one person, repeat steps 2 or 3. You can click the CC or BC buttons to designate some recipients to receive a carbon copy or blind carbon copy.

5 (Optional) To copy a new recipient's name into your address book, select the name on the Recipients list, then click <<Copy.

6 Click OK when you're finished addressing the message.

7 Type an appropriate title for the message in the Subject box.

 TIP **Some people receive hundreds of e-mail messages every day, so** make your subject line as informative as possible.

8 Type the body of the message in the message box.

9 Click Send Now.

TIP **You can go through this entire process before you log onto** CompuServe (which saves you connect charges). If you're not logged on when you click Send, CIM automatically logs you on and sends the message.

Sending files

Sending a file within an e-mail message isn't much different from sending a plain e-mail message. Just do this before you send the message:

1 Click the Attach button in the Create Mail window, then click the File button in the File Attachment window.

2 Find the file on your disk. Highlight it so its name appears in the File Name box.

3 Double-click the file's name, or click OK.

4 Type in some kind of explanation in the Additional Information box if you want, then click OK.

5 Type in a subject and (optionally) some information in the body of the Create Mail window, then click Send Now.

TIP **Only the most recent version of WinCIM (version 1.4) has the** capability to attach files to a message as I just described. With earlier versions of WinCIM, you have to send files separately, using the Mail, Send File command instead.

TIP **With this method, you can only send files to other CompuServe** members. To learn about sending files to people on other online services (like the Internet, America Online, or a BBS), see the "Sending files" section of Chapter 12, "Calling the Internet." CompuServe has promised that soon, their mail system will be able to support file-sending to other services, though, so watch for this feature.

Reading e-mail

When you log on to CompuServe, you'll know right away if you've received any e-mail—especially if you've got a sound card, that enables the CompuServe software to say "You have new mail waiting!" out loud. The CIM screen says "You have # new messages" if there's anything in your mailbox, and a mailbox icon appears at the far-right end of the ribbon.

To read your mail, click the mailbox icon on the ribbon. You'll see a list of the messages that have come in since you last read your mail. Double-click a message to read it. Then dispose of it by clicking File It, Delete; Reply to it by clicking the Reply button; or just click Close to leave the message in your New Mail list to dispose of later.

Plain English, please!

 You might think that your list of new mail is in your Inbox, but it's not. The **Inbox** is a separate place that holds mail you've moved there by clicking the Get or Get All button when reading new mail sent to your account. You can open your inbox by clicking the Inbox button in the ribbon.

Finding other people's addresses

To send someone e-mail, you have to have their CompuServe address or Internet address. If you have a friend on CompuServe, but you don't know his or her user ID, you can find it with CompuServe's Directory of Members:

1 Select Mail, Member Directory.

2 At the prompts (Last Name, First Name begins with, City, Country, State or Province) type in whatever information you know about the person.

3 Click Search. A list of IDs that match the information you entered will show up. Double-click the one you want to see more details about.

4 Information about that person appears. Click the Address button if you want to copy the information to your address book.

5 When you've made a note of the ID or copied it to your address book, click Cancel to close the window. Then click Cancel again to return to the search program, and Cancel once more to leave it.

 TIP **If you have trouble finding a friend this way, don't be afraid to** use a less-technical method of finding their user ID: for example, calling them on the phone or writing them a paper letter. You'll probably save time in the long run.

Sending e-mail to other online services (and other places)

Your friends don't have to be on CompuServe to exchange e-mail with you. You can swap messages easily with people who use:

- America Online
- The Internet

- GEnie

- MCIMail

- Postal mail (outgoing only)

 TIP **Even if you know someone who uses an online service *other* than** those just listed (Prodigy or The Microsoft Network, for example), they probably have access to the Internet through their service. Have them find out from someone at their service how they can exchange messages through the Internet.

As of this writing (September 1995), you won't be able to use CompuServe's File Attach function when sending messages to another online service, but you can use an Internet trick to make files pretend to be regular text: see the "Sending files" section of Chapter 12. However, CompuServe has promised that it will soon be possible to send files to other services directly, so watch the What's New area on CompuServe for this new feature.

The only real difference between sending messages to other CompuServe members and sending them to people at other online services is the address. Instead of using just their ID in the To field, like this:

75667,1443

you use a more complicated name that tells CompuServe the message is for someone on another service, like this one for the Internet:

INTERNET:dgibbons@bigcat.missouri.edu

Each online service has its own address format, listed in table 8.1. The table also shows you how the other person can send messages back to your CompuServe account from their online service. None of the information in the addresses is case-sensitive, so you don't need to worry about getting the capital letters in all the right spots. You can also get help by selecting Help, Address Book, Electronic Address Formats.

Table 8.1 Exchanging e-mail with other online services

From	To	Recipient's address	What to do
CIS	AOL	**DaveWriter**	Type **INTERNET:** followed by the AOL screen name and **@aol.com**, like this: **INTERNET:davewriter@aol.com**
CIS	GEnie	**BobUser**	Start with **INTERNET:** and add **@genie.geis.com** to the end of the account name, like this: **INTERNET:bobuser@genie.geis.com**
CIS	Internet	**bob.user@bobs.com**	Start with **INTERNET:** and use the regular Internet address, like this: **INTERNET: bob.user@bobs.com**
CIS	MCIMail	**BUser**	Start with **MCIMAIL:** and type the recipient's user name, like this: **MCIMail: BUser**
CIS	Paper	any mail address	Use **POSTAL:** as the address and put the full address at the beginning of the letter's body.
AOL	CIS	**75667,1443**	Change the account number's comma to a period and add **@compuserve.com** to the end, like this: **75667.1443@compuserve.com**
MCIMail	CIS	**75667,1443**	Use MCIMail's X400 gateway. For U.S. CompuServe subscribers, the address looks like this (with different IDs at the end, of course): **X400:(c=us;a=compuserve;p=csmail;d=ID:75667,1443)**

Chatting with other users

CompuServe's chat functions are in the CB Simulator, named for the Citizens' Band radios that were so popular around the time of CompuServe's birth. Like a CB radio, the CB Simulator is divided into **channels** (36 for each of three **bands**). The current bands are:

- General
- Adult I
- Adult II

The general band is for families and new participants, and the Adult bands are open to those eighteen and over. Adult II is an overflow for Adult I; it's not usually used unless Adult I gets full.

To check out the CB simulator, follow these steps:

1 In CIM, choose Go and use **CB** as the GO word.

2 Choose Access CB General Band.

3 In the Change Handle window that pops up, type in a name you'd like others to see when you send messages. Keep it short—for instance, your first name works well.

4 Click Channel 2 (called "Welcome Newcomers"). Check the CBers number in the upper-right corner of the Channel selector (see fig. 8.10). If it's 1, it means you're alone; click the Status button to find an active channel (one with other people in it), then click Tune to move to that channel.

Fig. 8.10
If the "CBers" number is 1, try another channel or you'll be talking to yourself.

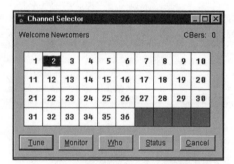

5 At the top of the Welcome Newcomers window, you'll see messages coming in from other people on that channel. Don't be surprised if some of the messages don't make sense—you're probably jumping into the middle of ongoing conversations. Type a greeting to the group (like **Hello all,**) and press Enter. You should get some responses, as long as your greeting is friendly enough.

6 When you're done conversing, click the Leave icon to get back to CompuServe's main system.

While you're in the CB Simulator, you'll see a floating palette of buttons on the right side of your CIM screen. They mean:

 Channel Selector

 Who's Here? (which shows you the handles of all the people on this band)

 Change Handle

 Update Group (which lets you add user names from your address book to your list of "CB Friends", people that you talk with frequently in CB Chat whose names you want to remember)

 Invite (which you can use to ask someone to join you on a channel or a private room)

 Squelch (which lets you ignore messages from specific senders—great for the occasional moron who won't leave you alone)

TIP **Have you ever tried to carry on a private conversation in a public** place? It's hard, because other people keep interrupting (or even listening in for that matter).

To talk privately with someone, click their name in the Who's Here list, then click the Talk button, and type your private conversation.

I knew this was too cool to be free

Ever take a casual read through the U.S. tax laws? If you have, you've seen something *almost* as complicated as CompuServe's pricing structure used to be. Recent price cuts are helping CIS shake its "CI$" nickname, and they've also made the pricing system much, MUCH easier to understand.

As of this writing, CIS has two main plans:

The Standard Plan

The Standard Plan has a $9.95 per month fee. You get five hours of service for that price per month, and then you pay $2.95 an hour after the first five hours. For instance, if you spend seven hours online in a month, you'll pay $15.85.

All e-mail costs are included in your connect time, so there's no extra charge for sending e-mail, even to different online services or the Internet.

There are a few special services on CompuServe that cost extra—they're called "Premium" features. Some of the more high-powered research tools are premium. These features usually assess a per-use charge. For instance, you might use one to locate abstracts of magazine articles, and then pay a $2 fee for each article you choose to read. These extra-cost services are always very clearly labeled.

 **CAUTION**   **These rates are for calls from the 48 contiguous states in the US. If** you're in Alaska or Hawaii, you can count on paying prime time communications surcharges no matter what time of day you call, and charges in other countries vary widely.

The Super Value Club

The Super Value Club is a great deal for people who use CompuServe a lot. For $24.95 a month, you get twenty hours of usage. (Twenty hours would cost over $54 under the Standard plan.) Plus, it's only $1.95 per hour more for each hour above twenty. And as with the Standard plan, almost everything you do online is included in your connect time charge. (Premium services, as usual, cost extra.)

Surcharges for using other networks

Sometimes there's a "communications surcharge" for using certain phone numbers that belong to certain networks to dial into CompuServe. You know CompuServe is a huge computer network, but you probably don't know that you're usually talking to *two* networks when you call CompuServe. When you call a local modem number to get to CompuServe, you're actually calling a computer network that then calls CompuServe for you, so your modem is talking through the first network to get to the second. That *first* network is usually owned by one of these companies:

- CompuServe

- SprintNet

- Tymnet

or any of dozens of other smaller players. If the network you call into for your local number is owned by anyone *other* than CompuServe, you can expect to pay an extra charge (the communications surcharge) for every minute you're online. There is usually a prime time charge for calls between 8 a.m. and 7 p.m. your time (SprintNet and Tymnet charge $11.70 per hour prime time) with a much reduced rate for non-prime time calls ($1.70 per hour for SprintNet and Tymnet). If you have a choice in your area, try to always use the CompuServe network's access numbers. For a list of access numbers in your area, **GO PHONE NUMBERS**.

Ways to save money on CompuServe

The cardinal rule with saving money on online services is: *Spend as little time online as possible.* You can accomplish this on CompuServe several ways:

- Get the fastest modem you can find. It'll pay for itself very quickly in online savings if you use CompuServe more than a few hours a month.

- Always compose your e-mail offline. Before you sign on, choose the Create Mail option in CIM's Mail menu. Write the message or messages, then log on to send them.

- If you just want to check your mail and/or send new messages (as opposed to using CompuServe's other services), use the "Send/Receive All Mail" option in CIM's Mail menu. When the dialog box pops up, make sure there's an X in the Disconnect When Done box and choose OK. This puts you online the absolute minimum amount of time to send and retrieve your mail.

- When you get an article, choose the File It button at the bottom of the window. This puts the article on your disk so you can read it when you're offline—that way you don't needlessly pay for the time you spend reading.

- Consider an automated logon program like TAPCIS (GO TAPCIS) or OZCIS (GO OZCIS). These are like robots. You tell them what you want done (for instance, "log on, go to the Pets forum, and copy all the new messages, then log off"), and they do it, much more quickly than you could, saving you lots of money.

Another way to save money with CompuServe is to understand its strengths. CompuServe is a great place for research and getting technical support— probably the best. If you'll be using Internet services, however, you can find much better (and/or cheaper) alternatives. Why pay CompuServe's hourly charges for the same Internet functions you can get with dedicated Internet services or BBSs for much less?

9

Calling America Online

● In this chapter:

- How do I join AOL?

- Signing on and signing off

- Where to go for help

- How do I use AOL's features?

- How AOL relates to your wallet—and how to save money online

Discover America Online—one of the biggest and best online hangouts. How can over 3 million people be wrong?. . . . . ❯

America Online (AOL) is the fastest growing of all the online services. Though it's been around for about ten years, it didn't catch on until the past few years—but then it caught on with a vengeance. Now the largest online service in America (CompuServe's still the largest worldwide), AOL has gained over 1.5 million members (almost half its subscriber base) in the past year.

This chapter explains most of the things you might want to try on America Online. The chapter doesn't pretend to give you a whole virtual trip through America Online like a coffee table book about the jungle. This chapter is more like the field guide—I'll just machete through the thicker vines so you won't get stuck.

TIP **A copy of the software you need to join AOL is included in the** Using your Modem CD, which you'll find in the back of this book. For more information, see Appendix D.

AOL Lingo

America Online uses a few terms you might not be familiar with:

screen name—Your user name, which is also your e-mail address. My screen name, for example, is DaveWriter.

Go To—This is what you do to use different features of AOL, and it's named for the menu you use—the Go To menu. For example, if you want to check out the Windows forum, you open the Go To menu, choose the Keyword option, and type the keyword **Windows**. It's similar to the Go feature in CompuServe.

keyword—The name of a service you can use. For example, to find the amount of your current bill, use the keyword **Billing**. These are like the Go words in CompuServe.

IM—Instant Message. You can send Instant Messages to anyone who's signed on. Immediately after you send it, your message pops up in a new window in front of whatever they're viewing (unless they're transferring a file).

AOLer—Someone who spends time on America Online (AOL). Kind of like a farmer is someone who spends time on a farm.

Favorite Places— When you visit an area of AOL you would like to visit again, you can add it to your Favorite Places list, so you can easily find it again.

A look at the America Online for Windows screen

America Online's screen offers all the usuals you'd expect from a Windows program (or a Mac program, for that matter). There's a toolbar, some menus, and lots of stuff to click.

All the commands you need are contained on one of these drop-down menus.

The toolbar offers point-and-click shortcuts for the most popular menu commands and online locations

The Main Menu lets you browse AOL by choosing a category.

Click here to go to the "Administration Desk" of AOL, where you take care of billing, passwords, technical assistance, and the like.

As you might guess from looking at the screen, the toolbar is the real gem of this program. Here's what you can do with it:

 Open your mailbox and read your incoming mail

 Compose and send a new mail message

 Reopen the Main menu, if you've closed it

 Go to Member services (help)

continues

Open a Directory of services

 Enter People Connection (chat)

 Get stock quotes and portfolios (financial services)

 Read today's headline news

 Visit Center Stage (online events)

 Use Internet services

 Check out what's new online

 Enter a keyword to go to

 Open Download Manager, where you can download files you've chosen

 Search for files to download

 Check the online clock to see how long you've been connected

 Edit your Personal Choices (screen names, passwords, etc.)

 Print the document that's currently displayed (if any)

 Save the current document

 Open your list of Favorite Places

Becoming a member

Ready to try out AOL? The first thing you'll need is a sign-up kit. There are versions for DOS, Windows, and Macintosh, and you can get one free by calling (800) 827-6364. America Online is famous for giving the software away freely—you may find a copy included with a computer magazine you buy, with your new modem or PC, or in the back of a book you buy.

 CAUTION **If you acquired your startup kit more than a few months ago (for** instance, if it came in the box with your modem several years ago), you probably do not have the latest version. You can go ahead and use the older version to sign up, but you should call AOL at (800) 827-6364 to request the latest version as soon as possible (it's free.) Without the latest version of the software, you may not be able to use some of AOL's features. You can download the update online if you prefer, but it takes a long time (an hour or more).

The next thing you'll need is a way to pay. Everyone who joins America Online gets a free trial (usually ten hours online) to try out the service. Even though there are no charges during the trial period, you'll need one of these to sign up with America Online:

- A credit card

    or

- A checking account (for automatic payments)

To start the free trial period, you go through the actual sign-up process. If you decide you don't want to keep AOL, remember to cancel your membership within a month of your sign-up—monthly fees are automatically charged to you after that first month *even if you don't use the service*. If you accrue more than ten hours your first month, you'll be charged for them as well. And believe me, it's easy to rack up ten hours fast on such a jam-packed service!

First, install the software

Once you get your startup kit, becoming a member is a fairly easy process. Follow these steps:

1 Assemble your materials. You'll need the startup disk, your startup certificate with a registration number and password, and a credit card (or information about your checking account).

2   Place the startup diskette in your floppy drive.

3   In Windows 3.1, select File, Run from the Program Manager. Or in Windows 95, click the Start button, then click Run. A Run dialog box appears.

4   In that box, type **A:\setup.exe** (assuming A: is your floppy drive.) and press Enter. The setup program starts.

5   Click the Install button. (Or click Review to change the directories used, then Install.)

6   Wait for the setup program to copy the needed files to your hard disk.

7   When you see You're ready to use America Online!, click OK.

Calling yourself names

Waol.exe

After you install the software, you'll need to register. I won't take you through every excruciating detail of this rather lengthy and self-explanatory process, but I will get you started:

Double-click the America Online icon, if its visible. If it's not, open the America Online program group (in Windows 3.1) or search the Start button's Programs menu (in Windows 95) to start the program.

Since this is your first time, you'll need to tell AOL something about your equipment, and read some information and reminders. Read them, and click OK or Continue (whichever appears).

Eventually, it will dial a toll-free number. When asked, enter your area code. A list of phone numbers in your area appear, with that number's maximum speed next to it (for example, 2,400 or 14,400). Choose the fastest local number that your modem will handle. For example, if you have a 14.4 Kbps modem, select a 14.4 Kbps or 28.8 Kbps number. You will also get to choose an alternate number, in case the first number is busy or has technical problems.

Continue reading information and typing the data that the program requests. You'll enter your certificate number and signup password, and your personal info such as name, address, and phone number. You'll also be asked to specify the credit cart type you're going to use to pay, along with its number and expiration date.

Finally, you'll be asked to select a screen name. Keep in mind that this first screen name you select is permanent—you can never change it. (You can change other screen names you create later, as I'll explain later in this chapter.) Type in the screen name you want, and click Continue. You probably won't get your first choice—a message will appear saying it's not available. Keep trying until you're prompted for a password. That means you succeeded in picking a unique screen name! Choose the password you want to use, and enter it twice (this safeguard prevents mistakes from typing errors), then move on through a few more information screens and you're done!

Signing onto America Online

If you just went through the registration process, you're already signed on— GO! But if you didn't, you'll need to start the AOL program and issue the sign on command:

1 Double-click AOL's icon in its program group (in Windows 3.1), or use the America Online shortcut on the Start menu (in Windows 95).

2 At the Welcome window that appears, select your screen name from the list in the middle of the Welcome window (see fig 9.1). (If you only have one screen name, it automatically appears in the Screen Name box.)

Fig. 9.1
Choose your screen name from the list. You probably have only one screen name at this point, so it's a no-brainer!

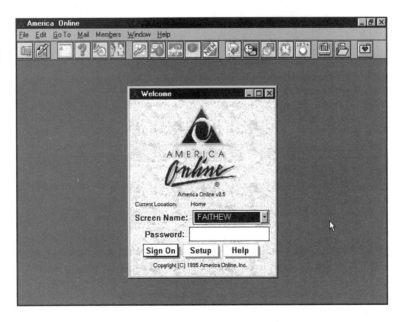

3   Type your password in the Password box. Don't worry about anyone else seeing it over your shoulder—each letter you type shows up as an asterisk (*) onscreen. Of course, you can't read it either, so you have to trust your fingers.

4   Click the Sign On button.

The software then calls the local America Online number, signs you on and opens two windows: the Main Menu (which has buttons for most major areas—see the graphics page earlier in the chapter) and the Welcome window (see fig. 9.2).

 TIP   If you don't want to type your password every time, select Members, Edit Stored Passwords and type your password in the box. Click OK. From now on, you won't have to enter your password when you sign on. Be careful, though—don't do this if other people use your computer.

Fig. 9.2
America Online's Welcome/Spotlight window shows you whether you have new mail, gives you access to Reuters and Time news, and "spotlights" three other services.

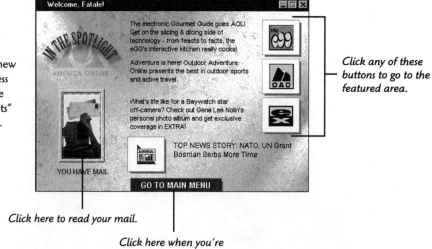

Click any of these buttons to go to the featured area.

Click here to read your mail.

Click here when you're done being welcomed.

The Welcome window covers up the Main Menu at first, so you can check your mail, read the news, and check out the three featured services, if you want, before really diving into AOL's web of other services.

The **featured services** change at least once a day, giving you a chance to see areas of AOL that you'd probably miss if you had to dig through all the menus to get to them. The first few days of each month, one of the featured services is a letter from AOL's CEO Steve Case documenting (usually) the phenomenal growth and new offerings.

When you're done with the Welcome screen, click the Go To Main Menu bar at the bottom.

Q&A *Why would I ever want to sign on as "guest" rather than as my own screen name?*

Well, you wouldn't, if your screen name was listed. The Guest feature is for other people who may be using your computer. Your AOL software stores all the user IDs that get billed to you (i.e. all the aliases you and your family make up), but it can't store IDs for more than one billing group at a time. So let's say your Uncle Henry stops by and wants to check his e-mail from your computer. Uncle Henry's screen name isn't on the list, so he needs to choose Guest. Then, once connected, a box will appear asking him for his own screen name and password. Uncle Henry can do everything from your computer that he could do from his own, except work with his Favorite Places list or add or edit screen names.

My connection seems to be awfully slow.

Maybe AOL isn't set up to use your modem's top speed. From the Sign-On screen, click Setup, then click Edit Location. A Network Setup dialog box appears. Make sure that your modem's maximum speed is selected in the Modem Speed drop-down list on the left side of the dialog box, then click OK.

The modem keeps hanging up on me.

It could be that you don't have the right modem settings for the modem you're using. From the Sign-On screen, click the Setup button, then click Setup Modem. A list of modems appears. Make sure that the modem selected on the list is the one you actually have, then click OK.

Signing off

In the rest of this chapter, you'll learn about using the various features of America Online. But at some point, you'll probably get tired and want to leave.

To sign off America Online at any point:

1 Select File, Exit. You'll see a dialog box asking `Are you sure you want to sign off?`

2 Click Yes to sign off but stay in the AOL program (to read files you've just downloaded, or whatever), or Exit Application to sign off and leave the AOL software at the same time.

The only time you won't be able to sign off this way is when the AOL software is busy transferring a file (see "Receiving a file," later in the chapter) or displaying a large amount of text. In both cases, the mouse pointer will look like an hourglass as you move it around—when it changes back to an arrow shape, you should be able to sign off normally.

Where do I get help?

America Online offers technical help several ways:

- Over the telephone, at (800) 827-3338. Automated information is available at all times; people are there from 6:00 a.m. to 4:00 a.m. Eastern time seven days a week.

- Through a FaxLink service. You call the voice number, and use the automated system to request certain information by fax. Then you enter your fax number and hang up, and AOL's fax machine calls you and transmits the information. The voice number to call to request a fax is (800) 827-5551.

- Through an America Online BBS. This is a private BBS, separate from America Online, where you can get technical support and download the latest version of the AOL software. Connect time is free, and so is the call. Use your terminal software to dial (800) 827-5808, and the settings N-8-1. (See Chapter 13, "Calling BBSs" for information about calling BBSs.)

- Online, through a variety of member services (which I'll describe momentarily).

You can get information about all the various kinds of help, including the fax and phone support, by entering Member Services online. To enter this area, click Member Services at the bottom of the Main window. You'll be asked if you realize you're entering a Free area—click Yes, and you're in. You'll see a screen resembling figure 9.3.

Fig. 9.3
Member Services offers several types of online help.

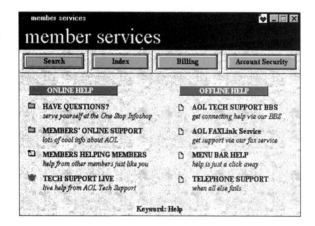

At the Member Services screen, you can click any of the Offline Help buttons (on the right side of the box) for information about any of those services.

If you click any of the Online Help buttons (on the left side of the box), you're taken immediately to that area online. The online help you can receive includes:

- **Q&A.**   This is the place to ask questions by posting a public message. You can also read messages others have posted, and benefit from the answers that have already been given.

- **Members Online Support.**   This takes you to a general "administration" area where you can change your password, set parental controls, cancel your account, and so on.

- **Members Help Members.**   This is a forum where you can post questions and have them answered by other members—not AOL representatives. The pros: sometimes you'll get a quicker response here than through Q&A, and sometimes you'll get "unauthorized" workarounds and information. The cons: the information may not be accurate (but it usually is).

- **Tech Support Live.** This is exactly like attending a live conference (discussed later in this chapter), only the person on stage isn't (necessarily) a star—they're a technician from AOL. You can type questions to a real person, in realtime, and get answers typed back to you.

While you're in the Member Services area, you don't incur any online charges other than long distance charges, if any. That makes Member Services an excellent place to hang out while you're gaining experience with AOL!

TIP   **Notice in figure 9.3 that there are two other features in Member** Services: Billing Information and Account Security. You can click either of those buttons from Member Services to investigate your options in those areas. I'll talk more about billing at the end of the chapter.

AOL's special interest groups

America Online has dozens of special interest groups, forums, and conferences, from genealogy to Star Trek, TV networks to rock bands, and gardening to the Gadget Guru. Sometimes they're hosted by a big company, like Microsoft; other times it's just a casual get-together place for individuals interested in a particular topic. In most of these, you can:

- Chat with others who share your interest

- Get files (programs, information, sounds, and pictures) that relate to your interest

- Attend scheduled auditorium events where you can chat with experts

- Post messages, questions, and comments related to the group's theme

Taking a look at special interest groups

Some groups are very organized and have a good-looking opening page, like the Homeowners Forum shown below. Such groups usually have a big budget and are sponsored by a business. Others are less polished but still fun, like the Star Trek group shown.

A folder contains any number of other icons. Double-click to open it.

When you double-click an interactive link, almost anything can happen. The most likely thing is that you'll see another window with more icons.

File search. Double-click here to open a window that lets you enter keywords you're interested in, and then find files to download that match.

Some forums have these big, convenient buttons that provide links to related services or take you to a popular area of the forum.

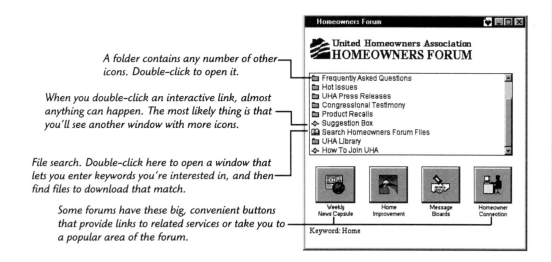

If you decide you want to visit here again, just click the heart icon to add it to your Favorite Places list.

Double-click one of these text icons to see an article, schedule, or other bit of information about the forum.

Message boards are places where people "chat" without necessarily being there at the same time. You post messages, and other people post responses.

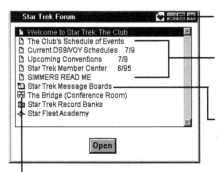

When you see this icon, you know you'll find live chat. It's sometimes called a "Live Discussion" or "Conference," but it's just a big chat room (see "Chatting with other users," later in the chapter).

How do I do e-mail?

America Online's e-mail system lets you exchange e-mail with people all over the world, whether they're AOL members or members of another service or the Internet. We've talked quite a bit about e-mail in previous chapters, so let's just jump right in and see how AOL handles it.

Sending e-mail

To send an e-mail message from AOL, follow these steps:

1 Choose the Compose Mail option from the Mail menu, or press Ctrl+M.

2 In the To field, type the screen name of the person you want to send the message to. If you want to send the message to more than one person, put a comma between the individual screen names. Press Tab twice to move to the subject box.

3 Type an appropriate title for the message in the Subject field. Hit the Tab key to move to the message box.

TIP **Some people receive hundreds of e-mail messages every day, so** make your subject as informative as possible. Otherwise, your message might be ignored.

4 Type the body of the message in the message box. Figure 9.4 shows a sample one, all filled out.

Fig. 9.4
Fill in the blanks to create an e-mail you can be proud of.

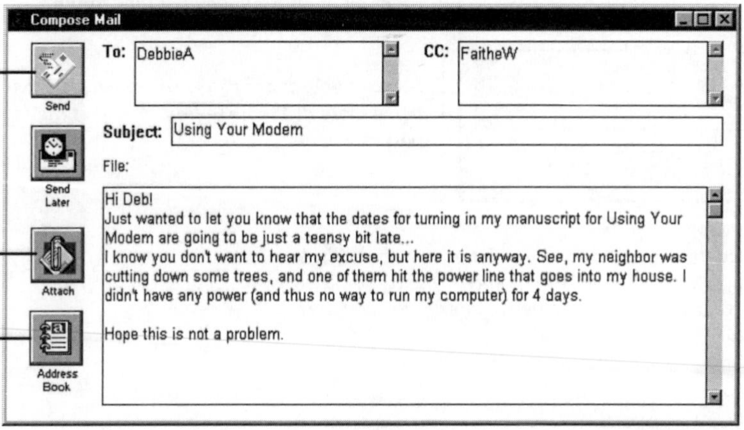

Click here when you're ready to send.

Click here to attach a file to the e-mail if you like.

You can choose addresses from your address book.

Compose Mail		
To: DebbieA	**CC:** FaitheW	
Subject: Using Your Modem		
File:		

Hi Deb!
Just wanted to let you know that the dates for turning in my manuscript for Using Your Modem are going to be just a teensy bit late...
I know you don't want to hear my excuse, but here it is anyway. See, my neighbor was cutting down some trees, and one of them hit the power line that goes into my house. I didn't have any power (and thus no way to run my computer) for 4 days.

Hope this is not a problem.

Send
Send Later
Attach
Address Book

5 Click Send. Or, if you are composing offline, click Send Later to send the message the next time you're connected to AOL.

 You can create all of your e-mail messages offline, to save money. Just click the Send Later button after you create each message. Then, when you sign on, click Send. We'll talk about FlashSessions, a feature that enables you to do most of your e-mail work offline, in "Save even more: FlashSessions," later in this chapter.

Sending files

Sending a file within an e-mail message isn't much different from sending a plain e-mail message. Just do this before you send the message:

1 Click the Attach icon in the Compose Mail window (refer to fig. 9.4).

2 Find the file on your disk. Highlight it so its name appears in the File Name box.

3 Double-click the file's name, or click OK.

 With this method, you can only send files to other AOL members. To learn about sending files to people on other online services (like the Internet, CompuServe, or a BBS), see "E-mail" in Chapter 12.

Reading e-mail

When you log on to AOL, you'll know right away if you've received any e-mail—especially if you've got a sound card, which enables the AOL software to say "You've got mail!" out loud. The Welcome screen says You have mail if there's anything in your mailbox.

 To read your mail, click the Mail icon, either in the Welcome screen or on the toolbar. You'll see a list of the messages that have come in since you last read your mail. Double-click a message to read it. If there's a file attached to the message, you'll see a Download File button. Choose Download Now to copy the file from AOL to your disk.

Finding other people's addresses

If you have a friend online, but you don't know their address, you can find it with AOL's Member Directory:

1 Choose Member Directory from the Members menu.

2 Choose Search the Member Directory.

3 In the Search Member Directory screen (see fig. 9.5), type in whatever information you know about the person. If the person you're searching for has a unique name, you may be able to get it by just typing that, but you'll probably have to use additional information like their hometown or one of their hobbies.

Fig. 9.5

Type in as much information as you can think of to identify the member you're looking for. With over 3 million members on AOL, using a name alone often brings up a huge list of matching names.

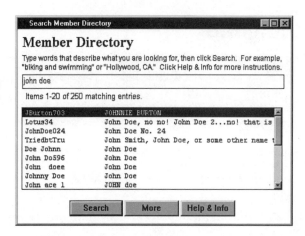

4 Click Search. If you come up with too many names, try another search with more information.

The Address Book helps you remember

Once you find the address you're looking for, you'll want to add it to your Address Book, so you don't have to type it every time you want to e-mail the person. Follow these steps:

1 Select Mail, Edit Address Book.

2 Click the Create button.

3 If you want to create a group of screen names (so you can send mail to the entire group by just typing the group name), enter the group name on the Group Name line. Otherwise, enter the name by which you know the person.

4 In the Screen Names area, enter the person's screen name, or multiple screen names separated by commas if you're creating a group.

5 Click OK to create the new entry, then OK to close the Address book.

As you saw in figure 9.4, there's an Address Book button when you compose mail. To pull a name from your address book at that time, just click that button.

 TIP **You can add any address to your address book, not just AOL ones.** This comes in handy—especially when you're working with long and complicated Internet addresses (see the next section).

Sending mail to other online services

Your friends don't have to be on America Online to exchange e-mail with you. You can swap messages easily with almost any service, including:

- CompuServe
- Internet
- BIX
- GEnie
- MCIMail
- Most BBSs (through FidoNet)

 TIP **Even if you know someone who uses an online service *other* than** just those listed (Prodigy, for example), they probably have access to the Internet through their service. Have them find out from someone at their service how they can exchange messages through the Internet.

You won't be able to use AOL's File Attach function when sending messages to another online service, but you can use an Internet trick to make files pretend to be regular text. See "Sending files" in Chapter 12.

 TIP **You can exchange files between different computer types, such as** PCs and Macintoshes, by mailing them through AOL. Some file types, such as some sounds, graphics, and text, can be used on both PCs and Macs, but other file types (like most programs) will only work on the computer type for which they were designed.

The only real difference between sending plain messages to other AOLers and sending them to people at other online services is the address. Instead of using just their screen name in the To field, like this:

> DaveWriter

you use a more complicated name that tells AOL the message is for someone on another service, like this one for the Internet:

> dgibbons@bigcat.missouri.edu

Each online service has its own address format, listed in the following table. The table also shows you how the other person can send messages back to your AOL account from their online service. It doesn't matter if you use upper- or lowercase letters, because e-mail addresses are not **case-sensitive**. You don't need to worry about getting the capital letters in all the right spots.

Exchanging e-mail with other online services

From	To	Address	What to do
AOL	BIX	**BobUser**	Add **@bix.com** to the end of their account name, like this: **bobuser@bix.com**
AOL	CompuServe	**75667,1443**	Change the account number's comma to a period and add **@compuserve.com** to the end, like this: **75667.1443@compuserve.com**
AOL	GEnie	**BobUser**	Add **@genie.geis.com** to the end of the account name, like this: **bobuser@genie.geis.com**
AOL	Internet	**bob.user@bobs.com**	Use the regular Internet address, like this: **bob.user@bobs.com**
AOL	MCIMail	**BUser**	Add **@mcimail.com** to the user's account name, like this: **buser@mcimail.com**
CompuServe	AOL	**DaveWriter**	At CompuServe's *Send to (name or user ID):* prompt, type **>INTERNET:** followed by the AOL screen name and **@aol.com**, like this: **>INTERNET: davewriter@aol.com**

MCIMail	AOL	**DaveWriter**	Use the recipient's full name at the To prompt and **INTERNET** at the EMS prompt. At the Mbx prompt, type the screen name followed by **@aol.com**, like this:
			`To:   Dave Gibbons`
			`EMS:  INTERNET`
			`Mbx:  DaveWriter@aol.com`

TIP **For more details on sending e-mail to other systems, open the** Mail menu, select Mail Gateway, and click the Can I Send Mail to Other Services? icon. There you will find a big list of services with really good help info in each one.

Getting software

Most of AOL's software is in the Computing section's Software Center, but individual forums often have file libraries as well. The process for downloading files from AOL is the same wherever you find them. It's also very simple. Let's look at the Computing area as an example:

1 Choose the Computing button from the Main Menu.

2 Select the Software Center.

3 Some of the best files (not surprisingly) are in the Best of Computing & Software folder. Double-click it.

4 Select the file area (Games, Windows, etc.) you want to list, then click Open.

5 You'll see a list of files, each with the date it was made available, a title and short description, the number of people who've downloaded the file so far, and the date of the most recent download (see fig. 9.6). You can scroll through this list with the scroll bar on the right side. If the List More Files button is available, you can click it to see the next twenty files in the list.

Fig. 9.6
Downloading files from AOL is a simple, intuitive process.

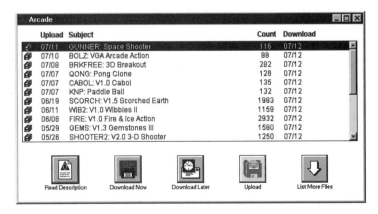

6 When you see a file you want to download, select it and choose the Download Now button.

TIP **Try the Hall of Fame button (or Go To keyword HOF) for another** good selection of files.

To learn more about an individual file, click it and choose the Read Description button, or just double-click it.

If you'll be downloading several files, you can set up a list of them with the Download Later feature. This lets you look for and select all the files you want before downloading anything. To add a file to your list, select it and click the Download Later button. When you're finished finding files, select the Download Manager icon on the button bar (see fig. 9.7). Click the Start Download button to download all the files you've selected.

Fig. 9.7
The Download Manager lets you prune files from the list if you change your mind.

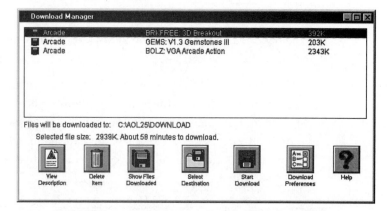

For more about finding and using programs and files, see Chapter 16, "Finding Software Online."

How can I find what I want fast?

With AOL boasting such a huge pool of software and information, you could hardly expect anyone (at least anyone with a life) to find all their files and information by reading long, boring file lists. AOL makes file searching easy:

1 Select the File Search icon on the toolbar.

2 In the Software Search window (see fig. 9.8), select All Dates and whichever categories you want to search (I usually select All Categories, since you can find some files in unexpected places).

Fig. 9.8
Be as specific as possible when you choose the words to search for—you're dealing with thousands of files.

```
┌─────────────────────────────────────────────────────────────┐
│ Software Search                                     _ □ ✕    │
│ List files released since: (Click one)                       │
│         ⦿ All dates        ○ Past month        ○ Past week   │
│ List files in the following categories: (Click one or more)  │
│                       ☑ All Categories                       │
│     □ Applications  □ Games            □ OS/2                 │
│     □ Development  □ Graphics & Animation  □ Telecommunications│
│     □ DOS           □ Hardware         □ Windows             │
│       □ Education   □ Music & Sound                           │
│ List files pertaining to the following keywords: (Optional)  │
│ │airline                                                    │ │
│        [ List Matching Files ]        [ Get Help & Info ]     │
└─────────────────────────────────────────────────────────────┘
```

3 In the List Files Pertaining to the Following Keywords box, type keywords that relate to the files you want to find. For example, to find all the files about airlines, you might type **airline**.

4 Choose List Matching Files.

5 You'll see a list of files that match your keywords (see fig. 9.9), or a message telling you that no files matched the keywords you tried. If you see the latter, start over with simpler keywords (like **bartending** instead of **recipe for the best extra dry Tanqueray martini**).

Fig. 9.9
The File Search Results window works just like any other file list on AOL, allowing you to download files directly from the list.

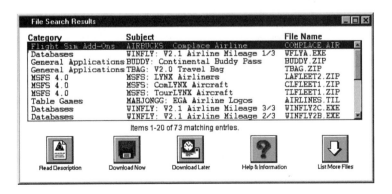

Chatting with other users

Chatting is one of AOL's most popular features. You can chat with a group of people (either in the People Connection or in one of the special interest group chat rooms) or with one person at a time.

For more about chatting, see Chapter 17, "Finding Like-Minded Users."

The People Connection is the hub of group chat. Any time of day or night, you're sure to find hundreds or thousands of other AOLers chatting about every topic imaginable—and some you wouldn't have imagined in the first place.

You'll find four general kinds of chat rooms on AOL:

- **Public rooms**, which are set up by AOL for everyone's use. If you're online with your family (or you have a delicate constitution), stick to the public rooms.

- **Member rooms**, which are set up by individual members. You can find rooms geared for every kind of special interest (there are usually several rooms for musicians and fans, book junkies, quilters, etc.), but you'll find some pretty off-beat interests as well.

 CAUTION   **If you do wander into the member rooms, use care when deciding** on a room based on its name. A good rule of thumb is: If a room title could have more than one meaning (especially if one is lewd), assume the worst. For instance, do not let your eleven year old Dungeons and Dragons fan wander into any room with the word "dungeon" in the title!

- **Private rooms**, which are member rooms that aren't open to the general public. To get to them, you click the Private Room button and type the name of the room.

- **Conference rooms**, which are large public rooms accessed only through certain forums and special interest groups. For instance, you can access The Bridge (the Star Trek Forum conference room) only through the Star Trek forum. There are usually scheduled times for the big meetings in these rooms, but you may find people hanging out in them at all hours.

To find a public room, follow these steps:

1 Enter the People Connection. You'll automatically be dumped into an arbitrary room (usually a lobby without a specific topic). You'll see a chat window (see fig. 9.10).

Fig. 9.10
You'll start your journey into the chatting world through a lobby.

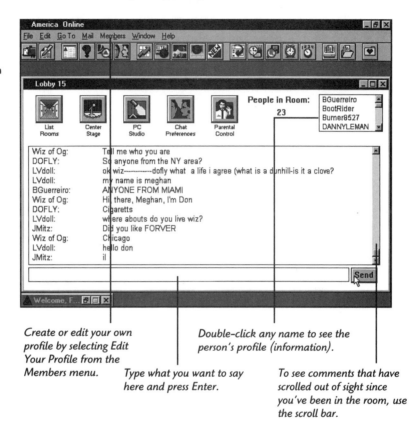

Create or edit your own profile by selecting Edit Your Profile from the Members menu.

Type what you want to say here and press Enter.

Double-click any name to see the person's profile (information).

To see comments that have scrolled out of sight since you've been in the room, use the scroll bar.

2 Choose the List Rooms button. You'll see the first twenty chat rooms.

3 Scroll through the list of rooms until you find one that looks interesting. If you get to the bottom of the list, click the More button to see the next twenty (if the More button is gray, there are no more rooms).

TIP To see who's already in a room, select the People button at the bottom of the window. AOL opens a window that lists all the screen names of the people in the room.

4   Look at the number in the Members column. It tells you how many people are already in the chat room. If the number is 23, the room is full. (An exception is conference rooms, accessed through forums. These can typically hold lots more people.) If it's less than 23, click the room name and choose Go.

TIP   **To see the Public rooms that no one is in right now, click the** Available Rooms button.

Finding a member room works just about the same way. First select the List Rooms option, then click the Available Rooms button. The Available Rooms window has a button for Member Rooms, which takes you to the list.

In both the Public Rooms and Member Rooms windows, you'll see a Private Room button. Click the Private Room button only if you've already arranged to meet one or more people in a private room, and they already know what it'll be called, because everyone won't be able to find it otherwise. Type the name of the room in the Private Room window, then choose Go.

TIP   **Use uncommon names for your private rooms, or you're likely to** collide with other people who've already thought of your room name. Avoid things like "Hidden," "Secret," "Private," and "My Room," which are sure to cause collisions.

If the private room name you've chosen *is* being used, you'll show up in someone else's chat. If this happens, netiquette dictates you must go to another room *immediately*. Send an Instant Message to the people you were going to meet and figure out a new room name.

To chat with just one person, you also can use Instant Messages (IMs). To send an IM, follow these steps:

1   Choose the Members menu, then the Send an Instant Message option. (Alternately, you can press Alt+I.)

2   In the Send an Instant Message window, type the recipient's screen name in the To box.

3   Type the text you want to send, then click the Send button.

TIP **If you're in a chat room, and you see the person there who you** want to send an instant message to, just double-click the name, then click the Message button. In the dialog box that appears, type your message, then click Send. It's much easier than wading through the menu system.

The text you send will pop up on their screen in new window with "Instant Message from *your screen name*." They can then choose to send you an Instant Message in reply with the Respond button, or close the window with the Cancel button.

I want to attend a live conference

America Online hosts several online events every month, where media stars, authors, politicians, and experts appear live in a virtual auditorium to take questions from AOL subscribers. If you happen to sign on during an online event, it'll probably be one of the featured services in the Welcome screen, but if you show up early, you'll have to get there the hard way (actually it's not *very* hard—you just select Go To, Center Stage, or press Ctrl+6). AOL has several major virtual auditoriums, which you'll see when you click the Auditoriums button from the Center Stage screen. Figure 9.11 shows a the list of events and auditoriums on the day I logged on.

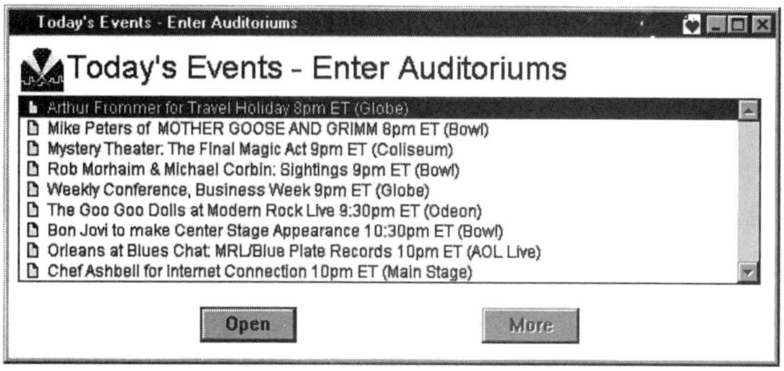

Fig. 9.11
Choose Center Stage to get to AOL's auditorium list.

```
Today's Events - Enter Auditoriums                    [controls]
┌─────────────────────────────────────────────────────────────┐
│ ▼ Today's Events - Enter Auditoriums                         │
│  ▶ Arthur Frommer for Travel Holiday 8pm ET (Globe)          │
│  □ Mike Peters of MOTHER GOOSE AND GRIMM 8pm ET (Bowl)       │
│  □ Mystery Theater: The Final Magic Act 9pm ET (Coliseum)    │
│  □ Rob Morhaim & Michael Corbin: Sightings 9pm ET (Bowl)     │
│  □ Weekly Conference, Business Week 9pm ET (Globe)           │
│  □ The Goo Goo Dolls at Modern Rock Live 9:30pm ET (Odeon)   │
│  □ Bon Jovi to make Center Stage Appearance 10:30pm ET (Bowl)│
│  □ Orleans at Blues Chat: MRL/Blue Plate Records 10pm ET (AOL Live) │
│  □ Chef Ashbell for Internet Connection 10pm ET (Main Stage) │
│                                                              │
│            [  Open  ]            [  More  ]                   │
└─────────────────────────────────────────────────────────────┘
```

Once you've chosen an auditorium, you'll be able to see who's on stage (they're listed in the upper-right corner). One of them will be the online host, who's something of an emcee. (If there's nobody on stage, you're either too early or in the wrong auditorium.)

Each virtual auditorium is a lot like a chat room—actually, it's more like a *collection* of chat rooms. The auditorium is divided into rows (just like the real thing), each of which is like its own chat room. Everything you type in the chat window goes to the other people in your row—*not* to the people on stage. To remind you of this, everything someone types from your row has the row number in parentheses, like this comment from someone else in row 4:

```
(4)DaveWriter:  Anyone know what this guy's talking about?
```

You won't see chat from people in other rows, nor will the people onstage see anything you're chatting about. When the people on the stage type something, it'll look normal:

```
OnlineHost: We're about to start the interview. Hang tight.
```

So if they can't read what you're typing, how do you ask your questions? Click the Interact button and type your question there. When you're done, click the Ask a Question button and it'll be transmitted to the folks onstage.

 TIP **Don't worry about asking a stupid question in an auditorium. The** other people in your row don't see the question you've typed in the Interact window unless the people on stage choose to answer it. Contrary to most people's fears, the auditorium doesn't show *all* the questions that come in—just the ones chosen by the people onstage.

What it costs

It's hard to say any online service is less expensive than its competition at any point, because the industry is involved in a fairly bloody price war. However, AOL is *currently* one of the best bargains in the business:

- $8.95 monthly fee, which includes five hours of online time

- $2.95 per hour charge after the free hours, with no surcharge for daytime calling

- $2.00 per fax, and $2.50 per U.S. Postal letter

This could change at any time, with competition intensifying and its huge subscriber base giving it more flexibility.

Saving money on AOL

Saving money on AOL means spending less time online. So how do you do everything you want in less time? There are six main ways:

- If you're going to get up from your computer for a few minutes (to get a sandwich maybe), enter a Free area if you want to stay connected to AOL while you're done. For instance, enter Member Support (Go To, Member Support). You aren't charged for your time in a free area.

- If you live in an area with high speed access (14.4 Kbps or higher), get a modem that can handle the higher speed—it'll pay for itself in online savings over a short period.

- Compose your mail messages offline if possible. To do this, double-click the AOL icon but don't sign on to the service. Select Compose Mail from the Mail menu and write your message. When you're finished, select the Send Later icon. When you're online, select Read Outgoing Mail from the Mail menu, then select the Send All button. Or use a FlashSession (described in the next section).

- Before you sign on, open a log of the session (choose File, then Logging, choose the Open button under Session Log, give the file a name, then select OK). When you open articles, mail, and any other text, it'll be captured to that log file. *Don't take the time to read the articles while you're online*, just open one and move right on to the next. Sign off when you've gone through all the things you want to read (so the meter stops running), then open and read the log file with your word processor.

- Log off whenever you leave the computer, even if only for a moment. It's not like a long distance telephone call, where the first minute costs more than everything after it. You pay for all the time you're online—even if you're not doing anything.

- If you're planning to download several files, use AOL's Download Later feature to get them all at the end of your session, and choosing the Hang Up When Transfer Completed option on the download window. This saves you a bit of online time by automatically naming the files rather than giving you a few seconds per file to come up with a name of your own. You'll save a few seconds with this procedure—plus you can leave the computer or do something else in Windows during the download process.

If you like to chat online, it's tough to decrease your bill. Most of the time when you're chatting, you're just staring at the screen, and that costs the same no matter how fast your modem is. The part of chatting that really eats up your money, however, is that it's so easy to lose track of time. *This* you can do something about. Try scheduling your chat time, even setting an alarm clock to remind you when your time is up. If you're really hooked, try to mix in some chatting on local BBSs, which almost always costs less than using a major online service.

 TIP You can check to see how long you've been online this session by clicking the Online Clock icon on the toolbar (the one that looks like an alarm clock).

Save even more: FlashSessions

If you get a lot of e-mail, or send and receive a lot of files, a FlashSession can save you scads of time (and therefore money). A FlashSession logs on, performs certain pre-defined tasks, and then logs off again. With a FlashSession, you can:

- Send e-mail you've composed offline

- Receive all the e-mail in your inbox, for later reading offline

- Retrieve any files you've marked in Download Manager

- Send and receive newsgroup messages

You don't have to be signed on to set up a FlashSession. Just select Mail, FlashSessions. You'll see the FlashSessions box, shown in figure 9.12.

Fig. 9.12
Schedule your
FlashSessions to
minimize your
online time.

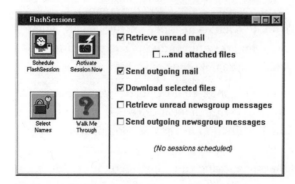

The easiest way to set up FlashSessions is to click the Walk Me Through button on the FlashSessions screen. You'll be asked a series of questions—just answer them.

Then, when you're ready to activate your FlashSession, select Mail, Activate FlashSession Now. Your software connects to AOL, does its business, and disconnects. You can read the incoming messages that were retrieved by selecting Mail, Read Incoming Mail. If you're on a tight budget, or participate in a lot of e-mail or newsgroup activities, a FlashSession can mean the difference between a $20 a month bill and a $100 a month shocker.

10

Calling Prodigy

● **In this chapter:**

- How do I join up?

- Signing on and signing off

- I need help!

- Working with special interest groups, e-mail, and files

- How do I chat with someone else online?

- How Prodigy relates to your wallet

How do you combine "family values" with the big, bad online world? Prodigy knows . . . . ▶

Prodigy markets itself as "The Family Service." It boasts the most stuff for kids, the most conservative editorial policies, and the most censorship of PG- and R-rated language and discussions. If you're looking for a safe place to turn your kids loose online, unsupervised, Prodigy is probably your best bet.

Not only is Prodigy the most family-oriented major online service out there, it's a close second to America Online for ease-of-use. You can do anything you want by clicking your mouse on the nicely labeled buttons, articles, and pictures, and it's almost impossible to get lost.

Another nice thing about Prodigy is its Internet offerings. Not so long ago, Prodigy users couldn't even hope to exchange e-mail with anyone on other online services, but Prodigy has pulled off something of an Internet coup recently. It was the first major service to offer a World Wide Web browser (and a pretty good one at that), giving its two million members access to one of the Internet's most popular functions.

 Plain English, please!

Through the **World Wide Web** (**WWW**, or simply **the Web**), people around the globe are able to create graphical **pages** (documents) dealing with whatever special interest their Web site is dedicated to. There are Web sites for popular (and obscure) bands, politics, news, sports, games, television and radio shows, hobbies, and literally everything else you can think of. For more information on the World Wide Web, see Chapter 12, "Calling the Internet."

On the downside, Prodigy frequently donates the bottom fourth of your screen to advertisements for cars, magazines, travel services, and mutual funds, among other commercial interests. You even receive "important announcements" (ads) in your electronic mailbox. In time, you learn to just ignore them, like you do magazine ads.

 Q&A   *Is there a way to turn off the ads?*

You can choose to get out of receiving *mail* ads (yes, it's online's version of junkmail). Use the Jump word **OPT OUT** (more on Jump words shortly), then click Take Me Off the List.

TIP **A copy of the software you need to join and use Prodigy is** included on the *Using Your Modem CD*, which you'll find in the back of this book. For more information, see Appendix D.

How do I sign up?

Call 1-800-PRODIGY to get a free trial offer, including Prodigy's software. Though the first ten hours of online time are free (maybe more or less hours, depending on the offer you get), you'll need a credit card to sign up. (Unlike most of the other services, Prodigy does not offer automatic checking account deductions.)

Installing the Prodigy software

Installing the Prodigy software is really simple. You get a diskette, a service ID, and a temporary password when you order a startup kit. Just pop the diskette into your floppy disk drive, then run the Install program.

- For the DOS version, you type **a:\install** at the DOS prompt, and press Enter

How to speak Prodigy

Prodigy uses a few terms you might not be familiar with:

*P. An abbreviation for the word "Prodigy." Sometimes switched around to **P*** or ***P***.

Jump. What you do to get from one place on Prodigy to another. For example, to find out more about online charges you might be instructed to **Jump Fees**. This means you open the Jump menu, choose Jump To, and type in the Jump word (**Fees** in this case— see the next item for more information).

Jump Word. The word or phrase you type to go to a Prodigy service. For example, when you **Jump Fees, Fees** is the Jump word.

BB. No, that's not "BBS," but it does mean "Bulletin Board." Prodigy's BBs are areas where you can discuss special interests with other Prodigy members.

Hot List. A list of services you use often. To create your own hot list, open the Jump menu and select Hot List. Then choose the Change Hot List button in the Hot List window that pops up.

Path. The trail you follow through your hot list. When you click the P or Path button at the bottom of the Prodigy window, or select Jump, Path, you're moved to the first (or next) place on your hot list.

A Look at Prodigy for Windows

There are versions of the Prodigy software available for DOS, Mac, and Windows, but the Windows version is by far the most popular. Let's take a look at a typical Prodigy for Windows screen.

As in all Windows programs, there's a menu bar, from which you can select menu commands.

This is the Highlights screen. It's the first screen you'll see when you sign on, unless you specify otherwise.

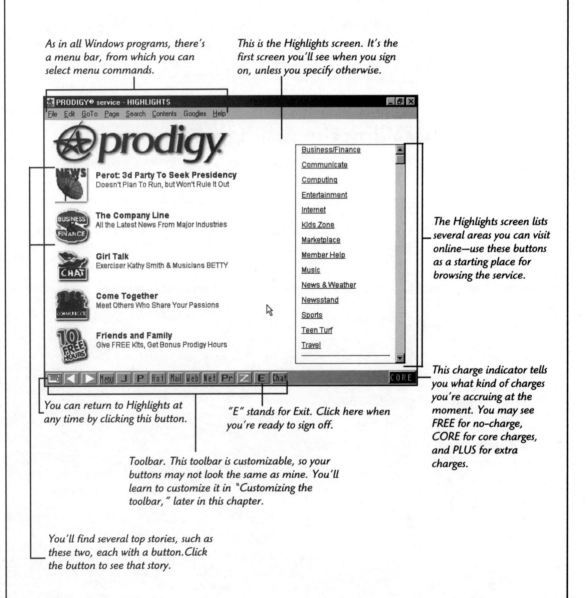

The Highlights screen lists several areas you can visit online—use these buttons as a starting place for browsing the service.

This charge indicator tells you what kind of charges you're accruing at the moment. You may see FREE for no-charge, CORE for core charges, and PLUS for extra charges.

You can return to Highlights at any time by clicking this button.

"E" stands for Exit. Click here when you're ready to sign off.

Toolbar. This toolbar is customizable, so your buttons may not look the same as mine. You'll learn to customize it in "Customizing the toolbar," later in this chapter.

You'll find several top stories, such as these two, each with a button. Click the button to see that story.

- For a Mac, just double-click the Install icon in the folder that appears when you insert the disk

- In Windows 3.1, select <u>F</u>ile, <u>R</u>un, type **a:\install**, and click OK

- In Windows 95, click the Start button, select <u>R</u>un, then type **a:\install** and click OK

First, you'll be asked what directory (a.k.a. folder) you want to put the files in; accept the default or change it, then press Enter (or click OK) to install.

You'll also be asked if you want it to search for the modem. Make sure your modem is turned on, then click Search and let Prodigy figure out the right modem settings. Then press Enter to start the file copying. When all the files are copied, you'll get a message to that effect—press Enter or click OK to move past it, and you're done.

Getting a Prodigy account

After you install the software, you'll sign on to Prodigy with the member ID and password supplied with your trial offer. The first time you start the Prodigy program (by double-clicking the Prodigy icon (Windows or Mac) or typing Prodigy at the DOS prompt (DOS), you'll be asked to verify your modem settings, and you'll be walked through the process of selecting a local access number. You'll also be asked for some personal information (such as name, address, phone number—nothing too personal).

One of the interesting quirks of the Prodigy signup is that you agree to the membership agreement without actually having read it. On the screen where you enter your personal data, there's a checkbox that you click to signal that you agree to the terms of membership. But to read the terms of membership, you have to click the Read Agreement button, then wade through more than ten separate sections of legalese!

CAUTION   **I don't know about you, but when a company makes it hard for** me to read the fine print, I wonder if they have something to hide. Before you accept Prodigy's membership agreement, read every section carefully!

You'll also be asked how you're going to pay for your membership—you'll need to enter a major credit card number and expiration date.

Once you've jumped through all the hoops, the setup program signals that it's finished with you, and you're ready to sign on like the full-fledged member that you now are.

Signing on

Once you've installed the software and have gone through the signup process, Prodigy's Windows software offers two ways to sign on:

- Manually

- Autologon

To sign on manually:

PRODIGY_R_
software for
Windows

1 Start the program PRODIGY_R_software for Windows. If you're using Windows 3.1, that means opening its program group and double-clicking the icon; if you're using Windows 95, click Start, Programs, Prodigy, then select the Prodigy for Windows program.

2 At the PRODIGY Network - Sign-On screen, type your User ID in the User ID box and your password in the Password box (see fig. 10.1).

Fig. 10.1
Here's where it all begins—at the Network - Sign-On screen.

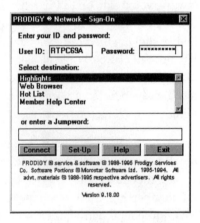

3 Click one of the places in the Select Destination box. For example, if you want to see Prodigy's main screen, select Highlights. If you like to start off in one of Prodigy's other areas, don't select a destination—instead, type a Jump word in the Or Enter a Jumpword text box.

4 Click Connect. The software dials the number, logs you on, and shows your selection.

Prodigy's IDs aren't exactly intuitive—on AOL, I'm "DaveWriter," but on Prodigy, I'm "YMES44A"—but you don't have to keep your cryptic ID on a sticky note on your monitor to remember it. Autologon lets you skip typing your ID (and password, if you choose) every time. To use Autologon:

1 Dial Prodigy with the manual procedure, and **Jump Autologon**. (That is, select Jump, Jump To, type **Autologon**, and press Enter.)

2 The AUTOLOGON screen (see fig. 10.2) lets you choose to have your ID *and* password entered automatically (option 1) or just your ID (option 2). Select the option you want.

Fig. 10.2
If you have problems with others using your Autologon feature, **Jump AutoLogon** and choose option 3.

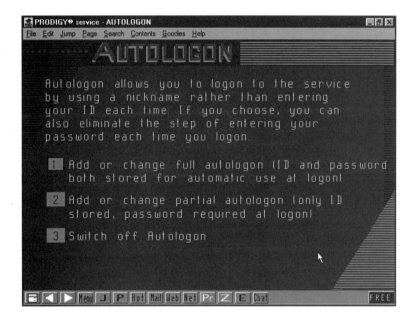

3 Type your password and press Enter if asked. (If you picked option 2 in step 2, you won't be asked for your password.)

4 Enter a nickname for your account (in case more than one person in your household wants to use autologon) and press Enter.

Autologon

5 Read the information that appears, and press Esc. You're done! You can now move to any other part of the service. The next time you log on to Prodigy you can use Autologon by selecting the Autologon icon istead of the Prodigy icon.

CAUTION Use full Autologon (option 1) *only* if you trust everyone who could possibly have access to your computer. With Autologon, *anyone* who can get to your keyboard can sign onto your Prodigy account. In the worst case, they could order software or equipment on your credit card and send e-mail using your name. At the very least, they could rack up extra online hourly fees.

TIP Even if you always use Autologon, you might want to write down your user ID and password and carry it with you in your wallet. That way, if you're ever using someone else's computer and want to log on to Prodigy, you'll have your information handy.

Signing off

When you're done, sign off one of these ways:

- **Jump Exit** (that is, select Jump, Jump To, type **Exit**, and press Enter.)

- Double-click the control menu box (the box with the dash in the upper-left corner of the Prodigy window, in Windows 3.1, or the P logo in that same corner in Windows 95).

- If you're using Windows 95, click the Prodigy window's Close button (the X in the top-right corner).

- Choose File, Exit

- If you have an E button on your toolbar, click it.

No matter which method you choose, you'll see Prodigy's Exit menu, which lets you choose to close Prodigy entirely (option 1), hang up and let another member sign on (2), or stick around for a couple of other services, which vary from time to time (see fig. 10.3).

Fig. 10.3
Prodigy's Exit screen seems to plead, "Aw, can't you play a little longer?"

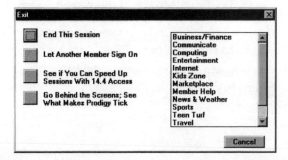

Moving around in Prodigy

There are a lot of ways to move around in Prodigy, and no one method is the best. You'll need to experiment with the various methods to see which one is best for you.

TIP **The first time you sign on to Prodigy with your new account, you'll** have to wade through some friendly "Welcome!" screens. Just read the info and move on through them.

Jumping around

As you may have figured out by now, one way to get from place to place on Prodigy is to Jump there. It's the same principle as the Go words on America Online and CompuServe—you type the name of an area, and you're whisked away to it.

To open the Jump window (where you type the Jump word), do any of the following:

- If you have a J button in your toolbar, click it.

- Open the Jump menu and select Jump To.

- Press Ctrl+J.

The Jump window is very simple—there's a single text box where you type the Jump word. Type it, press Enter, and you're off.

As you may have noticed, in this chapter, I abbreviate the procedure for using a Jump word to just **JUMP** and then the word. For instance, if I tell you to **JUMP BILLING**, that means to open the Jump window, type **BILLING**, and press Enter.

Q&A *How do I know what the Jump word is?*

Sometimes you don't know. In those cases, you'll use the A-Z Index (press F7 to see it). The index is covered in "Finding the areas you want to explore" later in this chapter. Wherever possible in this book, I'll tell you what Jump word to use. Once you're viewing an area of Prodigy, you can see its Jump word plainly—it's the word in all-caps on the toolbar, next to Prodigy® Service.

Customizing the toolbar

Prodigy has always had a toolbar at the bottom of the screen, but recently they've made it customizable. This is great, because you can choose the commands you use most often, and put them neatly at the bottom of your screen.

To choose which buttons you want on your toolbar, select Goodies, Toolbar Setup. You'll see a list of all the available toolbar buttons. You can use this screen to make changes, and also to see what each toolbar button does.

When you start out, your toolbar is probably full, like this one. The first thing you need to do is clear one or more buttons.

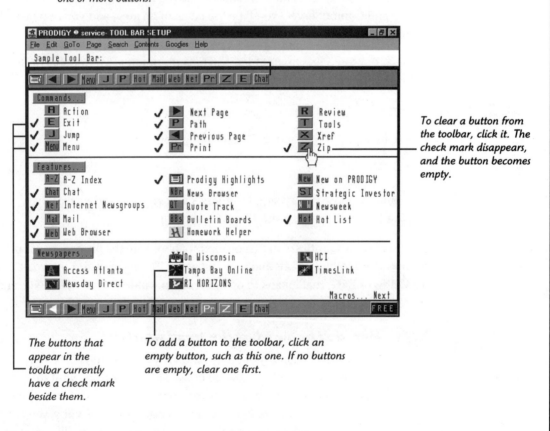

To clear a button from the toolbar, click it. The check mark disappears, and the button becomes empty.

The buttons that appear in the toolbar currently have a check mark beside them.

To add a button to the toolbar, click an empty button, such as this one. If no buttons are empty, clear one first.

Moving forward and backward

Most areas on Prodigy have more than one page. You start on its first page, and work your way through. Here are some ways to navigate:

To move forward:

- Click the right-pointing arrow button on the toolbar, if your toolbar shows this button

- Press the Page Down key on your keyboard

- Open the Page menu and select >

To move backward:

- Click the left-pointing arrow button on the toolbar

- Press the Page Up key on your keyboard

- Open the Page menu and select <

TIP **When you're reading an article, you'll** *sometimes* **see a [>] sign** telling you to press PgDn (Page Down) to see the next page. This convention is used inconsistently, so don't rely on it. Check the arrows on the toolbar instead. If there's more to the article, the right-pointing arrow will always be black.

Sometimes you choose options from menus in Prodigy. To get back to the last menu you used, or to move back to the previous page if there's no menu, use the Menu command by taking one of the following actions:

- Press Ctrl+M

- Click the Menu button in your toolbar, if your toolbar shows that button

- Open the Page menu and select Menu

Returning from an ad

Those ads that appear at the bottom of almost every screen can be seductive. They flash LOOK, and sometimes you can't help but click the LOOK button to see the full ad.

When you're done, you may find yourself lost in no-man's-land. You need to get back to what you were doing before that ad caught your eye! Simple—just use the Zip feature. Do any of the following:

- Click the Z button on your toolbar, if you have that button displayed

- Open the Page menu and select Zip

- Press Ctrl+Shift+Z

TIP   **If you want to return to an ad that you saw earlier at the bottom** of your screen, select Jump, Ad Review.

Adding members and controlling access

Since Prodigy really shines in the area of protective censorship, it's only appropriate that we should spend a bit of time talking about it here.

Many people view censorship as universally bad. These people are usually not parents. As a parent, you may want to turn your kid loose online without having to worry about what mischief he or she is getting into. Prodigy can help.

First, you'll need to create separate IDs for each person in your household. Then you can customize access for each ID. The use of Plus Features is the biggie when it comes to controlling access, because nearly all of the adult-oriented parts of the service are Plus features. Turn off Plus access for a member, and you've done two things:

- You've prevented that member from racking up huge bills with hourly charges

- You've prevented access to the majority of the adult material online

To add a member and set Plus feature use, follow these steps:

1   **Jump Add Member**. The Household Member Access screen appears.

2   Click Add/Manage IDs. You'll see Manage Household IDs screen, shown in figure 10.4.

Fig. 10.4

By managing your household IDs, you can control who gets to use what online.

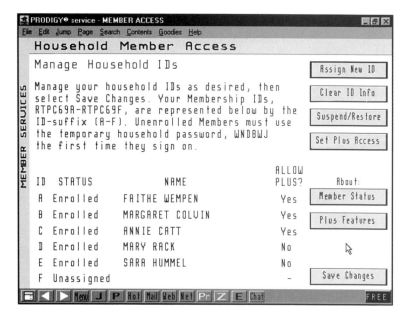

```
PRODIGY® service - MEMBER ACCESS                    _ □ ×
File  Edit  Jump  Page  Search  Contents  Goodies  Help

Household  Member  Access

Manage Household IDs                          ┌─────────────┐
                                              │ Assign New ID│
Manage your household IDs as desired, then    └─────────────┘
select Save Changes. Your Membership IDs,     ┌─────────────┐
RTPC69A-RTPC69F, are represented below by the │ Clear ID Info│
ID-suffix (A-F). Unenrolled Members must use  └─────────────┘
the temporary household password, WNDBWJ      ┌──────────────┐
the first time they sign on.                  │Suspend/Restore│
                                              └──────────────┘
                                              ┌──────────────┐
                                              │Set Plus Access│
                                 ALLOW         └──────────────┘
 ID  STATUS       NAME           PLUS?        About:
 A   Enrolled     FRITHE WEMPEN   Yes         ┌─────────────┐
                                              │Member Status│
 B   Enrolled     MARGARET COLVIN Yes         └─────────────┘
 C   Enrolled     ANNIE CATT      Yes         ┌─────────────┐
                                              │Plus Features│
 D   Enrolled     MARY RACK       No          └─────────────┘

 E   Enrolled     SARA HUMMEL     No
                                              ┌─────────────┐
 F   Unassigned                   -           │ Save Changes│
                                              └─────────────┘
 ◄ ► Menu J P Hot Mail Web Net Pr Z E Chat              FREE
```

3 Click Assign New ID.

4 Enter the person's first and last names, then click OK.

5 When asked if you want the member to be able to use Plus features, click Yes or No.

The new member's name shows up on the list. They're unenrolled, so the first time they sign on, they must use the password listed in the top paragraph, above the list.

You can also turn the use of Plus features for existing members ON and OFF. Just click Set Plus Access, and type the letter for the ID you want to change. This setting is a toggle—doing the same thing again will change it back to its original setting.

❝❝ *Plain English, please!*

> A **toggle switch** is one that turns something alternately ON or OFF each time you activate it. For instance, the power button on your computer's monitor is a toggle—press it once to turn it ON, then again to turn it OFF. **❞❞**

With some online features, such as Pseudo Chat and some of the adult-themed BBs, the first time you access these, you're asked to specify which IDs should have access to the feature, and which should be locked out of it. Very handy for the parent who wants to have adventures that Junior should not be messing with!

I need help!

If you get stuck on Prodigy, **Jump Member Services**, or click the Member Help Center button on the Highlights screen. The Member Help Center will appear, shown in figure 10.5.

Fig. 10.5
The Member Help Center is your one-stop help connection. And your time spent in this area is free!

From here, just click the type of help you want. For instance, to chat with a real live help representative online, click the Chat icon. Or, to see the questions that other people have asked, and Prodigy's answers to them, click the BB icon. Sometimes Prodigy also offers special help topics on this screen, which may vary from time to time—for instance, if there's a new version of the software, there may be extra help available to learn how to use it.

TIP **Some of the member support options (the ones marked PLUS)** cost extra. For free help, try the e-mail option if your question isn't urgent, or use Prodigy's telephone support (800-PRODIGY).

Finding the areas you want to explore

Prodigy offers somewhere around 3,000 different services. If you have an extra day or two, you might want to read through them all (**Jump A-Z Index**, or press F7). The A-Z index is shown in figure 10.6.

A quicker way to find what you want is to choose one of the categories on the left of the A-Z Index screen (see fig. 10.6). To read a brief (sometimes *very* brief) description of a service, click it once and type a question mark.

Fig. 10.6
Page through 275 pages of services, or choose the bite-sized chunks on the right.

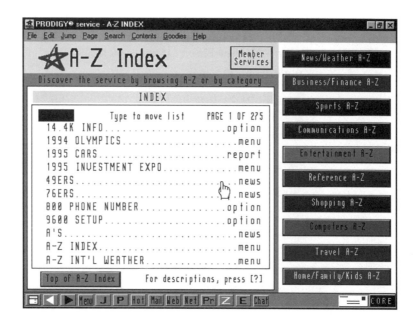

TIP **You might notice the Quick Search and Power Search features on** the Search menu in Prodigy. These won't help you find areas of the service that interest you—they're strictly tools for finding news articles.

Each area of the service looks different, but you can count on a few things:

- There will be at least one button onscreen that points you to the next logical step to take.

- The frame around the most popular button will be blinking

Most of Prodigy's services do a good job of explaining their options, so pay attention to the instructions on each screen. You probably won't see all the services Prodigy has to offer, no matter how much time you spend online, but you'll stumble across some interesting ones if you look around:

- **Jump Games** for some interesting online diversions

- **Jump CR** for Consumer Reports' online profiles of cars, electronics, consumer-oriented legislation, and more

- **Jump Encyclopedia** for Grolier's frequently-updated encyclopedia

- **Jump Weather Maps** for quick pictures of national and regional conditions

- **Jump Baby-Sitters** for an online convention of *Baby-Sitters Club* fans, including interactive adventures, letters to and from Ann Martin (author of the series), and new stories

- **Jump Make It!** for step-by-step instructions for family-style crafts

- **Jump National Geographic** for an online adventure guided by the experts

- **Jump Web** to try out the Internet's World Wide Web

If you get into a screen and you don't know how to get back out, click the Menu button on the toolbar or press Ctrl+M—it'll take you to the previous menu. If you want to go all the way back to the beginning, click the Highlights button at the far left of the toolbar, or press F5 if the button isn't visible.

 TIP **If you like the service you're using, open the Page menu and** choose Xref. It'll show you a list of related services.

TIP **If you accidentally stumble upon a service you like, and think you** won't remember how to get there in the future, check the title bar—it lists the current service's Jump word beside the word PRODIGY.

Keeping a list of your favorite places

Prodigy maintains a unique hot list for each user, so you can keep the Jump words handy for the areas you visit most often. To view your current hot list, press F3 or select Jump, Hot List. Just click any item on your hot list to go to it immediately.

To add a Jump word to your hot list, click the Change Hot List button. The Change Hot List area appears. Click the Add button, and follow the directions that appear to add a hot word. You can delete any hot word by clicking the Delete button and following the instructions.

TIP **Clicking the P button on the toolbar or selecting Jump, Path will** move you to the next area on your hot list, so you can move through your hot list quickly without bringing up the list each time you want to make a move.

Using BBs

Prodigy's bulletin boards (BBs) are the gathering places for people who share common interests. **Jump BBs** to see the main bulletin board screen.

CAUTION **Bulletin Boards are PLUS features. That means there's an hourly** charge to use them. There's more discussion about billing and charges at the end of this chapter.

To browse the BBs:

1 Click either the Boards A-Z button or the Topics A-Z (BB names are sometimes only marginally related to their topics).

2 Scroll through the list with the PgUp/PgDn keys or the arrow keys on your keyboard.

3 When you find a BB you'd like to visit, click it. You'll see an opening screen for the BB, as in figure 10.7.

Fig. 10.7

Here's the first thing you'll see when you visit a BB. There's a welcoming message, and an opportunity to select the topic and subject you want.

Click here to choose a topic

Click here to choose a subject

BBs are arranged by topic area. Within each topic area, there are subjects, and people post messages under subjects. It's not as complicated as it sounds, and it saves you from having to read messages on topics and subjects in which you have no interest.

Once you're in a BB:

1 Look for the Choose a Topic box on the right side. Click Choose a Topic to see a list of the topics being discussed on the BB.

2 Click a topic.

3 Choose the Begin Reading Notes button to see the subjects in that topic. If it's a popular topic, you'll have to page through many subjects. You can type the first few letters of the subject in which you're interested, to move quickly to that place on the list. (I did this in fig. 10.8.)

4 Select a message you'd like to read.

When you've read a message, look at the bottom of the screen. If other people have replied to the message, the Next Reply button blinks, otherwise the Next Note button blinks. If you'd rather go back to browsing the messages, choose the Subjects button at the top of the screen, or switch topics with the Topics button. You also can choose to reply to the current message, either publicly (with the Reply button) or privately (with E-mail Reply, which sends a note to the message's author).

Fig. 10.8
You can use Page Up or Page Down to move through the subjects, or type some letters to move quickly in the list.

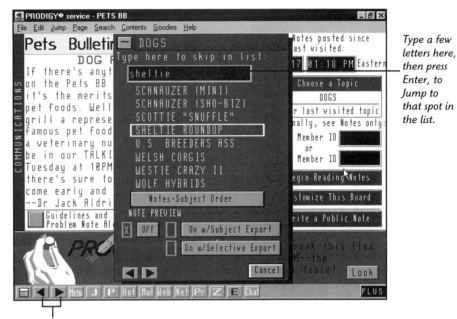

Type a few letters here, then press Enter, to Jump to that spot in the list.

These buttons work the same as pressing Page Up and Page Down.

Where can I find software?

Prodigy doesn't have a huge file section like most online services, but one of their affiliates does: ZiffNet is available through Prodigy (for an extra charge), and their software library is huge enough to satisfy almost any software aficionado. **Jump ZiffNet Selections** to check them out.

When you're in ZiffNet's software library, you can search through the files by category or title. When you get to a file list, you see the title, size, and *cost* of each file. That's right—as soon as you download a file, ZiffNet chalks up that fee on your Prodigy bill.

Because it's so expensive, Prodigy is not the best online service for downloading files. The same program that costs you $3 to download on ZiffNet can usually be found on another service, such as America Online or CompuServe, and you'll only have to pay the per-hour connect charge, not the extra fee.

CAUTION   **If you have a slow modem (2400 bps, say), it might take more** than an hour to download a big program. If one service lets you download it for free, but charges $5 an hour general connect time, and ZiffNet charges $3 for the entire file, which is a better deal? You need to look carefully at the total charges involved in your online activities, and decide what's best for your individual situation.

Sending and receiving e-mail

E-mail is a popular feature on any online service, and Prodigy is certainly no exception. The first thing most people do when they log on is check the bottom of the screen for that little envelope (if the envelope is there, you've got new mail).

TIP   **E-mail is one of Prodigy's big bill-inflators. E-mail is a PLUS** feature, so when you're reading or typing, you rack up hourly online charges, even though it's your brain and fingers that are working hard, not Prodigy itself. If you plan to use e-mail a lot, check out Prodigy's E-mail Connection software (available directly from Prodigy, currently $14.95), which lets you read and write messages while you're offline. **Jump E-mail connection** for details.

Prodigy's mail is handled through a program called Prodigy Mail. (Clever title, eh?) You enter that program automatically when you open your mailbox. To open your mailbox, follow these steps:

1 Click the picture of the envelope at the bottom of the screen, if you have new mail, or **Jump Mail** if you don't see the envelope there.

2 If you get a message saying you have no new mail, and asking if you still want to go to your inbox, click Yes.

Prodigy Mail opens, showing a summary of the mail in your inbox, as shown in figure 10.9.

Fig. 10.9
Prodigy Mail helps you manage your incoming and outgoing mail.

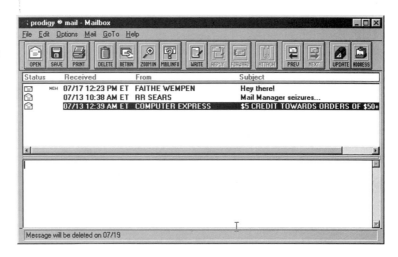

Sending e-mail

To send an e-mail message on Prodigy, start Prodigy Mail (as just explained), then follow these steps:

1 Click the Write button. A blank message screen appears.

2 In the To box, type in the address(es) to where you want the message to be sent. (If you don't know the address, see "How do I find my friends' addresses?," later in the chapter.)

TIP It's easy to send e-mail to any other online service—just type that person's Internet address. For instance, my addresses are **DaveWriter @aol.com** (America Online), **75430.174@compuserve.com** (CompuServe), **JoeUser@geis.com** (Genie). Of course, you can send mail to actual Internet addresses as well, as in **fwempen@iquest.net**.

3 Tab to the subject field and type a subject.

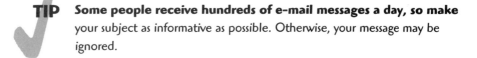

TIP Some people receive hundreds of e-mail messages a day, so make your subject as informative as possible. Otherwise, your message may be ignored.

4 Tab to the message area and type away. A finished message is shown in figure 10.10, in case you want to compare it to your own.

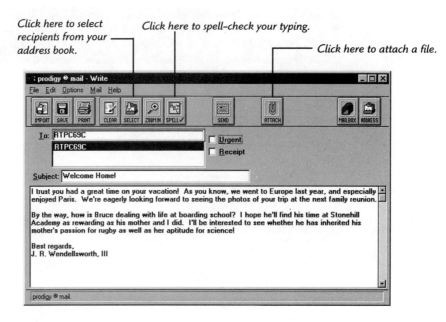

Click here to select recipients from your address book.

Click here to spell-check your typing.

Click here to attach a file.

Fig. 10.10
Here's a sample message you could send—but it might be better if you created your own instead.

TIP You can send a file attached to a message easily—just click the Attach button and specify a file to attach.

5 When you're finished, click Send.

If you prefer to write messages in your word processor, you can still send them with Prodigy. This saves you the time (and money) you would spend connected to Prodigy while composing your thoughts. Follow these steps:

1 Before you connect to Prodigy, save the files in your Prodigy directory (plain text format is best—check your word processor's documentation for instructions on saving a file as plain text).

2 After you address the message, click the Import button.

3 Select the file you want to use in the message.

4 Click Send.

Reading e-mail

It doesn't get much easier than this. Enter Prodigy Mail, then double-click the message you want to read. It appears in the lower pane of the Prodigy Mail window (see fig. 10.11).

Fig. 10.11
When you double-click a message, it appears for your perusal.

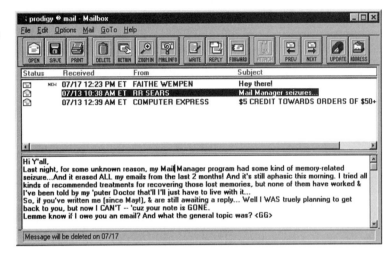

From here, you can click any of the toolbar buttons to act on the message—save it, print it, delete it, retain it, reply to it, and so on.

How do I find my friends' addresses?

If you can't remember someone's e-mail address (and as we've already pointed out, Prodigy addresses are tough to remember anyway), try the Member List.

To find a Prodigy member's ID, you have to exit Prodigy Mail and **Jump Member List**. (You can do this by selecting Mail, Member List within Prodigy Mail.) From there:

1 Click the By Name button to search for the person by name. You also could search by location, but your chances are pretty slim if you only know what *state* they're from.

2 Type in the last and first names, then click OK.

3 Select the state or province you think the recipient is from. If you don't know, select Search All.

4 The search begins, and Prodigy displays a list of members, with the name you chose at the top. (FYI, this is an alphabetical list of every member, so you can page through it if the name you typed didn't appear, to find perhaps a different spelling.)

5 Click the number next to the person's name to see their full ID and their city and state.

6 Click the Add button to add the person to your address book, or click Write to send this person a message now.

TIP **You may see a different message composition screen than Prodigy** Mail if you click the Write button—something more primitive, like in figure 10.12. Don't worry—just fill in the blanks and click Send. It works just the same. Prodigy Mail is a new feature, and it hasn't been tied in with all the features that use Mail as of this writing.

Fig. 10.12
If you choose to write a message directly from the member directory, you might see a mail composition screen like this, instead of Prodigy Mail.

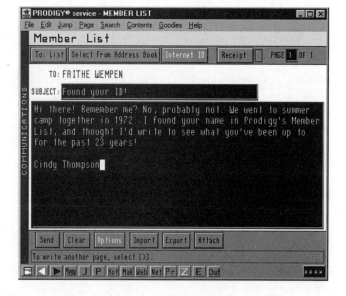

TIP **Not everyone is listed in the Member List, so you'll only find your** intended recipient if they've specifically requested to be listed.

Chatting with other users

Bulletin boards and e-mail simply don't satisfy that part of us that looks for immediate feedback—you know, the part that makes us run up 100-dollar phone bills instead of writing 32-cent letters. Online chat is about as close as you get to telephone conversation on Prodigy, and it's at least as addictive.

Jump Chat to talk with other Prodigy users. Any time you sign on, you're bound to find from 100 to 1,000 people (or more) chatting, in a wide variety of groups.

To start chatting:

1 **Jump Chat**. You'll see a welcome screen.

2 Click either Prodigy Chat or Pseudo Chat, whichever suits your interests. (See the following sidebar for more information.) Since this is a family-type book, we'll go with Prodigy Chat for the examples.

3 In the window that pops up (see fig. 10.13), you'll see the Select an Area box with dozens of choices. Each area has a collection of topics, which you see when you click an area. Since I'm a writer, I'm going to look for other writers. I'll click the Common Interests area.

There's Chat, and then there's CHAT...

There are two chat areas on Prodigy:

- **Prodigy Chat**. A mostly clean and wholesome place for both kids and adults.

- **Pseudo Chat**. A virtually uncensored and often lewd and lascivious place for adults.

The first time you enter Pseudo Chat, you're given all kinds of warnings, and given the opportunity to block some or all of the IDs in your membership from using the feature. This is for the benefit of parents who want to keep their kids out of the racy stuff.

For more rooms and areas, click a different room type.

Fig. 10.13
Find a room that strikes your fancy, then click Go to Room to get there.

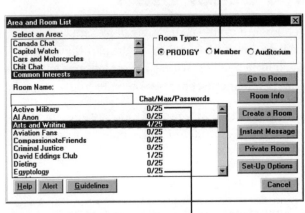

Select a room with a number larger than 0 in the Chat column; 0 means there's no one there.

4 Click the room name that matches your interest. We're going for the Arts and Writing room. We're in!

5 Do your chatting thing. (The graphics page that follows these steps can help you figure out what to do.)

How do you decipher the Chat/Max/Passwords info in Prodigy's chat rooms?

The Chat/Max/Passwords column tells you if there's anybody in the room. For example, if it says 3/25 it means there are 3 people in the room that holds up to 25 people. If it says 25/25 (or any other equal numbers), it means the room is full. If you see the words Entry and/or Text in the Chat/Max/Passwords column, it means you have to have a special password to get in.

CAUTION **Prodigy's chat rooms are uncensored, and though all of the truly** adult topics show up only in the Member rooms, nobody (not even Prodigy) can guarantee the content of any chat areas, just like no one can guarantee your kids won't hear swearing on the street. If you want to exclude a member of your household from using Chat, see the section "Adding members and choosing access" earlier in this chapter.

A typical Prodigy chat

There's a lot to see and do in Prodigy Chat, and it all moves fairly briskly. Beginners can miss out on a lot just trying to figure out the controls! The following figure can help.

Click here to set some chatting options. You can choose whether to have your ID number displayed, among other things.

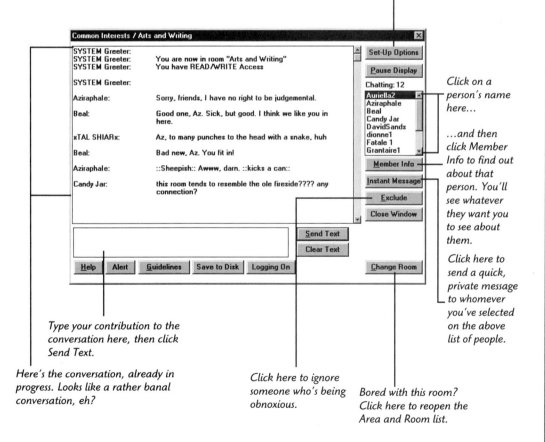

Click on a person's name here...

...and then click Member Info to find out about that person. You'll see whatever they want you to see about them.

Click here to send a quick, private message to whomever you've selected on the above list of people.

Type your contribution to the conversation here, then click Send Text.

Here's the conversation, already in progress. Looks like a rather banal conversation, eh?

Click here to ignore someone who's being obnoxious.

Bored with this room? Click here to reopen the Area and Room list.

What's all this talk about World Wide Web?

As you'll learn later (in Chapter 12), the World Wide Web (WWW or the Web for short) is part of the Internet. Prodigy offers a great, easy-to-use Web browser as part of its Plus services. To access it, **Jump Web**, then click the Browse the Web button.

 Plain English, please!

A **browser** is a program (or in Prodigy's case, a program-within-a-program) that enables you to view text and graphics found on the World Wide Web.

 CAUTION **The World Wide Web is uncensored, and therefore unpredictable.** In general, it's not for kids. To limit who in your family can use this feature, click the Enrollment button and follow the instructions there. You must have set up IDs for each member of your household beforehand, as explained earlier in this chapter in "Adding members and controlling access."

Then what? Once you see the Prodigy Home Page (as shown in fig. 10.14), just start clicking parts of the page, and you're off to all kinds of interesting spots on the Internet. See Chapter 12 for many more details about the Internet and World Wide Web.

Fig. 10.14
Prodigy's Web browser will take you all over the Internet!

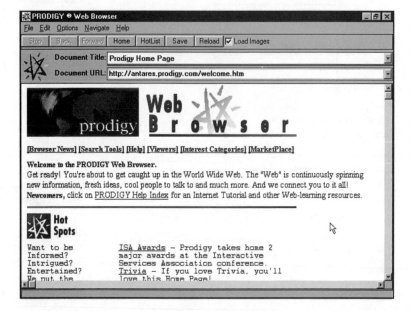

How much does Prodigy cost?

Prodigy currently has three membership plans, but in the quick-change atmosphere of online service charges, they may be wildly different by the time you read this. (Call 800-PRODIGY or **Jump Fees** for current charges.)

The Basic plan (which is the default) costs $9.95 per month. It includes five free hours of Core and Plus services, with each additional hour billed at $2.95. Table 10.1 shows the service types on Prodigy.

The Value plan costs $14.95 month. It gives you free time in all Core services (which include most of the services on Prodigy) and charges you $2.95 for each hour of Plus services (past the first five, which are free). If you use Prodigy more than five to seven hours a month, this is the better plan.

The 30/30 plan costs $30 a month and gives you 30 hours, with which you can use for both Core or Plus services. This is a good deal for the hardcore user.

Table 10.1   Prodigy Services

Area type	Description
Free	Information about Prodigy, online help, etc. is free of online charges. When you're using a Free service, you'll see the FREE buttonlike icon in the lower-right corner of the screen.
Core	The majority of Prodigy's services are Core services. When you're in a Core service, CORE appears in the lower-right corner.
Plus	Many of the most popular services are Plus, including E-mail, Chat, BBs, and airline reservations. When you're in a Plus service, the box in the lower-right corner shows PLUS.

In addition to the regular charges, Prodigy offers Custom Choices. These are extra-special (supposedly) features for which people (allegedly) don't mind paying extra. Certain news retrieval services and games are Custom Choices. The exact extra cost depends on the service, but some games, for instance, cost about $30 for twelve weeks of play.

Saving money on Prodigy

The cardinal rule with saving money on all online services is *spend as little time online as possible*. You can accomplish this on Prodigy several ways:

- Get the fastest modem you can find. It'll pay for itself very quickly in online savings if you use Prodigy more than a few hours a month.

- Whenever possible, compose and read your e-mail offline. The E-mail Connection program may be of help to you if you use e-mail a lot—**Jump E-mail Connection** to find out about it.

- When you view an article, choose the Copy option from the Edit menu. When the Copy window pops up, choose Story. Click Save As in the Copy window and enter a filename. This puts the article on your disk so you can read it when you're offline—that way you don't needlessly pay for the time you spend reading.

11

Calling the Microsoft Network

● **In this chapter:**

● What's so special about the
Microsoft Network?

● Signing up and signing on

● How do I find my way
around this place?

● Files, chatting, and other fun stuff

● Keeping track of your favorite areas

*The Microsoft Network may be new, but with a company like
Microsoft behind it, you just know it's going to be good. . .* **>**

As if you needed another reason to upgrade to Windows 95, after the cool stuff I showed you in Chapter 4, "Going Online with Windows 95," here's another reason: The Microsoft Network.

The Microsoft Network (MSN) is definitely the new kid on the block in the online services game. As of this writing, it's been up and running for less than two months. My preliminary impression of it, I have to admit, is less than outstanding. It's a little bit harder to use than America Online, and certainly doesn't have the volume of stuff that the other big three services have accumulated over their years of operation. But check with me in a year or so, and I may have changed my mind. It's possible. With the aggressive Microsoft Corporation behind it, The Microsoft Network may soon become the "in" place to be online.

 **CAUTION** **Because the service is just starting up, it's going through some** changes, and will continue to do so for its first year or so. Like the ugly duckling, most services go through an awkward phase. So by the time this book gets published, some of the instructions in this chapter may not work exactly the same anymore. There'll probably be newer and greater features available than the ones I'm describing here, too. But you should be able to find your way using the basic procedures you'll learn here, no matter what changes come about.

To use The Microsoft Network (MSN), you need Windows 95. In fact, that's how you get the startup software for MSN—it's included with Windows 95. Since you can't run MSN without Windows 95, and since every copy of Windows 95 comes with MSN, there's no phone number to call or two to three week wait for software to arrive by mail. It's all right there at your fingertips.

Becoming a member

No, there's no secret handshake required to become a member of MSN. All you need to do is install the software (if it's not installed already), double-click the Microsoft Network icon, and follow the onscreen instructions. Anyone (that is, anyone with a major credit card) can do it. Like the other online services, they want your money.

When you installed Windows 95, if you used the default settings, MSN did not install automatically. You had to specifically choose it. If you did, you'll see a Microsoft Network icon on your desktop, like so:

If you don't see that icon there, that means you'll need to install the software. (I'll explain that in the following section.) If you see the icon there, you can jump right to "Signing up for MSN" later in the chapter.

Installing the software

Installing MSN is as simple as installing any other Windows accessory or component. Just dig out your Windows 95 installation disks or CD, then follow these steps:

1 Click the Start button, and then choose Settings, Control Panel. Double-click the Add/Remove Programs icon.

2 Click the Windows Setup tab, and use the scroll bar to move through the list until you find The Microsoft Network (see fig. 11.1).

Fig. 11.1
Here's where you can choose which Windows components you want installed. In this case, we want The Microsoft Network.

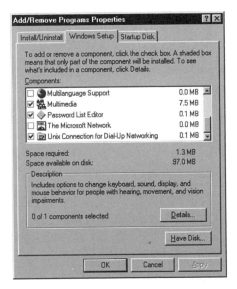

TIP **While you're at it, check out the other Windows 95 accessories** and options that you may not have installed yet. If you see something else you want to check out, go ahead and click its checkbox to select it too.

3 Click the checkbox next to The Microsoft Network to select it.

4 If Microsoft Exchange isn't installed yet, you'll get a dialog box asking if it's okay to install it too. (MSN needs it.) Click Yes to continue.

5 Click OK. You'll get a message telling you what disc or diskette you should insert into your computer. Do it, then click OK to continue.

6 If you installed Microsoft Exchange, you'll be asked some questions about your setup. Just click your answers then click Next to step through the procedure.

When you're done, you should see the Microsoft Network icon on your desktop. You're ready to go on to the next step, which is signing up for MSN.

Signing up for the goodies

Even if the software is installed, it doesn't do anything until you sign up for MSN. To sign up, you go through a fairly simple procedure where MSN asks you questions and you answer them, like so:

1 Double-click the Microsoft Network icon on your desktop. You'll see a welcome screen. Click OK to move past it.

2 Next, you're asked about your area code and the first three digits of your phone number. Enter these in the appropriate blanks, then click OK.

3 The installation program comes back at you with a phone number that will be used to make a very brief call. This call will retrieve the latest sign-up information and phone number list. Click Connect to let it happen.

4. MSN connects, does its business, and disconnects, all in less than 30 seconds. Then you'll see the Sign Up screen displayed in figure 11.2.

5 Click the Tell Us Your Name and Address button, the first one on the screen. A screen appears with blanks for all the pertinent information about you—name, address, phone number, and so on.

6 Enter your information into the blanks, then click OK.

Fig. 11.2

Here's where you enter the information that MSN needs to sign you up.

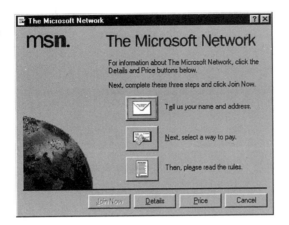

7 Click the Next, Select a Way to Pay button. A screen appears with several major credit cards listed in a box at the top.

8 Select the type of credit card, and blanks appear below for you to provide the information about your card. Enter the information, then click OK.

9 Finally, click the last button on the start-up screen, Then, Please Read the Rules. A policy statement from MSN appears. Click the I Agree button after you've read it (assuming you do agree).

10 Click the Prices button to find out what the current pricing system is, then click OK to return.

11 Notice that now the Join Now button is available. Click it to send your information off to MSN.

12 MSN has selected phone numbers for you from its directory. You'll see them on the next screen that appears. Click OK to accept them.

13 Click the Connect button to sign on for the first time.

14 The first thing you'll see is a request for a Member ID and Password (see fig. 11.3). Enter the name of your choice (your real name or an alias) and a password in the corresponding blanks, then click OK.

Fig. 11.3
Choose a unique member ID and a hard-to-guess password.

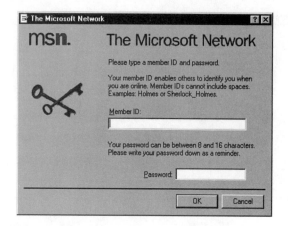

CAUTION **All the usual precautions apply to selecting a password—jumbles** of letters, numbers, and other characters are best, and the longer the better. Make sure you write it down after you type it in! Unlike some services, MSN will not ask you to type it twice to confirm it.

As soon as you enter your Member ID and Password information, MSN disconnects again, and you'll see the regular Sign In screen that you'll deal with from now on. We'll look at it in the next section.

Signing on

Once you're signed up for the service, connecting (a.k.a. **signing on** or **logging on/in**) is a snap. Just double-click the Microsoft Network icon on your desktop, and you'll get the Sign In screen shown in figure 11.4

Fig. 11.4
Here's where you sign in, with your member ID and password. You did write them down, didn't you?

Enter your Member ID and Password in the appropriate blanks, then click Connect, and you're off to the races.

TIP **If you're the only one who ever uses your computer, you can save** time by checking the Remember My Password checkbox. That way you won't have to type your password each time. On the downside, though, anyone who sits down at your computer will be able to sign in, impersonating you and running up charges.

The first thing you'll see when you connect is the MSN Central screen, shown in figure 11.5. A window might also open displaying the MSN Today news, shown in figure 11.6. You can close or minimize the window to get it out of the way.

Fig. 11.5
MSN Central is your home base for all MSN activities.

Click here if you want to see the MSN Today screen.

Click this house icon to return here, MSN Central, at any time.

If you don't see this toolbar, select View, Toolbar.

TIP **You can turn off MSN Today, so it doesn't pop up automatically,** from the MSN Central screen. Select View, Options, and click the General tab. Deselect the Show MSN Today title on startup checkbox, then click OK.

Fig. 11.6
MSN Today is the daily
update for what is
happening around the
Microsoft Network.

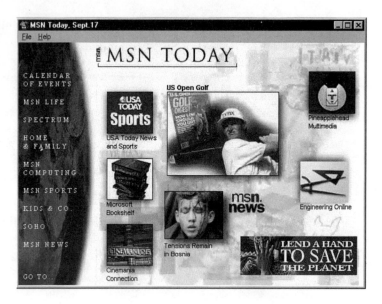

Signing off

When you want to leave, any of the following will work. Figure 11.7 shows
them.

- Click the Sign Off button on the toolbar
- Double-click the MSN window's control-menu box
- Click the MSN window's Close button
- Open the File menu and select Sign Out
- Double-click the tiny MSN icon next to your clock in Windows' taskbar

Double-click the control-menu box.

Fig. 11.7
The many ways of
leaving MSN.

Select File,
Sign Out.

Click the
Close button.

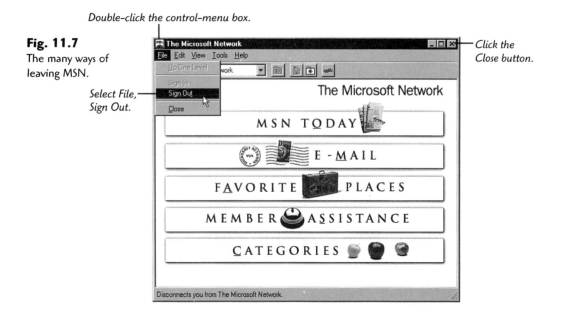

How do I get help?

There are several ways to get help with MSN. One of the best is the online
help system. Like all reputable Windows programs, the MSN program has a
great online help system that you can browse or search for whatever subject
you're confused about. To access it, select Help, Help Topics, and use it as
you would any Windows 95 help system.

TIP **Need Help using Help? Sounds like one of those unsolvable**
paradoxes... But seriously, there's information about using Windows 95 style
Help systems available throughout Windows 95. Click the Start button, then
select Help. Click the Contents tab, then double-click the book labeled
How To. Find Using Help on the list that appears and double-click it. You'll
see a list of documents that will help you figure out the Help system.
Double-click any document to read it.

Another way to get help is through MSN's Help forum. It's called Member
Assistance, and you can access it right from MSN Central (refer to fig. 11.5)
by clicking the big Member Assistance bar in the middle of the screen. When

you do so, you're whisked away to the Member Assistance area, where you'll find lots of help possibilities, as shown in figure 11.8. Actually, your screen will probably look different from the one shown in figure 11.8, because the Help system is in a constant state of flux—they're always adding to and improving it.

Fig. 11.8

MSN's Member Assistance information is constantly changing, so you may see different choices here than I have displayed.

To check out a help topic, double-click its icon. Here are some places you might want to stop:

- Reception Desk—This is just like a reception area in a business. Here you'll find the most basic information about and guidelines about MSN—kind of like waiting-room reading.

- Maps and Information—A great stop for first timers. You'll find a directory of the services offered, an explanation of how MSN is organized, and even a place to sign up for a personal guided tour of MSN.

- Member Agreement—This is a text version of what you agreed to when you signed up with MSN, for your reference.

- Accounts and Billing—To find out your current bill totals, or learn more about the payment plans available, check this area out.

- Activities and Promotions—Look here for what's hot and new on MSN.

The Member Assistance area is constantly improving, so you may find even more assistance available than shown in figure 11.8. Just double-click what you find, and go!

Getting around in MSN

If you know how to navigate the Windows Explorer program that comes with Windows 95 (under Start, Programs), you're well on your way to understanding MSN, because they operate on the same principle. MSN is a big maze of folders and shortcuts, and all you have to do is double-click what you want.

In MSN, everything is broken down into categories. To see the list of categories, click Categories in the MSN Central screen. The categories are ever-changing, but the ones that were available the day I tried it are shown in figure 11.9.

Fig. 11.9
Almost every topic imaginable, from bowling to computer hardware, is contained in one of these categories.

To check out a category, just double-click it. You'll get another group of icons, with which you can further narrow your interest. Double-click again, and keep double-clicking icons until you arrive at something interesting to read, do, or download. I'll talk about the various types of activities you'll find in the remainder of this chapter.

TIP **Sometimes you can't tell what type of activity you're getting into** by looking at the icon. Most folder icons look more-or-less like folders, but with many others, you won't know if you're jumping to a different area of MSN or reading a text file. You just have to double-click and see what happens. Online time is cheap, so you can explore!

Reading text files

A text file is a text file is a text file. (Take *that*, Gertrude Stein!) In other words, reading a text file in MSN is the same as reading a text file in Windows 95 itself. You double-click its icon, and the text file opens in whatever program you've specified for viewing.

 Plain English, please!

MSN's text files are in RTF (Rich Text Format). This is better than plain text, because the files can include special formatting and colors that make them more attractive and easier to read. Almost all word processing programs can open RTF files, so you can use your favorite word processor to view MSN's text files. **99**

 Q&A **How do I choose a different program to view text files in?**

Keep two things in mind: 1) MSN text files are RTF format, which means they have .RTF extensions, and 2) Windows 95 enables you to choose which program is associated with which file extensions. Do you see where I'm headed?

To change which program opens RTF files, open Windows Explorer. Select View, Options, and click the File Types tab. Find Rich Text Format on the list of file types, and select it. Then click the Edit button. Click the word Open in the Actions list, then click the Edit button. In the Application used to perform action text box, type the full path to the program you want to use to open the file. Then click OK, Close, and Close again to exit.

Reading and posting to bulletin boards (BBSs)

If you've explored other online services already, you're familiar with the concept of **bulletin board systems**, or **BBSs** for short. They're areas where you can post public messages on a variety of subjects, and other people read them and post public replies to your messages. Like their name conjures up, it's sort of like leaving a note tacked to a bulletin board in your office, and then coming back later to find that someone has read your note and written a response on it, and perhaps tacked up a new note of his own.

Almost all of the areas you'll find in the categories have their own BBSs. Unlike other services, where each BBS is broken down into subcategories, each MSN BBS is just one big list of notes, so naturally there have to be a lot of separate BBSs, so people interested in computer hardware don't have to page through any messages about computer software.

Usually (but not always), BBSs will be identified as such, so you'll be able to see what you're getting into, like so:

Pagemaker &
Quark BBS

Double-click a BBS icon to see a list of messages, as shown in figure 11.10.

Fig. 11.10
Here's a typical BBS on the Microsoft Network. Amazing, isn't it, how so many people have so much to say?

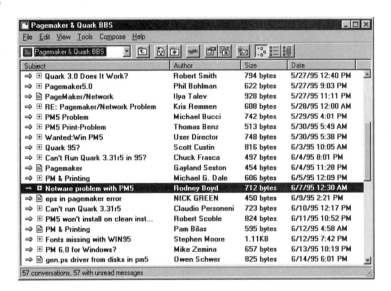

As if the list of messages in figure 11.10 isn't daunting enough, let me tell you that there's more. Lots more. Each note that has a plus sign next to it has replies. Click the plus sign to see the replies listed. When you do that, you'll see that some of the replies have plus signs next to them, indicating replies-to-replies! Sometimes there are many levels of replies-to-replies-to-replies in a BBS.

❝ *Plain English, please!*

Whenever you've got a message with at least one reply to it, you've got a **conversation**. ❞

Reading a BBS message

Don't let all those levels scare you—it's actually fairly easy to move through them. Double-click the message you want to read. It'll appear, as shown in figure 11.11.

Fig. 11.11
Double-click a message to open it in a viewing window like this one.

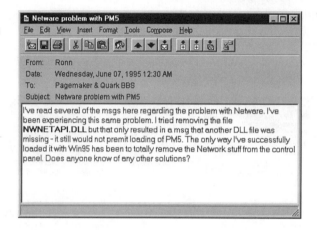

Here are some of the things you can do with a message once you've read it:

 Save this message to disk. You're prompted for a file name and a location.

 Print this message.

 Reply to the message. A blank message composition screen appears, but with the subject already filled in.

When you're ready to move on to another message, you don't have to go back to the BBS list of conversations—you can use one of the following toolbar buttons to see another message:

 View the previous message (or response, if you're reading responses).

 View the next message (or response, if there are more responses to the original message).

 View the next unread message. Same as above, except it skips the ones you've already read.

 View the next conversation. It skips the replies and proceeds directly to the next original message.

View the previous conversation. Same as above, except it goes backwards.

 View the next unread conversation. Skips over replies, and any original messages you've read already.

Replying to a message

 When you click the Reply button, a window opens where you can type a reply to the message. Figure 11.12 shows my reply to the message in figure 11.11—notice that the Subject line has already been filled in for me. (I could change it if I wanted to, and thereby start a new conversation, but it sums up the topic fairly neatly, so why bother?)

Fig. 11.12
Do you have something to say about a message you read? Reply to it!

Click here to send.

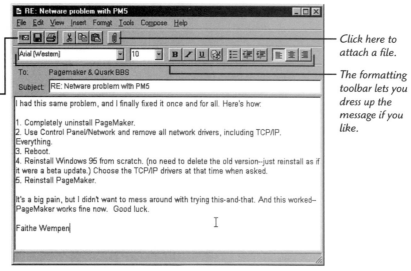

Click here to attach a file.

The formatting toolbar lets you dress up the message if you like.

 TIP **Reading Internet newsgroups works exactly the same way as** reading any other BBS—you just click a message, and it appears. You can print it, save it, or respond to it, like always.

Where do I find software?

Yes, Virginia, there's software available on MSN. You might have noticed that when you are writing a BBS message, you have the option of attaching a file to it. Well, that's how software arrives at MSN—people attach it to messages.

So technically, any BBS message could have a downloadable file attached. There's a lot more information about software available in Chapter 16, "Finding Software Online."

Fortunately for anyone who is looking for files to download, it's not the custom to attach interesting files to BBS messages, where they can be easily overlooked. Instead, files are normally attached to messages in a File Library area.

Let's look at an example: my favorite area, Computer Games. To find it, go through Categories, Computers and Software, Software, Electronic Games, and Computer Games Forum. Double-click the Computer Games File Library icon, to see the list of computer games folders.

TIP **MSN changes so frequently that I can't guarantee that the** Computer Games area will be exactly where I described it, or that it'll be there at all. If it's not, work with what you can find—the instructions I'll give in this section will work with any File Library area.

Double-click any folder to open it, and you'll see a message list that probably looks very familiar—it's just like the message list you saw back in figure 11.10, structure-wise. The only difference is that each file has a paper clip icon next to it, indicating that there's a file attached.

Double-click any message to open it, and you'll see text describing the game, plus an icon for the game itself (see fig. 11.13).

Fig. 11.13
Downloadable files are attached to regular-looking messages in MSN.

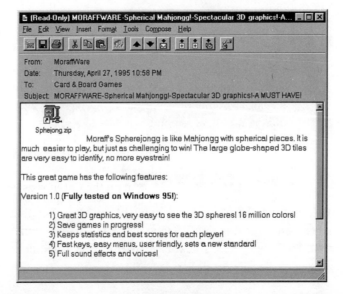

Double-click that icon, and you'll see a description of it, along with two buttons: Download File, and Download and Open. Click Download File, and a File Transfer Status window opens up, where you can see the file being downloaded (see fig. 11.14).

Fig. 11.14
Use this window
to control your
downloads.

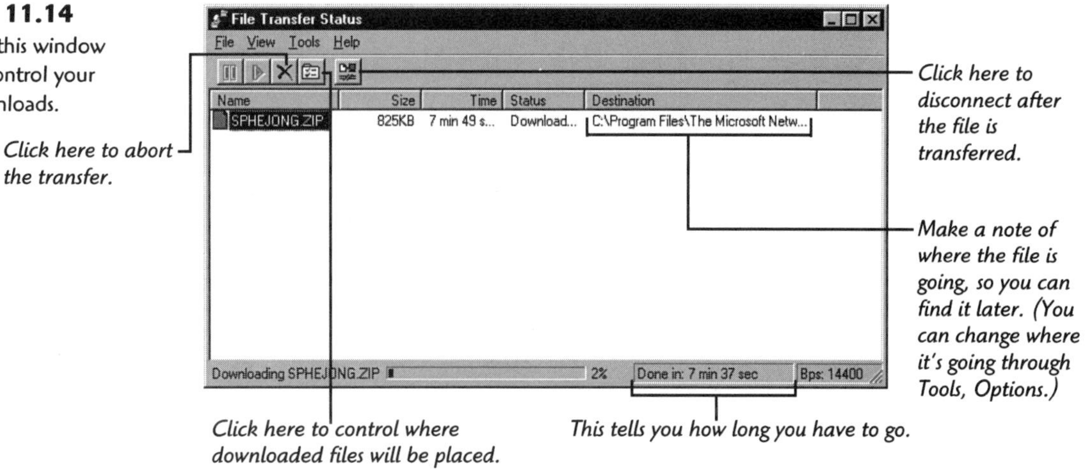

Click here to abort
the transfer.

Click here to
disconnect after
the file is
transferred.

Make a note of
where the file is
going, so you can
find it later. (You
can change where
it's going through
Tools, Options.)

Click here to control where
downloaded files will be placed.

This tells you how long you have to go.

Use Exchange to send e-mail

MSN doesn't have its own e-mail system *per se*—it uses Microsoft Exchange, a mail program that comes with Windows 95. I covered it pretty thoroughly in Chapter 4, so refer there now if you will.

To open Microsoft Exchange while you're in MSN, all you have to do is click the E-Mail bar in the middle of MSN Central (refer to fig. 11.5). From there, you just read your mail and reply to it in the same old Microsoft Exchange ways.

Online chatting

MSN's chat area is called Chat World. It's structured like a big hotel, with all kinds of meeting rooms (both public and private). You can get to it by double-clicking the Chat World icon on the Categories list.

TIP **There are many other chat rooms on MSN than the ones listed in** Chat World. One way to find all the chat rooms is to use the Find feature. Select Tools, Find, On the Microsoft Network. Set Of Type to Chat, and leave the Containing field blank. Click Find Now, and a list of all chat rooms will appear. You can go to any chat room on the list by double-clicking it.

You enter a chat room the same way you activate any feature—by double-clicking it. Once you're in the chat room, you'll see something like figure 11.15.

Fig. 11.15
Here's a lively chat room where folks are discussing their Windows 95 problems.

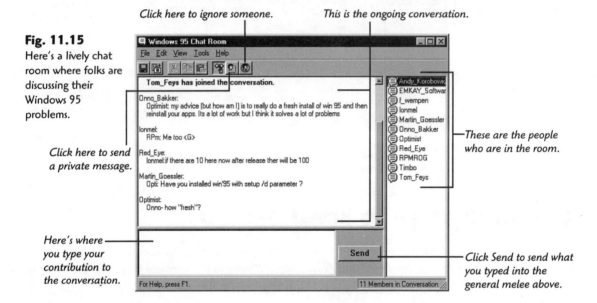

Click here to ignore someone.

This is the ongoing conversation.

Click here to send a private message.

These are the people who are in the room.

Here's where you type your contribution to the conversation.

Click Send to send what you typed into the general melee above.

Finding good stuff

Wading through category after category is all well and good if you've got lots of time, but if you're looking for something in particular, it can be maddening. Would religion be under People & Communities, or under Home and Family? Or maybe it's considered an interest, in which case it would be under Interests, Leisure & Hobbies? It's enough to drive even a patient person mad—mad, I tell you.

Fortunately, there's a fix. You can look for your particular interests with the Find feature. Follow these steps:

1 Select Tools, Find, On the Microsoft Network. A Find screen appears, as in figure 11.16.

Fig. 11.16
Find your favorite stuff quickly and painlessly here.

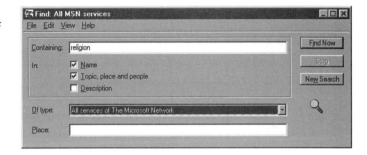

2 Type the word or phrase you're looking for in the Containing field.

3 Select checkboxes to tell MSN where to look:

Name: searches in the name of each area

Topic, place and people: Searches by the text listed in the topic, by location (for instance New York), and by the people using that feature

Description: looks in the area's description

4 Choose the type of area you're looking for from the Of Type drop-down list to narrow your search, or leave it set at All Services of The Microsoft Network to find it all.

5 Click the Find Now button. A list of all the places online that match the criteria appears. You can double-click any of them to go there immediately.

TIP **You can add any item that Find shows on its list to your Favorite** Places list by right-clicking the item and then selecting Add to Favorite Places from the shortcut menu that appears. You'll learn about Favorite Places in the following section.

Keeping track of your favorite places

Once you've found an interesting area, you'll probably want to visit it again. But who wants to wade through countless levels of folders and categories to get there each time, or search again for it with Find? Ugh, not me.

Fortunately, you can keep track of the places you like with your Favorite Places list. Almost all the online services have this feature, so you may already be familiar with it. The Favorite Places list is a collection of shortcuts to the areas you choose. You can open the list, then double-click any of the shortcuts to go directly to that area.

As you're working with MSN, you can add a location to your favorite places list at any time. When you arrive at an area you want to add, just open the File menu and select Add to Favorite Places, or click the Add to Favorite Places button on the toolbar. You won't see anything special happen, because MSN doesn't want to interrupt you, but rest assured that the shortcut has been placed on your Favorite Places list.

To access the Favorite Places list at any time, just click the Go to Favorite Places icon in the toolbar, or select Edit, Go To, Favorite Places. A window containing all your favorite places icons appears, as in figure 11.17. Just double-click any icon to go to that area!

Fig. 11.17
As you can see by my favorite places, I have some fairly diverse fascinations.

MSN's Internet connection

One nice feature of MSN is the seamless integration of all things Internet-related into the service. Use the Go To word **Internet** to see all the Internet offerings in one place, or discover them as you go along under various categories.

As I mentioned earlier, Internet newsgroups are treated like regular BBSs, with lists of conversations. You read and reply to them exactly as you would with a BBS. Internet e-mail is also integrated—you can send an e-mail to an Internet address as easily as a message to another MSN member.

As a MSN member, you also have access to Microsoft Internet Explorer, a World Wide Web browser. (You have to set up the software for it first, but MSN walks you through this process the first time you access it.) To use it, use the Go To word **Internet** to reach the Internet Center, then double-click the World Wide Web icon and follow the directions that appear.

What does it cost?

At this writing, there are a few different subscription plans available to MSN. The plan that you start with is the Trial Plan. It gives you up to ten hours the first month absolutely free. This gives you a bit of time to play around and decide whether MSN is for you. This plan expires 30 days after your first sign-on, so you have to pick another plan within 30 days. If you go over your ten hour allotment, each additional hour is $2.50.

The most economical plan is the Charter Member plan, which Microsoft says will only be available to the first 500,000 people. (They haven't said what they'll charge for a regular subscription after that.) The Charter Member plan is $39.95 a year (that's right—you buy a whole year in advance) and includes three hours per month. Additional hours are $2.50 apiece. There are no restrictions or special charges—everything you can do on MSN is covered in the price.

The other plan hasn't been officially announced at this writing. It's going to be some sort of economy plan, for people who use MSN a lot. It'll include twenty hours a month for a fixed rate. No word yet on how much it'll cost, but you can get the latest details about it online.

To examine details about the various subscriptions available, and to change to a different plan, select Tools, Billing, Subscriptions. Then click the Subscriptions tab in the dialog box that appears to see the various subscriptions available. Select the one you want, then click the Change button to change to it.

TIP **There's a special area on MSN Member Assistance just for the** financial end of the stick—from the Member Assistance screen, double-click the Accounts and Billing icon. Here you'll find text files that describe the latest billing procedures and subscription offers.

12

Calling the Internet

● **In this chapter:**

- **So just what exactly *is* the Internet?**

- **Tell me the basics of the Internet**

- **What can I do?**

- **Tell me all about the World Wide Web**

- **How do I use basic Internet tools like Telnet, FTP, and Gopher? And what are these things, anyway?**

- **How do I access the Internet? What's it cost?**

In the 1980s the cry was, "I want my MTV!" Today it's, "I want my Internet!" Just as MTV revolutionized how we get our music, the Internet, and the service providers who let us use it, are revolutionizing how we get our information . . . . ⊳

The Internet isn't run by the government. It's not owned by one company. You can't buy Internet stock (but you can buy stock on the Internet—but that's another topic).

Simply put, the Internet is really just a name. It's not one particular computer that you can see, or that you can blame when something goes wrong. (Unlike my own computer or the network at my office, the Internet itself has never been "down.") The term **Internet** simply describes what you don't see: the underlying network that all of the computers on the Internet participate in. It is a network of networks, if you will. Each entity on the Internet—be it a government agency, corporation, or commerical network—is responsible for maintaining its own systems and connections to other systems.

The Internet grew out of a 1960s US Department of Defense project aimed at linking together all of the institutions across the country that were doing military research, which included a number of government agencies and universities. First, it expanded to include all types of research—medical, scientific, and so on—going on at companies and institutions around the world. Over the past few years, it's expanded even more rapidly into general business and personal applications of all sorts. Today, the rush is on as companies strive to develop new Internet services that are beyond the imagination of even the most creative thinkers of the early days of the Internet.

You, too, can be a part of the Internet. People across the globe are rushing to "get on the Net." It used to be difficult and costly to get an Internet connection. Now, it's easy—and cheap (relatively speaking). And with all of the new capabilities being added to the Internet, it can become a very useful tool for both your business and personal life. If industry experts are right, the Internet of the future may, in fact, become an integral part of all our lives.

Finding your on-ramp

Although there is no Internet "organization" that you pay once you're on the Internet, accessing the Internet is expensive due to the necessary computers and networking hardware that must be bought. If you had to connect directly to the Internet youself, you could spend thousands of dollars doing so.

So, instead, many companies have sprung up that offer access to the Internet to people using modems. The companies pay for their expensive computers and networking hardware, and simply charge you for your use of those resources. These companies are generically called **internet on-ramps** or, technically, **Internet Service Providers (ISPs)**.

There are many ISPs available to connect you to the Internet. They range from small ISPs in your area to large companies like IBM, Microsoft, CompuServe, and America Online. All of these organizations sell you Internet access using a variety of different pricing schemes.

Different ways to connect

There are two different methods used to connect to the Internet through a service provider.

The first method is called a **shell account**. With this type of access, you dial into the ISP computer and your computer merely acts like a text-mode terminal of their system. Sometimes you end up running the UNIX operating system, which is just a bit like DOS, but much more complex. With this type of account, you type commands and use text-based programs to access the Internet. Shell accounts are usually the cheapest way to use the Internet, but can be very complex if the company doesn't use a friendly GUI interface (see fig. 12.1). If you're not a computer nerd, stay away from shell accounts that only use Unix.

Fig. 12.1

Here, you see me transferring a file from a system on the Internet to my ISP's system, and then transferring the file from the ISP's system to my computer.

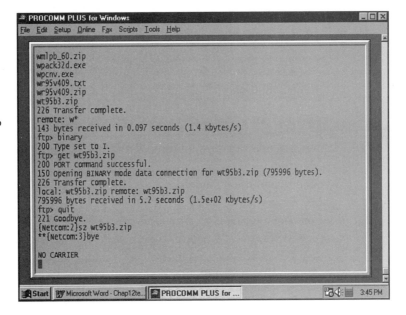

The second method lets your computer act as if it were connected to the entire Internet. This is called a **remote node**. With this type of access, you can use all the graphical tools available for working with the Internet, such as Windows-based programs like Netscape. Some companies even provide Windows-based programs along with their service. For example, NetCom, one of the fastest growing ISPs, offers subscribers its NetCruiser software to access all the various Internet features. Another example is CompuServe, which also offers graphical tools for accessing the Internet, as you can see in figure 12.2.

Fig. 12.2
Here, I'm transferring the exact same file from the same system on the Internet, but I'm using a much easier graphical file transfer tool that CompuServe offers. Just point and click to download!

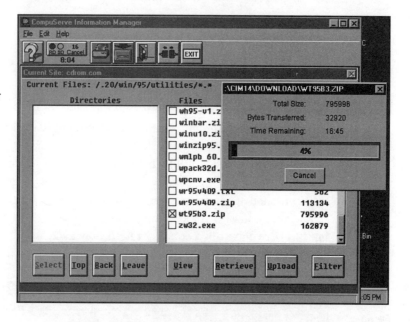

Remote nodes are by far the easiest and most powerful way to work with the Internet, although they generally cost a bit more than shell accounts.

SLIP? PPP? What's that all about?

There are two sub-types of remote node access: SLIP and PPP. Both refer to the underlying technology that's used to establish the connection between your computer and the Internet service provider. **SLIP** stands for **Serial Line Internet Protocol**, while **PPP** is short for **Point-to-Point Protocol**. At present, most service providers offer SLIP access through their consumer-oriented programs, while others are starting to move to PPP access. Basically, it doesn't matter which you use, so long as you have the matching software from your ISP.

How much does it cost?

Prices for access to the Internet vary considerably and change frequently. Here are a couple of examples of different programs:

Provider	Type of account	Charges
NetCom	NetCruiser (Windows)	$19.95 per month. Includes 40 free hours for prime time (9:00 a.m. to midnight). Unlimited hours after prime time. Additional prime time hours cost $2 per hour.
IBM	Getting Started (OS/2 Warp)	$14.95 per month. Includes three free hours; $3 per hour for additional hours.
IBM	Comprehensive (OS/2 Warp)	$29.95 per month. Includes 30 free hours per month. Additional hours billed at $2 per hour.
CompuServe	Standard and Super Value	Included with your CompuServe membership, billed at the same rates as normal CompuServe access.
Microsoft Network	Varies	Billed at the same rate as normal MSN access.

 CAUTION **There is a lot of competition between Internet service providers.** The prices just listed may not be accurate at the time you read this. Check with the individual service providers in question for up-to-date prices.

How do I find an on-ramp?

The best way to find an Internet provider is to ask around in your area. Talk to your computer salesperson, or the salespeople at a software store. People at work can be good sources of information, as can the local newspaper. Different areas have different providers, and there are also some national services, such as NetCom, Microsoft Network, CompuServe, America Online, and IBM's Advantis.

Enough hype: What's it really good for?

The Internet is a very complicated place, but its power is easy to tame if you know what to do and where to look. You can send and receive e-mail, hunt for information, talk to other people, download software, and much more. How you do all this depends on the tools you're using, and what area of the Internet you're looking in. This section will give you an overview of the Internet, including a little about the different tools available to you.

World Wide Web

Imagine that you have to catalog all of the information stored on hundreds of thousands of computers and create a way for people to find the information easily. What a nightmare! It's a lot like looking for a needle in a haystack.

The World Wide Web is a tool that was developed to meet this need. It's a relatively new development on the Internet, but it has quickly become the most popular. Using it, you can browse through hundreds of thousands of documents on the Internet, called **pages**. Each page has **links** to other pages, and these links are usually related to the topic you're viewing (see fig. 12.3).

How do I know which ISP is right for me?

There are several key things that you'll want to take into account when choosing an ISP for yourself:

- How often will you be using it?
- During what hours will you normally access the Internet?
- Does the ISP have an access number that's in your local calling area? (You want to avoid long distance phone charges if at all possible to keep your costs down.)

- Does the ISP offer the software you'll need?
- Do you need other services besides access to the Internet? For instance, do you need to access CompuServe so you can use their research databases? Do you want to use AOL or The Microsoft Network?

Given these factors, you should be able to examine the different pricing plans and features of the ISPs in your area and choose an appropriate service provider that meets your needs and budget.

Fig. 12.3
When you use the Web, you'll first see a home page that's the "home base" for your use of the Web. Here, you see MSN's home page.

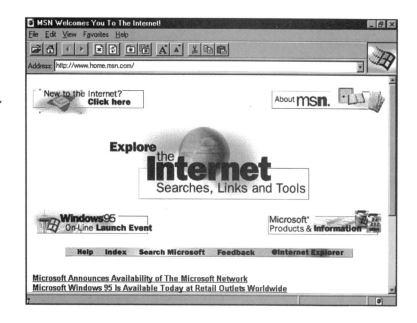

The World Wide Web is a graphical tool, and so all of these pages and links are represented with a combination of text and pictures, making it easy to use. For instance, you might be looking at a page on sailboats, and there might be a link to another page that shows sailboat manufacturers. The links will be represented either as highlighted text, or as pictures. Click the highlighted text or the picture, and you're instantly whisked to the page that the link connects to. Just keep clicking links to jump to all sorts of connected pages on the Web. Figure 12.4 shows you how this works.

Where are all these Web pages, anyway?

The beauty of the World Wide Web is that it's truly world-wide. When you click a link on a Web page, you jump to a different computer that stores that new page you just jumped to. And the computer might be just down the street, or on the other side of the world. So not only are you jumping from page to page on the Web, but you're doing it by jumping from computer to computer, state to state, and country to country—and there's no jet lag! And it's all automatic! Plus, there are no long distance charges for accessing computers all over the world; you just pay for telephone access to your ISP, and you can instantly access all of these other computer systems.

Fig. 12.4
Here's an example of a Web page, shown using the Microsoft Network's Web Explorer.

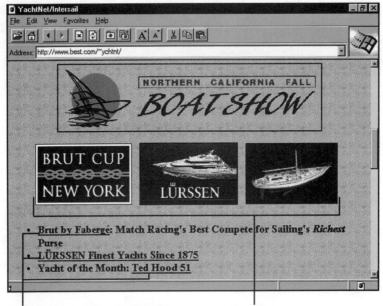

You can also click these highlighted names to jump to their Web pages.

You can click these three pictures to jump to the pages to which they're linked.

You access the World Wide Web through a program called a **Web browser**. Most Internet providers that offer World Wide Web access can tell you how to get Web browsing software that you can use as part of their service, or they'll include it along with their other access software.

Gopher this, gopher that!

Another tool that aims to make the Internet easier to use is **Gopher**. Gopher puts a menu system onto the Internet, in which each menu option links to Internet resources. You can follow the menu tree and use it to browse the contents of computers all over the world. Figure 12.5 shows Gopher being used through a shell account.

A tour through some Gopher tunnels

Let's say you're on the Internet using Gopher, and just want to explore around and see what you can find. Using the menu shown in figure 12.5, you choose option 6, Other Internet Gopher Servers. Choosing this shows you the screen shown in figure 12.6. Figures 12.7 through 12.11 show some more options.

Fig. 12.5
The Internet's Gopher puts a menu onto Internet resources. Gopher is an early predecessor to the World Wide Web. While primitive in comparison, it's still useful.

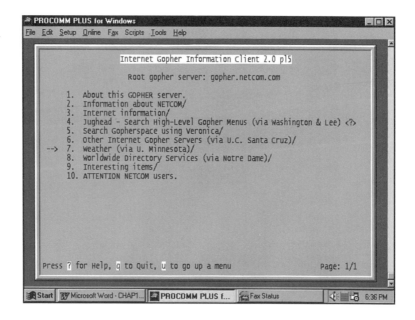

Fig. 12.6
After choosing a menu option, we see a new menu. This one lists Gopher servers by country. Hmmm, let's see what the Russians are up to by choosing option 12.

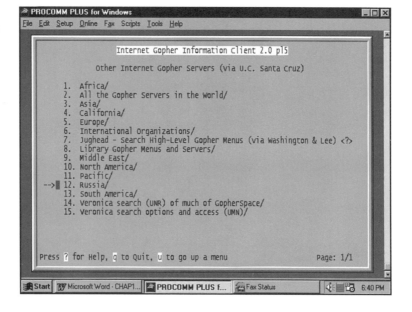

Fig. 12.7

Another menu! Let's keep on going, and check out the Global Ukraine Inc. Gopher, option 2.

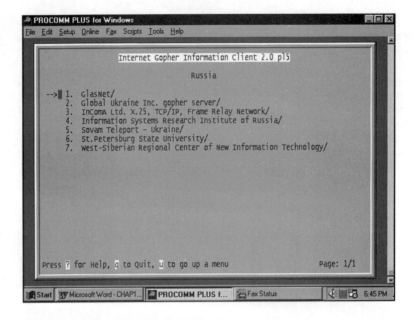

Fig. 12.8

I'm in a fun mood, just exploring. So I think I'll check out Anekdotes and other fun!, option 5.

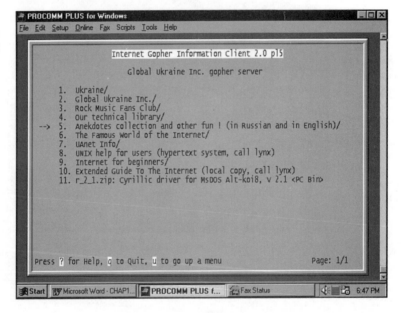

Fig. 12.9
Do these Gopher menus ever end? OK, I like a good cup of coffee. Let's see what's behind menu option 4.

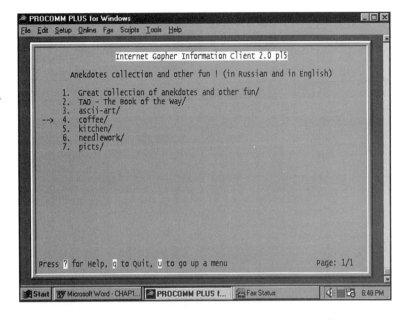

Fig. 12.10
Hmmm. Two of these menus look like they might be in Russian, which isn't going to do me any good. But the coffee.faq entry looks interesting...

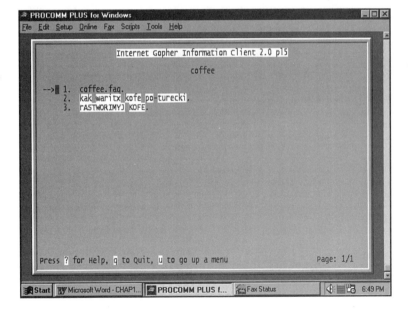

Fig. 12.11
Hey, cool! The FAQ
(Frequently Asked
Questions) has all kinds
of great information
about coffee in it.
After reading it, I know
more about coffee
than anybody on my
block.

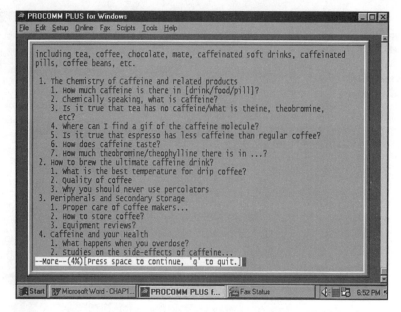

```
including tea, coffee, chocolate, mate, caffeinated soft drinks, caffeinated
pills, coffee beans, etc.
  1. The Chemistry of Caffeine and related products
     1. How much caffeine is there in [drink/food/pill]?
     2. Chemically speaking, what is caffeine?
     3. Is it true that tea has no caffeine/what is theine, theobromine,
        etc?
     4. Where can I find a gif of the caffeine molecule?
     5. Is it true that espresso has less caffeine than regular coffee?
     6. How does caffeine taste?
     7. How much theobromine/theophylline there is in ...?
  2. How to brew the ultimate caffeine drink?
     1. What is the best temperature for drip coffee?
     2. Quality of coffee
     3. why you should never use percolators
  3. Peripherals and Secondary Storage
     1. Proper care of Coffee makers...
     2. How to store coffee?
     3. Equipment reviews?
  4. Caffeine and your Health
     1. what happens when you overdose?
     2. Studies on the side-effects of caffeine...
--More--(4%)[Press space to continue, 'q' to quit.]
```

Q&A *How do I find anything in all these Gopher menus?*

There are over 5,500 gopher servers on the Internet, most of them containing many gopher menus. Finding anything in all this would be impossible without a couple of friends: Veronica and Jughead.

These two are the names of search tools for what is loosely called **gopherspace**. They let you find Gopher menus that contain a word or phrase that you're looking for. Both let you enter search words, and they will then go and find all of the gopher menus that contain the word you're looking for.

You can usually access both of these tools from the menu that first appears when you start Gopher. Or, your ISP may have a submenu that includes access to these searching tools.

Telnet

Remember that the Internet has been around for a long time—a lot longer than graphical computer interfaces, in fact. In the early days of the Internet, you had to connect to other computers in order to work on them. When you connected to these remote computers, you used a program called **Telnet** that let you access the remote system just as if you were sitting at one of its terminals, looking at its screen and typing on its keyboard. You became a remote terminal to the remote system, with the Internet acting as the underlying go-between. Using Telnet, you can run programs on the remote computer.

Telnet is still alive and well on the Internet, and some Internet services require its use. In order to use Telnet, you have to know several things:

- The Internet address of the computer you're trying to connect to—sometimes you also need a port number

- A valid username on the remote system

- A password for the username

How you use Telnet will vary, depending on how your ISP implements it. Some may include graphical versions of Telnet that let you connect to remote systems, as CompuServe does. Others require you to use the actual Telnet program (as you would with a shell account, for instance).

From a shell account, you connect to a remote system with a command like **telnet server1.ibm.net**. Sometimes, you also have to specify a port number on the remote system, for example: **telnet lostsouls.org 3000**. The number at the end is a port number that automatically connects you to a program running on the remote system, rather than a general login screen.

FTP

Another program that's been around for a long time on the Internet is FTP, which stands for **File Transfer Program** Using FTP, you connect to remote computers on the Internet and can transfer files both from and to them. In order to do this, you need to know:

- The address of the computer to which you're connecting

- The user name on the remote system

- The password on the remote system for whatever user name you're using

 TIP **FTP servers on the Internet often allow something called anonymous ftp.** In this case, you use the word **anonymous** for the user name on the remote system, and enter in your e-mail address in place of the password. This lets anyone connect to the server in question and transfer files.

Earlier in the chapter two figures show two different methods of using FTP (refer to figs 12.1 and 12.2). In figure 12.1, you can see FTP being used with a command line interface while figure 12.2 shows a graphical interface being used through CompuServe.

When you use the real FTP program through a shell account, you need to know certain commands, as detailed in the following table.

Command	What it does
ftp	When typed from a Unix command prompt, this starts the FTP program. You typically also add on the name of the computer to which you're connecting, such as **ftp cdrom.com**, and press Enter.
ls	**ls** is short for list, and is the Unix equivalent of DOS's DIR command. Typing **ls** and pressing Enter displays a list of files and directories on the remote system.
cd	**cd** works the same as its DOS equivalent: It lets you change the directory that you're viewing on the remote system. For instance, you can type **cd /pub** to switch to the remote system's /pub directory.
binary	This command forces FTP to transfer files in binary mode, rather than in text mode. You want to use binary mode for just about every file you transfer; binary mode ensures that you get an exact copy of the file from the remote system.
get *filename*	The command **get**, followed by a filename on the remote system, copies the files from the remote system onto whatever system you're using. If you're using a shell account, the file is placed in a directory on your ISP's computer. If you're using some kind of remote node connection, the file will be placed on your computer.
mget *filename*	Here, the "m" stands for "multiple," as in "multiple files that you want to retrieve." When you want to grab a whole bunch of files from the remote system, you can type **mget** followed by a filename containing wildcards (usually asterisks, just like DOS uses). So, **MGET A*** will retrieve all files that start with the capital letter A.
quit	To end your FTP session and return to your regularly scheduled session, type **quit**.

CAUTION **The Internet, being mostly based on Unix computers, uses the** forward slash (/) to separate directory names. DOS uses the backslash (\). Keep this in mind when using FTP over the Internet, or when using Unix commands in general.

UseNet newsgroups

No matter which way you choose to get online, be it CompuServe, Prodigy, Microsoft Network, or whatever, you will no doubt run across discussion groups, or **special interest groups**. They go by many different names (forums, groups, SIGs, and so on) but they all serve the same purpose. In these groups, people with similar interests exchange messages and electronically discuss issues that are important to them. They're great fun, and oftentimes very educational to boot.

The Internet has discussion groups, too, and they're called **UseNet newsgroups**. These discussion groups range from very serious scientific discussions to fun discussions about the best computer games.

At the time of this writing, there are over 14,000 different newsgroups, each one focusing on a different topic and containing anywhere from just a few to thousands of messages. It's really, really huge, so finding what you're looking for might take some time.

CAUTION

The Internet, as mentioned before, has no controlling body or central authority. Because of this, there is nobody who censors or controls UseNet newsgroups on the Internet. Some of these groups will offend you. (It's guaranteed, no matter how hard you are to offend.)

UseNet newsgroups vary considerably in tone and content from group to group. Some are restricted to scholarly dicsussions, while others contain lots of **flames**. (A flame is a message attacking another person.) Some people send these flame messages for fun. I wish I were making this up, but I'm not. So keep your eyes open and see what kinds of messages are posted in the groups you're interested in before participating. When you're using the Internet, you're on the Electronic Frontier, where there are very few rules, and not many sheriffs around to keep law and order.

You access UseNet newsgroups through a program called a **news reader**. News readers might be text-based, such as when you're using a shell account, or Windows-based if you're using a graphical interface to access the Internet. The Microsoft Network, for instance, just shows UseNet newsgroups as normal BBS sections that you can browse.

TIP   **If you're using a shell account, try using tin, my favorite news** reader. It has lots of nice features that I haven't seen in some of the other choices out there. See if your shell provider makes it available to you.

UseNet newsgroups are divided into major groups. Each group starts with a different name. Here are some of the major groupings:

Group name	What type of information it contains
alt	Alternate subjects
biz	Business subjects
comp	Computer topics
news	Internet news
rec	Recreation discussions
sci	Science topics

Newsgroups are broken into names seperated by periods. So, one group might be called **comp.os.ms-windows.win95.setup**, which would be devoted to setup issues for Windows 95. Another two examples are **sci.psychology** and **rec.motorcycles.harley**. As you can see, knowing what information different newsgroups contain is usually pretty easy with this system.

Using Microsoft Network, figures 12.12 to 12.16 show you how newsgroups appear.

Fig. 12.12
Here, you can see that MSN conveniently creates some folders that help categorize newsgroups above and beyond the name categories.

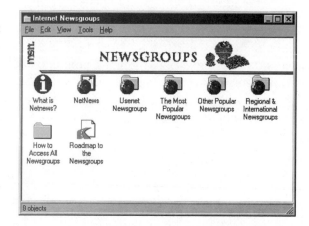

Fig. 12.13
After opening Usenet Newsgroups folder, you see the top-level folder that shows the main newsgroup categories.

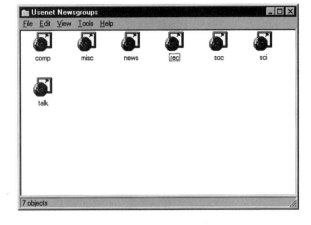

Fig. 12.14
Choosing the rec group lists all the groups in the **rec** category. Some of these folders contain other sub-folders.

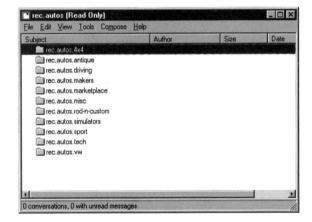

Fig. 12.15
Opening the **rec.autos** group reveals still more subdivisions.

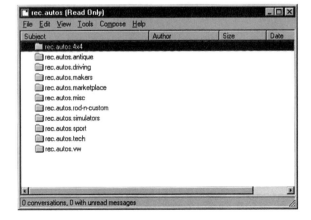

Fig. 12.16
Finally, after opening
rec.autos.4x4 you
see a number of
messages that are in
the newsgroup. MSN
conveniently organizes
all the messages by the
message title. Some
news readers don't do
this.

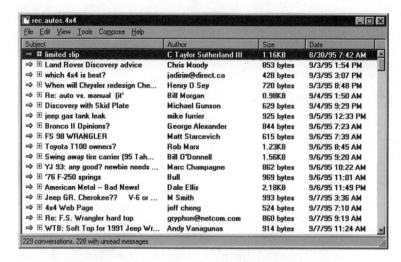

All the messages you see in the newsgroup shown in figure 12.16 are written by people just like you, who either have questions or answers about the subject contained in the header. Newsgroups can be an invaluable source of help and opinions on virtually any topic. In fact, I'll never forget the time I posted a question about general relativity in one of the physics groups and got about twenty responses over the next twelve hours in my e-mail, all of them from serious physicists who knew far more about the subject than I, and were willing to share their knowledge, just for the sake of helping someone understand something.

Q&A *What's a FAQ?*

Many newsgroups have a message that refers to something called a **FAQ**, which stands for Frequently Asked Questions. It's a file that contains answers to questions that people frequently ask. Sometimes, a message might just tell you how you go about getting the FAQ, and other times the whole FAQ is actually in a message.

You should always read a newsgroup's FAQ before posting a question to the newsgroup, as your answer may already be answered within the FAQ. One of the purposes of FAQs is to cut down on the number of unecessary messages in a newsgroup that are merely repeats of questions that people commonly ask. The FAQs contain the answers to those sorts of questions, and may have lots of other interesting information on the subject that will make interesting reading.

E-mail

One of the most useful services available through the Internet is e-mail. This lets you send electronic messages to other people who have e-mail addresses on the Internet or Internet access on other major online services like CompuServe and AOL. You can converse almost instantly with people that are next door, or across the world. All of the major online services now let you send and receive e-mail through the Internet. So, for example, you can send a message to joe@aol.com from CompuServe and your message will get through, by using the Internet as the underlying e-mail "tunnel." Thus, with an Internet account, you can send e-mail to just about anyone online.

In order to send an e-mail message to someone else online you need two things: an Internet e-mail program that works with your ISP, and the e-mail address of your intended recipient. Depending on who your ISP is, finding an e-mail program is usually easy: you typically just use the ISP's built-in e-mail program. For instance, I can use CompuServe's normal mail system to send e-mail to people on the Internet, just by giving it their Internet e-mail address. Other systems work similarly.

The other thing you need is the person's e-mail address. This will always be in the form **name@service.type**. So, for instance, if you're sending e-mail to someone who has the account name **larryv** and they have an account at **netcom.com**, their e-mail address is **larryv@netcom.com**.

 TIP **CompuServe uses commas in its account numbers. The Internet** doesn't allow commas in e-mail addresses, so periods are substituted. For instance, my CompuServe account is **76376,515**. From the Internet, it would be **76376.515@compuserve.com**.

 Q&A *Can I send files to someone over the Internet?*

Basically, the answer is yes, but it can be difficult. The problem is that Internet e-mail wasn't originally designed with file attachments in mind, and so creative ways were developed to overcome the problem.

The first method is the most difficult, but has been around the longest. Using a pair of programs called UUEncode and UUDecode, you can take a binary file, like a program file or a file from your word processor, and UUEncode it into a text file. The text file isn't usable or even understandable by you, it just looks like a bunch of gobbledygook. But it can be carried inside an e-mail message by cutting and pasting the results into your e-mail message. Then, the person on the other end can save the encoded text to a file and run UUDecode on their end, which reconverts the file to its original form.

The second, and far easier method, involves a fairly new technology that lets the Internet carry binary files attached to messages. This technology is called Multipurpose Internet Mail Extensions (MIME). In order to use MIME, both your e-mail program and the e-mail program that your recipient/sender uses must support MIME messages. While this is becoming more common, it's not universal by any means and so you need to check your e-mail program's documentation, and have your recipient do the same.

Internet Relay Chat

One of the fun programs on the Internet is **IRC**, which stands for **Internet Relay Chat**. IRC is sort of like the CB radio of the Internet, on which you can join realtime conversations with other users.

To enter IRC, using a shell account, type the command **IRC**. (If you're using a graphical method to access the Internet, you'll need to ask your ISP how to do this.) Once you've entered the IRC area, you can choose a nickname for yourself with the command **/nick** *nickname* (where *nickname* is your nickname, such as **Scooby** or **Jimbo**). I recommend that you use a nickname that does not identify who you really are.

There are lots of channels in IRC, and you can see them all with the **/list** command. Figure 12.17 shows a listing scrolling by on my system. To get help, type **/help**. To quit IRC, type the **/quit** command.

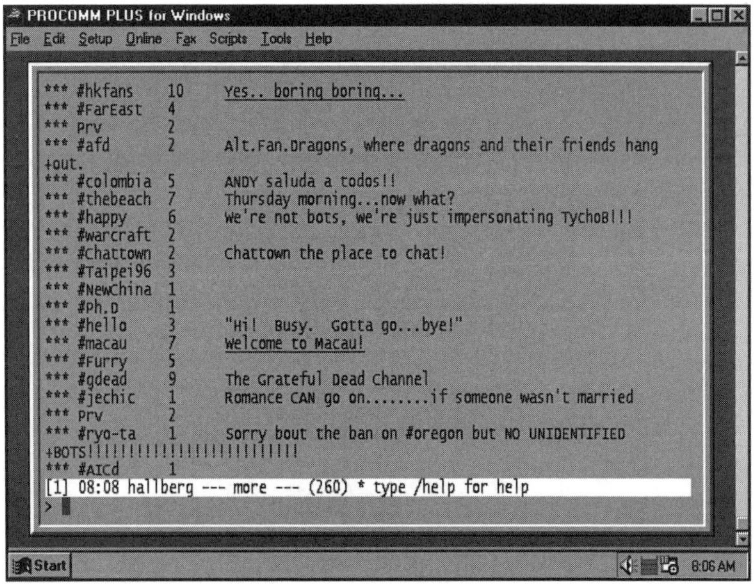

Fig. 12.17

A list of the channels open on IRC lists the channels' names, how many people are present in the channels, and in some cases a description of what sort of discussions the channels contains.

```
PROCOMM PLUS for Windows
File  Edit  Setup  Online  Fax  Scripts  Tools  Help

*** #hkfans    10    Yes.. boring boring...
*** #FarEast    4
*** Prv         2
*** #afd        2    Alt.Fan.Dragons, where dragons and their friends hang
+out.
*** #colombia  5    ANDY saluda a todos!!
*** #thebeach  7    Thursday morning...now what?
*** #happy     6    we're not bots, we're just impersonating TychoB!!!
*** #warcraft  2
*** #Chattown  2    Chattown the place to chat!
*** #Taipei96  3
*** #NewChina  1
*** #ph.D      1
*** #hello     3    "Hi!  Busy.  Gotta go...bye!"
*** #macau     7    Welcome to Macau!
*** #Furry     5
*** #gdead     9    The Grateful Dead channel
*** #jechic    1    Romance CAN go on........if someone wasn't married
*** Prv        2
*** #ryo-ta    1    Sorry bout the ban on #oregon but NO UNIDENTIFIED
+BOTS!!!!!!!!!!!!!!!!!!!!!!!!!!!!
*** #AICd      1
[1] 08:08 hallberg --- more --- (260) * type /help for help
>
```

Internet 101: Understanding addresses

One way to think of the Internet is as a complex street system. You have freeways, tollways, city streets, and even some dirt roads here and there. With a street system, how do you know who lives where? With addresses, of course. The Internet is no different, and every computer and person on the Internet has an address. These addresses are what allows your computer to connect to a computer on distant shores.

Computer addresses

At the most basic, computer-oriented level, all computers on the Internet are assigned a unique numeric **address** that has the form $xxx.xxx.xxx.xxx$, where each xxx is a number from 1 to 255. So, my computer might have an address of 192.1.45.255 while yours has an address of 128.64.12.5.

Now, this is all well and good, but it's not very useful as is. It would be a real pain if you had to type in a command like **CONNECT TO 192.1.45.255** every time you wanted to send an e-mail message to my computer. So a naming convention was developed that makes addresses easy for humans to use. These names are called **domain names**. The underlying numeric address is still there, but there's also an easy-to-use address that's made up of simple words, separated by periods. Examples of named addresses include **server1.ibm.net** or **barney.netcom.com**. Each part of the name has meaning, too.

Let's work backwards. The last part of the name is called the **top-level domain**. It broadly defines what sort of organization owns the computer you're connected to. In the previous examples, the top-level domains are **.net** and **.com**. Here are the six major top-level domains and what they stand for:

Top-Level Domain	Organization Type
.com	A company, or commercial site
.edu	An educational institution
.gov	A government entity
.mil	A military organization
.org	A miscellaneous organization, often non-profit
.net	A network resource

There are also top-level domains for most major countries. For example, you might see **.uk** for the United Kingdom, or **.de** for Germany.

The next part of the address, to the left of the top-level domain, is the **domain**. Broadly, this is the name of the actual organization you're connecting to. So, the address **whitehouse.gov** would define a government organization (the top-level domain), and specifically the White House (the domain).

The first part of the address, before the first period, is the actual name of an individual computer, also called a **host**. If you connect to **server1.ibm.net**, **server1** is the name of the actual machine to which you're connecting.

Just like it's easier to find "123 S. Main" than "house 16, street 7, area 19, district 28, city 12, state 38, country 5," the Internet's **domain naming system (DNS)** makes understanding Internet addresses much easier than all those numbers—and it gives you some clues about what, exactly, you're connecting to.

People addresses

Individuals also have addresses, and they are defined as part of a domain. For instance, one of my e-mail addresses is **BruceH1@ibm.net**. The first part of the address is my name on the system, while the address after the @ symbol defines what domain I'm a member of. To send me an e-mail message, you would address it to **BruceH1@ibm.net** or my other Internet account, **hallberg@netcom.com**. (Of course, if you really want to reach me, you should send a message to **76376.515@compuserve.com**—I check that daily.)

TIP **A couple of neat e-mail addresses to keep handy are president@whitehouse.gov and vice-president@whitehouse.gov.** You can actually send e-mail to them over the Internet! For a list of other interesting addresses to visit or write, see the "Places" file included on the CD that accompanies this book.

Web Addresses

Web pages are also accessed through addresses, although you usually don't need to know them if you're just following links between pages. However, sometimes someone will tell you about a neat Web page, or you'll read about one, and you'll need to use its address to access it.

Web pages use an address called a **Uniform Resource Locator**, or **URL** for short. Mostly, they follow the form: **http://www.servername/directory/filename.** Your Web browser will have a place to enter in a page's URL, often in a field at the top of the screen, or in a command that's called something like Open or Open Document. See your Web Browser's documentation for details on how it handles this.

13

Calling BBSs

● **In this chapter:**

● **Tell me about BBS systems**

● **How do I find BBSs?**

● **What do they cost?**

● **What can I expect to do with a BBS system?**

You don't have to limit your electronic horizons to the big services like CompuServe or Prodigy. Often, what you need is available just around the corner . . . . **>**

When you go shopping, you can choose between those huge superstores that carry everything from chain saws to diapers, or you can go to small, specialized "mom-and-pop" stores. Depending on what you need, both offer advantages. Want "one-stop shopping?" Go to a large department store. Do you want specialized products? Go to a smaller, specialized store.

The online world is no different. There are big "superstore" services, such as CompuServe, AOL, and GEnie. And there are smaller, specialized services, in the form of **bulletin board systems** (**BBSs**). Depending on what you need and want, both offer advantages. In this chapter, you learn about what makes BBSs unique.

What's a BBS?

Bulletin board systems are typically small, specialized services offered on computers run by individuals or small companies. In fact, with a computer, phone line, and modem, you can easily and cheaply set one up yourself. There are thousands of BBSs scattered all across the country, and probably some in your local area (see fig. 13.1).

Fig. 13.1
Here you see the main menu for a BBS in my area called Palladin BBS.

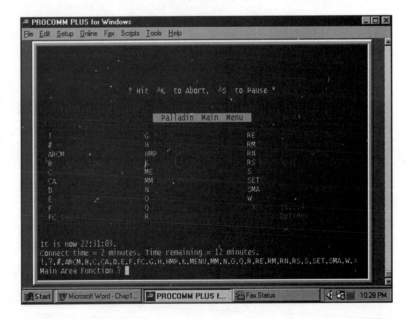

What can I do with a BBS?

BBS systems generally offer these services, although services vary considerably from system to system:

- File downloads and uploads—most offer shareware or freeware programs that you can download and use

- E-mail to other members of the BBS

- Discussion groups, where people post messages that are publicly available to all members

- Information files of all sorts

- Picture and sound files

- Discussion groups carried between BBSs across the world, called **echoes**, that you can participate in

- Online games, including some that you can play against other users of the system

- Many suppliers of computer hardware and software operate and maintain BBS systems for their customers where you will find updates to their products and sometimes areas for questions (and hopefully answers) pertaining to their products. Many require that you enter the serial or registration number as you sign up the first time so it's a good idea to make sure you have that information handy, as well as the product version or model number, before you call in

How do I find BBSs?

You can find local BBSs in a number of ways. Here are some suggestions:

- Get a copy of *Que's BBS Directory*, which includes over 2,000 local and national BBSs arranged by area code, topic, and various other configurations

- Ask people you know that use them

- Check your local newspaper's classified or computing section (BBS advertisements can sometimes be found there)

- If there's a local computer newspaper, there will be ads for BBSs in it

- Ask salespeople at your local computer or electronics store

- There are a number of national magazines devoted to online activities and BBSs that will contain many listings; check the magazine stand at your local computer or book store for the best selection.

- Once you find one BBS, it will likely have a listing of others in your area, or even nationally; often, this listing is contained in a bulletin that you can read, or in a file that you can download

How do I connect to a BBS?

You connect to BBSs using **terminal software** on your computer. Examples of this type of program include HyperTerminal (which comes with Windows 95), PROCOMM PLUS, Crosstalk, Windows 3.1 Terminal, Qmodem (a shareware program), as well as a host of others.

When you use this type of software, you define the BBS in the software's phone book, or dialing screen (see figure 13.2). You tell the software what phone number to use, what modem speed to use, and what other communications parameters are necessary. The **communication parameters** refer to:

- The number of data bits (usually 8, sometimes 7)

- The parity the remote system needs (usually None, sometimes Even or Odd)

- The number of stop bits to use, which is usually 1

- The terminal type the remote system expects—this is usually ANSI-BBS

See Chapter 3, "Installing Your Software," or the glossary (included on this book's CD) for more information on these terms.

I created the directory in figure 13.2 using a file called USBBS*xxx*.LST (where *xxx* is the version number of the document) that's available for download from many BBS systems.

Once you've set your parameters, you tell your software to dial the remote system, a connection is established, and the remote system walks you through its sign-up process and gives you menus to interact with it.

Fig. 13.2
Here's one of my
dialing directories in
PROCOMM PLUS
for Windows.

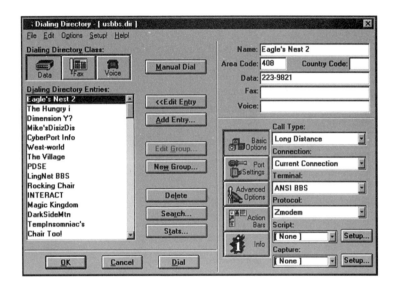

TIP **Almost all information services that tell you the phone numbers**
for BBSs also include the parameters that you'll need to connect.

How do I download files?

Once you connect to a BBS, it will show you menus that help you navigate
the system. Most often, it will also have lists of files that are available for
download. You access these lists of files, and the download function, through
your menu choices. You can browse the list of files and select ones that
you're interested in. Once you've found what you want, you tell the remote
system to download the file to you. Once it begins, you then tell your software to receive a file. During this process, you tell both the remote system
and your software what download protocol to use—they have to match.
Figure 13.3 shows a file download in progress.

TIP **Some software programs automatically sense when a remote**
system starts sending a file, and automatically start receiving it for you.
PROCOMM PLUS for Windows, for instance, will do this.

Fig. 13.3
Downloading a file
with PROCOMM PLUS
is easy. It automatically
senses when the
remote system starts to
send a file, and starts
receiving the file
automatically.

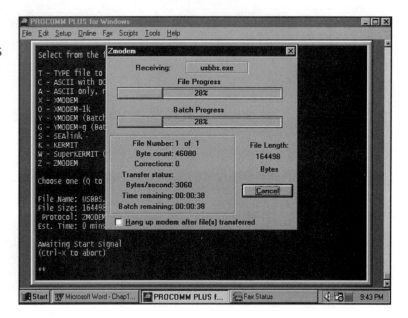

66 *Plain English, please!*

A **download protocol** defines how files are transmitted. The best all-around one to use is Zmodem. If that isn't available, Ymodem is another good choice.

Download protocols are like specialized languages that both computers must speak in order to transfer the file from the remote system to your computer without error. There are many different protocols that have been developed over the years, so there are almost always lots of choices to choose from on both the remote system and your system. Some other protocol names are Xmodem, Kermit, CIS B+, and IND$FILE. 99

Tell me what it costs

Since BBSs are operated by individuals and small companies, and because the services they offer vary widely, costs vary from system to system. Here's a summary of different pricing plans I've seen:

- Free, with no restrictions

- Free, but you're limited to a maximum amount of time each day or each call

- Free, so long as you upload files in which others would be interested and maintain a certain ratio between your downloads and uploads

- A monthly charge, which you pay either with a check or a credit card (see fig. 13.4)

- A combination of free and charged access. Free users are limited in what they can do, while paying members receive more connect time, or higher download limits, or whatever

Fig. 13.4

Oops! I overstayed my free trial time on this BBS. Now I have to pony up and use a menu option to enter my credit card information if I want to access the BBS anymore.

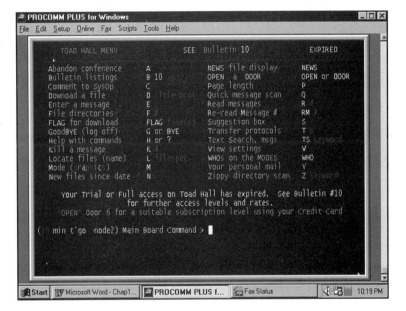

 CAUTION In addition to any charges that you have to pay to the BBS, don't forget that you also have to pay for your long distance telephone charges (if applicable) to access the system.

What's FidoNet?

Many BBSs participate in FidoNet, which is a network of BBSs that form various discussion groups. There are groups for almost every interest you might have. FidoNet **Special Interest Groups** (**SIGs**) are exchanged between the different BBSs on, typically, a nightly basis. That means that every night, any messages you write will be distributed to the other systems, and new messages from other systems will become available on your local BBS.

Protect yourself on the electronic frontier

There's a reason why communicating with your computer is often called "being on the electronic frontier." This is a new area for lots of people, and there is little policing done to protect people from unscrupulous BBS operators or hackers. Almost all BBSs are run and maintained by people who do it for the joy of it, and are careful, thoughtful people. But there are just a few who are not.

Follow these simple precautions when using an unfamiliar BBS:

- Think carefully about whether you want to subscribe to a BBS with your credit card. Perhaps sending a check or money order might be a better idea? It's not only an issue of worrying about the BBS operator, but other people accessing the system could, conceivably, break its security and access its member lists. This kind of thing is rare, but it doesn't hurt to be careful.

- Some systems don't carefully check programs available for download for computer viruses. There are many virus-checking programs on the market. These programs are available on most BBS systems, along with instructions for using them. Carefully check programs you download with a virus checker before running them on your system. Keep in mind, though, that BBS systems are considered to be one of the rarest places from which to catch a computer virus. Still, be careful.

- Some BBS systems contain copyrighted material that should not be available for download. These are often called "Pirate Boards." Downloading from them could mean that, if the owner of the BBS is prosecuted at some point, your name could come up as a user of the system and could therefore have additional, serious ramifications to you. Keep your nose clean on the electronic frontier.

- Follow the rules of the BBS operator. It's almost like you're visiting their home, and it's a good netiquette to behave as they ask. Most systems have rules that you can read with a menu command.

14

Faxing, with or without a Fax Modem

● **In this chapter:**

- **What kind of hardware do I need?**

- **Choosing the right fax software**

- **Receiving faxes on your computer**

- **How do I create cover sheets?**

- **Fax broadcasting—a high-tech mail merge**

- **Yes, you *can* fax without a fax modem *or* fax machine—no kidding!**

Your computer makes a great fax service. Once you start faxing with it, you'll never want to go back to that clunky old fax machine again . . . . **>**

Most people don't use the *fax* part of their fax modems. They use the modem part to connect to various online services and what-not, but they're scared of the faxing capabilities.

> ### 66 *Plain English, please!*
>
> A fax modem is nothing more than a modem with faxing capabilities. It's every bit as much a modem as any other. Don't let the word fax fool you into thinking that's its primary purpose. 99

There's no need to be scared, though. Fax machines and modems operate on exactly the same principle—they take digital information and convert it into audio signals that can be sent over the phone line. Then, at the other end, they convert it back to digital (computer) information. Nothing too mysterious about that.

As with a regular modem, a fax modem doesn't have a lot of complicated settings to fuss with—all the controls you need are accessible through your fax software. That makes it especially important to choose good fax software, as you can imagine. Once you've got your fax modem in place and your software installed, look out—you've got yourself a regular communications center.

In this chapter, I'll demystify the faxing process, and talk a bit about fax modems and software. Then we'll try sending and receiving some faxes.

 TIP This chapter uses the words *probably* and *usually* a lot when talking about your fax modem and fax software because there's such a variety of similar features out there. Don't worry that your modem or software will be *too* different, though. Everything in this chapter is universal except for the tiny details. Where there's a difference in your fax software or fax modem, it'll be pretty easy to spot—and I'll point out what to look for.

Where can I send faxes with my fax modem?

If you've been modem shopping recently, you've probably seen a lot of boxes and ads shouting things like "CLASS 1 AND 2 FAX CAPABILITY!," "Send faxes at up to 9,600 bps!," "14.4Kbps send and receive fax!," or maybe "Group I, II, and III fax!" Don't let these tactics confuse you—there are only a few real differences between all these features, and they mostly work with each other.

The fax machine came before the fax modem, evolutionarily speaking, so all fax modems are going to be able to *send* faxes to fax machines—no matter who made the fax modem, what kind of fax software you use, or what kind of fax machine you're sending to. If you only send faxes, and never receive them, the entire subject of classes, groups, and compatibility is completely moot.

Receiving is a different matter. Early fax modems (at least the ones normal people could afford) weren't able to *receive* faxes from *anything*—fax machines or other fax modems. These are called **SendFax modems**. Newer fax modems (let's say the ones made in the last few years), including most 9,600 bps fax modems and practically every 14,400 bps or higher fax modem, are able to send *and* receive faxes.

There are still some send-only fax modems on the market, but they're becoming more and more rare. Make sure that the fax modem you buy clearly says "send/receive" on the box.

Q&A *What does it mean when a modem's box has two numbers on it, like 24/48, or 24/96, or 96/14.4?*

The first number is the speed in bps of the modem part of the fax modem. The second number represents the fax speed. For instance, a 24/96 fax modem can communicate with your own line service at 2,400 bps, but can fax at 9,600 bps. Several years ago, these dual-speed fax modems were popular, but you won't see them much anymore. These days, almost every fax modem faxes and modems at the same speed.

Classes and Groups: what they mean

As you're shopping for fax modems, you may see designations like "Class 1 and Class 2 operation" or "Group I, II, and III fax." Here's a quick rundown:

Class 1 and Class 2: These classes are fax language standards. Most fax software will let you use either, and will work it out with the fax modem all by itself, without any intervention on your part.

Class 2, as you might suspect, is the newer of the two. It has some extra bells and whistles, but that advantage is offset by the fact that there was some confusion about the standard when it was first introduced, so there are some subtle differences between modems that advertise themselves as Class 2 and those that call themselves Class 2.0. Class 1 is less fancy and more stable.

There are lots of modems that support both Class 1 and Class 2—these are your best bet, for maximum flexibility.

Group I Fax: This is an old, obsolete standard that applied only to fax machines, not fax modems. I would wager a guess that you will never need to communicate with a Group I fax machine, because they're such old dinosaurs.

They took six minutes to transmit a single page! However, any fax modem you buy will probably offer support for Group I anyway.

Group II Fax: This is an old standard too, and it's almost obsolete. It also pertains only to fax machines, not fax modems. This type of fax machine transmits a page in about three minutes. Any fax modem you buy should support Group II, so you can communicate with Group II machines, of which there are still quite a few out there.

Group III Fax: This is the current standard, for both fax machines and fax modems. Any fax modem you see in a store today should advertise Group III compatibility.

Group IV Fax: This is a standard for fax transmission over ISDN lines. These are not standard telephone lines, and they don't use modems, so you will probably never encounter Group IV when shopping for a fax modem, unless you're specifically looking for an ISDN model. (For more information on ISDN, check out "ISDN: The New Wave of Online Communications, which you'll find on our CD.")

This table shows some common types of fax equipment (fax modems and fax machines) and what they're compatible with.

If you have...	You can send faxes to...	And receive faxes from...
SendFax modem (including most 24/48 and 24/96 fax modems)	Group III, Class 1, and Class 2 fax machines and fax modems	None
Online fax service	Group III, Class 1, and Class 2 fax machines and fax modems	None

If you have...	You can send faxes to...	And receive faxes from...
Group III, Class I or Class 2 fax/modem	Group III, Class 1, and Class 2 fax machines and fax modems	Any fax machine or fax modem (including Groups I, II, and III)

How do I pick the best faxing software?

The best fax software is like a traffic light—if it's doing its job well you don't even notice it, but once it malfunctions, you have a terrible mess on your hands.

Sending faxes is about as easy as printing a document on your printer, and receiving faxes is a matter of double-clicking an icon and leaving the computer on. The trickiest part of the whole process is usually the installation, and that's only if you're using cheap software—the high-end programs like WinFax PRO and PROCOMM PLUS for Windows even make that part automatic.

CAUTION **Your fax modem came with some free fax software. Don't use it!** You'll have a lot fewer headaches (and probably save money in the long run) if you spring for a real fax program right away. (Count on spending about $50 to $100.) The exceptions to this rule occur with data/fax/voice modems like the Complete Communicator, which include specialized software to handle all three functions, and some computer systems that bundle WinFax PRO or other high-quality fax software. MS Fax, which comes with Windows 95, is also a winner. (We'll talk about it in "Setting up Microsoft Fax in Windows 95," later in this chapter.)

Installing fax software (or one of the hybrid fax/modem programs like PROCOMM PLUS for Windows) is like installing regular modem software, which is covered in Chapter 3, "Installing Your Software." It'll ask you which COM port your fax modem is on, whether you want to use tone or pulse dialing, and where you want it to put the files, along with a few other standard questions.

If you're using Windows 95, you already have a fax program—Microsoft Fax. I'll talk a bit about this program later in this chapter, as it's a pretty good little program, considering the cost (it's free with Windows 95).

Are you Class 1 or Class 2?

The main difference between fax software and data software is that the fax installation program might ask you whether your fax modem is Class 1 or Class 2. You'll need to know this before you can install the fax software. (Some fax programs can detect the class themselves, but it's best to be on the safe side and know in advance.) This is where you dig up the fax modem's box or manuals to find out the answer.

If you don't have the box and manuals (and I know I don't have most of mine), you can find out the answer with a regular communications program like PROCOMM PLUS, WinComm, or Windows Terminal or HyperTerminal.

Issue whatever command you need to in your particular communications program to enter **terminal mode** (so you can type a command directly to your modem). In most programs (like Windows Terminal and PROCOMM PLUS), you're in terminal mode when you start—the most you might have to do is press Esc or click Cancel to clear away a dialog box.

TIP **If you're using Windows 95's HyperTerminal program, it's a bit** more complicated to type commands directly. HyperTerminal does not normally allow you to issue commands to your modem by typing them, so you need to trick it. Here's what to do:

1 Open one of your existing connections, and in the Connect dialog box, click the Modify button.

2 Click the Configure button. Click the Options tab, then select the Operator Assisted or Manual dialog checkbox.

3 Click OK twice to return to the Connect dialog box.

4 In the Connect dialog box, click Dial, Connect, Cancel.

Okay, now HyperTerminal should be in terminal mode, and you can enter commands to your modem. You're ready to do the following steps.

1 At the terminal screen (the blank window), type **AT** (uppercase) and press Enter. This is like tapping the modem on the shoulder to see if it's ready. If the modem and software are talking to one another, you'll see

the response OK. (If you don't see the OK response, or if some other unexpected thing happens, try again. Still nothing? check the Troubleshooting chapter at the back of the book.)

2 After the OK shows up, type **AT+FCLASS=?** and press Enter. This asks the modem what kind of fax capability it has. You'll see a response something like the one in figure 14.1, with OK after it. The highest number in that response is the one you want to use in the fax software. If you see ERROR, check to make sure you've typed **AT+FCLASS=?** correctly and try typing it again. If it still says ERROR, the modem is probably not a fax modem, or something's wrong with it—call the manufacturer or the store where you bought it for help.

Fig. 14.1

In Windows Terminal, this particular fax modem says it supports Class 1.

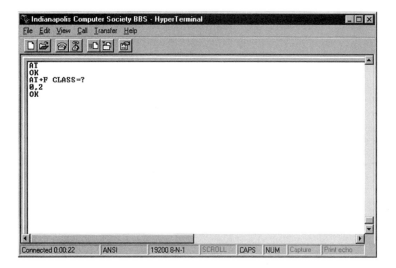

3 Use the Disconnect or Hang Up command in your program to terminate the connection. (There's no connection really, but some programs will think there is at this point.) Shut down the modem software and run the fax software's installation program, armed with your new information.

What the AT+FCLASS=? answers mean

Answer	Meaning
0,1	The modem supports Class 1 fax
0,1,2	The modem supports Class 1 and Class 2 faxes
0,1,2.0 or **0,1,2,2.0**	The modem supports Class 1 and Class 2 faxes, plus the final standard of Class 2, which is called 2.0.
ERROR	The modem doesn't know what **AT+FCLASS=?** (a standard fax command) means, so it's probably not a fax modem

Higher-end software, such as WinFax Pro, for instance, can figure all this out on its own, which is just another hassle you avoid by buying good software before you think you need it.

Setting up Microsoft Fax in Windows 95

Windows 95 users have a built-in, fair-to-middling fax program called Microsoft Fax, or MS Fax for short. It's not as powerful as a full-scale program like WinFax PRO—but on the other hand, it's free!

To see if MS Fax is installed, click the Start button, then select Programs, Accessories. If you see a program group labelled Fax on the menu, it means MS Fax is installed. If it's not installed, follow these steps in Windows 95:

1 Click the Start button, then select Settings, Control Panel. Double-click the Add/Remove Programs icon.

2 Click the Windows Setup tab.

3 Find MS Fax on the list of programs, and click its checkbox to place a checkmark in it.

4 Click OK, and follow the instructions displayed to install MS Fax. You will probably be asked to insert your Windows diskettes or CD to copy the program.

Microsoft Fax uses Microsoft Exchange, the Windows 95 e-mail inbox, to store received faxes, so you'll have to install Microsoft Exchange, too, if it's not already installed. (See "Sending and receiving e-mail with Microsoft

Exchange" in Chapter 4 for a long discussion on Exchange.) I'll explain how to use MS Fax to send and receive faxes in the following sections, as we go through those topics in general.

Sending a fax

With your fax modem, you can fax anything you can print or view with your computer. This is one of the big differences between a fax modem and a regular fax machine. With a desktop fax machine, you can fax anything you can fit into the fax machine—hand-written notes, photographs, newspaper articles, bar napkins, etc.—but a fax modem gets all its information from the computer. In fact, most computers treat the fax modem as a printer, such that faxing is the same procedure as sending a document to print.

But I want to fax handwritten stuff with my fax modem

You already know that information has to be in computerized form before you can fax it with your fax modem, right? Unlike regular fax machines, which have scanners built in, fax modems can fax only what a printer can print.

So how do you get something that's not computerized into your computer? There's a couple of ways:

One way is to use a scanner to put a computerized picture of whatever you want to fax on your disk. If you don't have a scanner, find a local do-it-yourself copy shop with a self-service desktop publishing setup—they'll have a

scanner. Warning, though—most cheap hand-operated scanners produce shoddy, hard-to-read scans.

The second way is to break down and go to a regular fax machine, and fax it that way. After all, fax modems can't be all things to all people.

Here's a trick for saving money—if you are paying by the page to use someone else's fax machine, and you need to send the same fax to more than one recipient, send the thing you want to fax to your fax modem at home. Once it's in your computer, you can send it out as a fax to as many different people as you like.

Because sending a fax is like printing something on your printer, most fax software actually *pretends* it's a printer. In Windows, OS/2, or Macintosh, the fax software shows up in your list of available printers. Along with your normal printer, you'll see something like "Microsoft FAX" or "WinFax" (see fig. 14.2). Your word processor doesn't know the difference, it just knows it has to dump all of its data to whatever printer you tell it to—it's up to the printer (or in this case, the fax software) to know what to do with it.

Fig. 14.2
Two fax programs are cunningly pretending to be printers in Windows 95.

It's easy to send a fax from Windows with this fake printer:

1 Open the document or create the document with whatever program you want to use—as long as the program is able to print to a regular printer.

2 Select Print Setup from the File menu, or whatever command opens up the dialog box where you can select the printer to use. (In some programs, you select File, Print, then click the printer from a drop-down list.)

3 Choose the fax software from the list of printers. (You may have to click OK after doing so, depending on the program.)

4 Print the document just as you usually would. Normally, this means choosing Print from the File menu; some programs have button bars with a button for printing.

5 You'll see a dialog box where you can fill in the phone number, the recipient's name, and other information (see fig. 14.3). Fill it in and select whatever button looks like it'll send out the fax (sometimes it's "Send," other times it's "OK").

Fig. 14.3
WinFax PRO's Send Fax dialog box gives you places to type all the information you'd normally put on a cover sheet.

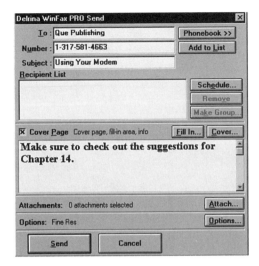

 CAUTION **Don't forget to change the chosen printer back to your regular** printer when you're done faxing.

Sending a fax with Windows 95

If you use Windows 95, you can send a fax in the way just described, but you also have Microsoft Fax, a fax program specially designed for Windows 95, at your disposal. Microsoft Fax comes with a Fax Wizard program that walks you through the steps for creating a simple fax, as shown in the following steps:

1 From Microsoft Exchange, select Compose, New Fax. Or, if you're not in Exchange at the moment, click the Start button, then select Programs, Accessories, Fax, Compose New Fax. Either way, the Compose New Fax Wizard starts.

2 If you get a screen asking about the location you're calling from, click Next.

3 When you come to the addressing dialog box shown in figure 14.4, fill in the information about the recipient, then click the Add to List button. When you're done adding recipients, click Next.

Fig. 14.4
In the Addressing dialog box, you specify who youre sending the fax to.

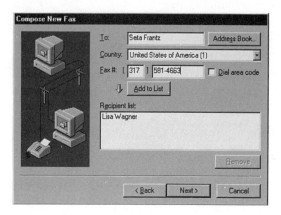

Compose New Fax

To: Seta Frantz   Address Book..
Country: United States of America (1)
Fax #: [317] 581-4663   ☐ Dial area code
⬇ Add to List
Recipient list:
Lisa Wagner

Remove

< Back   Next >   Cancel

4 Click Yes or No to choose whether you want to send a cover page. If you choose Yes, click the cover page you want to send from the list.

5 (Optional) Click the Options button to set a certain time for the fax to be sent, to choose a different cover page, or to set other options. When you're done, click OK to return to the main process.

6 Click Next, and you'll see a simple screen, with a Subject line and a Message area. The message will appear on the cover page. Type in the information you want to send in your fax, then click Next.

7 If you want additional pages, including graphics or material from another pre-written document, click the Add File button, find the file, then click OK. You can repeat this to add as many files as you like. They'll all be assembled into a single fax for you. Click Next.

8 Click Finish. MS Fax sends the fax without delay. You can view the fax later, for your reference, in the Sent Items folder in Microsoft Exchange.

Receiving and reading a fax

Your fax software must be running before you can receive a fax—the fax modem can't do it by itself. Just running the fax software, however, isn't enough. You also have to let it know that it's supposed to be answering the phone, or else it'll sit numbly by while the phone rings off the hook. (That's not necessarily a drawback—there's nothing more frustrating than running to answer a voice call, only to have your fax machine beat you to it and screech in your caller's ear.)

You can set most fax programs to receive two ways: automatically or manually. **Automatic Receive** means the fax modem answers every call and checks to see if it's an incoming fax. If it's not, the modem usually hangs up on the caller. If you're expecting a fax while you're away from the computer, this is the option you want.

All fax software is a little different, but you can usually start the Automatic Receive function with an option in the Receive menu or the Fax menu. WinFax PRO, for example, has an Automatic Receive option in its Receive menu.

With MS Fax, you can set it to automatically answer by doing the following:

1 In Exchange, select <u>T</u>ools, Microsoft Fa<u>x</u> Tools, <u>O</u>ptions.

2 Click the Modem tab.

3 Click the <u>P</u>roperties button.

4 In the Answer Mode area, click <u>A</u>nswer After, then fill in a number in the text box (for instance 3, to answer after 3 rings).

5 Click OK, then OK again to return to Exchange.

To turn automatic answering off, repeat the procedure, but select Manual or Do not answer. Some fax modems (like the Complete Communicator and many new high-speed modems) can tell whether incoming calls are data, fax, or voice, and launch the correct software to deal with the call.

 TIP **If you leave your PC on to receive faxes while you're away, turn** the monitor off *even if you have a screen saver*. Not only is it plain common sense (nobody's there to look at the monitor, so why have it on?), but computer monitors burn up a lot of energy, so leaving it off saves you money on your electric bill.

Manual Receive is for those times when you answer the phone and discover it's a fax call. You have quite a while to launch your fax software (most fax machines and fax modems will wait at least 30 seconds to a minute before they hang up), so even if you don't have your computer on, you may be able to start it up and catch the fax. Your odds are better, of course, if the computer's on and you're already running Windows, OS/2, or whatever other system you use.

Again, all fax software is different, but you should be able to receive a fax manually by selecting an option like Receive Fax Now, Manual Receive, or Answer Fax Now from your program's Receive menu or Fax menu. WinFax PRO, for example, uses the Manual Receive Now option in its Receive menu.

With Windows 95's MS Fax, from within Exchange, you can answer a fax manually by double-clicking the tiny fax machine icon in the right corner of your taskbar. This little picture appears there whenever MS Exchange is open, if you have MS Fax installed. When you double-click it, a status window for MS Fax appears. Click the Answer Now button to answer the phone.

 TIP **Incoming fax calls are easy to spot because the fax machine or** fax modem on the other end usually sends out a dull beep every few seconds until you hang up or launch your fax software.

Once you've got the fax, it'll appear in a list of incoming faxes in your fax program. This list is often called the "Receive Log," and you may have to hunt for it in your fax software. In most fax programs, you can simply double-click the received fax in the Inbox to view it. In Microsoft Exchange, faxes appear amongst all your regular e-mail, as you saw in Chapter 4.

Figure 14.5 shows a WinFax PRO viewer, and you saw the MS Fax viewer in Chapter 4, when you were learning to read e-mail and faxes in Exchange. Almost all fax viewers, including both of these, offer these options while you're viewing:

- **Flip** turns the page you're viewing upside-down (you never know which way people are going to feed pages into a fax machine). If there's a button for this, it's usually an upside-down picture or letter.

- **Rotate** turns the fax in 90-degree increments so you can read text on landscape pages (where the text runs along the long side of the page instead of the short side). "Rotate" buttons usually have a page turned sideways or a page with arrows pointing clockwise or counter-clockwise.

- **Invert** changes all the white to black and vice versa. If your software has an Invert button, it probably looks like a picture or letter that's white-on-black instead of black-on-white.

- **Magnify/shrink** probably looks like a magnifying glass on your fax viewer, with a plus (for enlarge) or minus (for shrink). Your viewer may also have a list of common sizes available (usually 25 percent, 50 percent, 100 percent, and 200 percent, but sometimes more), including a Fit in Window option, which shrinks the entire fax page to fit the current window, and Fit Horizontally, which shrinks or stretches the fax so its width matches the width of the viewer window.

- **Switch pages** enables you to move through multipage faxes. If your software has this feature on its button bar, it'll probably have one button with a page and a left-pointing arrow (for the previous page) and one with a right-pointing arrow (for the next page). Some fax viewers also have buttons that take you to the first and last pages of a fax.

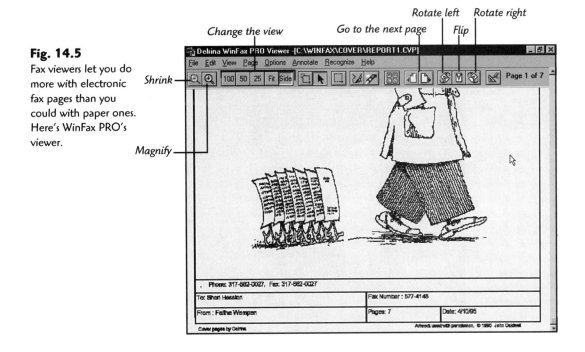

Fig. 14.5
Fax viewers let you do more with electronic fax pages than you could with paper ones. Here's WinFax PRO's viewer.

Using cover pages

In most offices, you'll find a tray full of blank cover sheets beside the fax machine. You fill one of these out and fax it as the first page of your fax message. Fax software uses the same concept in electronic form.

When you use the Print command to send a fax from your word processor or other program, the fax software pops up and asks you about the recipient's name, fax number, and other information. If you've already put a cover sheet in the document you're faxing, you can get away with just filling in the fax number. To let the fax software create the cover sheet, however, you should fill at least some of the other information (otherwise, why use a cover sheet at all?).

As you saw when you sent a fax with MS Fax or WinFax PRO earlier in the chapter, you're often prompted by the fax software to create a cover sheet as you build the fax. That's the easy way to go. But no matter which fax software you're using, somewhere on the fax software's window, you'll find a way to enable or disable its cover page feature. It'll probably be a checkbox that says "Cover Page." If you want to use the fax software's cover page feature, select that box. You'll also be able to choose which cover page you want to use, assuming your fax software offers more than one (see fig. 14.6).

Fig. 14.6
Most fax software includes a good sampling of cover pages. If you use one of the popular fax programs, you can get more cover sheets at the software store or download them from most online services.

Just look at all these categories of cover sheets!

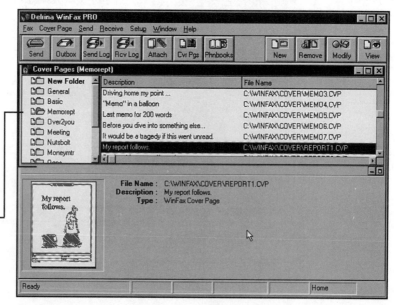

The fax software uses whatever information you enter in its Send Fax window to fill in the spaces on the cover page. There are usually spaces for the recipient's name, phone number, and comments. You probably won't have to fill in the information about who you are and what your fax number is, because your fax software should already know that from the initial installation.

TIP **Microsoft Fax comes with a Cover Page Editor, in which you can** create your own cover pages. From Windows 95, select Start, Programs, Accessories, Fax, Cover Page Editor. An editing screen comes up, with access to all kinds of drawing and formatting tools that enable you to make your own faxing masterpiece.

Fax broadcasting

If you have a message that has to go to multiple fax machines, you don't have to send each fax individually—your fax software can handle it for you. *Fax broadcasting* is sending a single fax to multiple people, and most fax software has built-in broadcast features.

1 Put all the names and numbers for the recipients into your fax software's phone book (sometimes called a **dialing directory**).

2 Create the fax as you normally would in your word processor or other program.

3 Select your fax modem as the printer in your program's Printer Setup screen.

4 Print the document.

5 When the fax software pops up on the screen, open up its phonebook function. In WinFax PRO, for example, select the Phonebook >>.

6 Select all the phone numbers you want to send the fax to. You may have to hold down the Control key on your keyboard as you click the numbers. Make sure you have the Cover Page function enabled.

7 Choose the Send button.

If you do a lot of fax broadcasting for business, you might want to consider using an outside company for your fax broadcasting. (You could do this to advertise, or send out coupons, or announce the location of a meeting, for instance.) Just about all mailing companies have some sort of fax service, and there are now some companies that specialize in fax. Delrina (the makers of WinFax PRO, which seems to be popping up a lot in this chapter) has a fax broadcast service for their customers which makes the process fairly easy.

Faxing without a fax modem

If you belong to CompuServe, America Online, or most of the other major online services, you can send faxes even if you don't have a fax modem. Unfortunately, you probably won't be able to send anything but plain text in your fax.

To send an e-mail message to an online service's fax system, you use a special format in the address. With CompuServe, for example, you replace the regular ID number with a fax number in this format (the first digit is the country code):

FAX: 1-317-555-5555

On America Online, use this format:

username@317-555-5555

For Delphi, enter FAX at the mail menu and enter the fax number at the prompt.

Part III: What Now?

15

Finding Information Online

In this chapter:

- **You won't believe all the stuff that's out there!**

- **Tips for information hunting**

- **Where to go on the online services**

The secret to writing great reports, making smart business decisions, and answering all of life's questions isn't knowing everything—it's knowing where to look everything up . . . . ⊙

orget stock brokers, research consultants, encyclopedia sales people, filing cabinets, and the Dewey Decimal System. The information resources of today and tomorrow aren't high-priced "experts" or ink-stained sheets of wood pulp, they're online services. Magazines, encyclopedias, and even some books are now just a few clicks away, along with information on everything from personal finances to pizza recipes.

It's *all* online. Really. Every bit of information (above the "Where'd I leave my keys?" level) is online somewhere. If you know where and how to look, you can find every argument's solution (or at least ammunition), every carefully guarded family recipe, every statistic, everything.

What kind of information do you want?

Online information usually comes in these flavors:

- Databases (collections of information in easy-to-search formats)

- Text files (including electronic books)

- Messages and instructions in special interest forums

Searching through a database

If information is buried in a database, digging it out is usually pretty easy: You just open the database's Search function, type the word(s) you're looking for, and (usually) click a Search button. Online versions of magazines, encyclopedias, almanacs, and other publications are really just databases of articles, usually with Search buttons somewhere on their main screens.

The main "problem" with online databases is that you often end up with more information than you want. Make sure you keep your database queries simple enough to get what you want, but specific enough to weed out what you don't. For example, if you're looking for information on Bud Abbott of Abbott and Costello:

- If you just used the keyword "Bud," the database would probably give you all information relating to everybody named "Bud," every kind of flower bud, every product with the letters "b-u-d" in its name, and so on

- If you used "Bud Abbott Lou Costello Comedy Team Movies" as your key words, you'd miss any information on Bud that didn't list the words "comedy," "team," or "movies"

- A good search would be "Bud Abbott," which would weed out all the extra "buds" from the first example, but catch all the relevant articles the second example might miss.

 Plain English, please!

Database queries are, more or less, the keywords you type in the database's Search window. You'll hear people say, "I did a *query* for 'Washington' in the history database," which means they used "Washington" as the keyword in their search. **"**

Text files, anyone?

Information text files include articles, electronic books, tutorials, and more. You can find these texts in online magazines, encyclopedias, and file libraries (usually special interest group libraries). For instance, on most online services, you will find text files mixed in with the downloadable files in various forums and special interest groups.

On some services, there are Search features that let you search for text files along with programs. You will probably find more binaries (programs) than text files, but you can try anyway:

- **GO IBMFF** on CompuServe to search most of its file libraries. This is the same file finder program that we will use in Chapter 16, "Finding Software Online," to find software.

- Choose Search the Libraries in AOL's Software Center. It too is the same search engine that finds software.

- Use Veronica to search several Gopher sites on the Internet (see Chapter 12, "Calling the Internet"). (On the Internet, there are separate search procedures for information and for software—Veronica is for information, and Archie is for software.)

Plain English, please!

Text files are computer files that are made up of text. You may hear them called ASCII files. There's no formatting—just text. A word processor file is not a text file, strictly speaking, because it contains formatting codes along with the text. **9 9**

 TIP **To search for information-oriented files on online services, try** using the keywords "Info" and/or "Text" in their file search features.

Forums and special interest groups

Sometimes the most up-to-date and honest information isn't contained in an official information file—it's heard "on the streets." If you're looking for information on a brand-new model of laptop computer, for instance, you could turn to the manufacturer for a spec sheet, but you might get a realistic, unbiased opinion of the product from another "average Joe" user like yourself.

Every major online service has areas where users can post public messages to one another—they're called **bulletin boards**, **forums**, **special interest groups**, and other, similar, names. On the Internet, they're called **newsgroups**. (There's more information galore about the individual services in Part II of this book.)

Let's say I needed to know if the manufacturer's claim about the longevity of the Lithium battery in the latest Toshiba laptop computer is true. I could post a message in an Internet newsgroup or on an online service forum or BBS, asking for opinions from people who have already bought one.

The great thing about getting information from other users is that it's totally honest—there's no Public Relations department screening each message. The un-great thing is that you never know whether the information is accurate. Sure, it's true to the best of the author's knowledge, but who is this guy, really, that he's so qualified to judge? You just never know.

Okay, I get the picture. Now what?

In the tables accompanying the following sections, I haven't tried to produce a comprehensive list of the online resources in each category, just a few highlights. I've intentionally stayed away from most commercial services (they can do their own advertising), except where they offer the most effective tools and information available.

Also note that the online world changes all the time, so there are bound to be new resources we haven't seen yet, and some of these services might not be available when you look for them.

Always read the FAQ first!

You can usually find good information—direct from the experts—in Internet newsgroups. Most of the experts who hang out in newsgroups genuinely enjoy their topics, but you'll often get a cold response from them if you just jump into an ongoing discussion with a **newbie question**. (Newbie questions usually imply that the questioner hasn't done their homework and wants somebody else to do it for them, like "What are the three main exports of North Dakota?".)

Online experts have come up with a crafty (and immensely helpful) way of avoiding newbie questions: the FAQ (pronounced *fack*). **FAQ** stands for **Frequently Asked Questions**, and it's one of the online community's most useful inventions. A FAQ is a text file that contains all the questions that people normally ask when they first show up.

For example, in a coffee enthusiasts group, newbies always ask "Is it true that Mountain Dew has more caffeine than espresso?" So, that question appears in the FAQ with a well-thought-out answer from the group's experts. FAQs almost always list resources (online and off) where you can learn more about a topic.

FAQs are more common on the Internet than on other online services, but groups on CompuServe, AOL, Prodigy, and other services are quickly catching up with their own FAQs.

To find FAQs for Internet newsgroups and mailing lists, try using Veronica (through Gopher) to search for the newsgroup or mailing list's title (not the word "FAQ," which would bring up thousands of FAQ files). For AOL, CompuServe, and Prodigy, try searching for the keyword "FAQ" in their file libraries. You might also search for "info" or "text."

Business and marketing information

Whether you're looking for a company to invest in or a market for your services, you can find the business and marketing information you need online. Demographic surveys and company profiles are just moments away, as are patent and trademark scans—any of which used to take days or weeks. Several resources online specialize in helping small businesses and entrepreneurs with startup and networking. Figure 15.1 shows the Business area on Prodigy. Table 15.1 tells you where to find business materials on other services too.

Fig. 15.1
Prodigy's Business section (**Jump Business**) is a gateway to lots of business features including stocks, profiles, and business news.

Table 15.1   Sources for business and marketing information

Service	How to get there	Description
AOL	Go To keyword **BW**	*Business Week* magazine
AOL	Go To keyword **CBD**	*Commerce Business Daily*, which provides information on government contracts
AOL	Go To keyword **COMPANY**	Hoover's company profiles
AOL	Go To keyword **NBR**	*Nightly Business Report*

Service	How to get there	Description
CompuServe	**GO ANALYZER**	Company Analyzer
CompuServe	**GO BIZALMANAC**	*Info-Please Business Almanac*
CompuServe	**GO BIZNEWS**	CNN Business Forum
CompuServe	**GO BUSDATE**	Business Dateline
CompuServe	**GO BUSDB**	Business Database Plus
CompuServe	**GO BUSDEM**	Business Demographics
CompuServe	**GO DATAQUEST**	Dataquest Online
CompuServe	**GO DEMOGRAPHICS**	State-County Demographics
CompuServe	**GO DMI**	Dun's Market Identifiers
CompuServe	**GO DYP**	*Dun's Electronic Business Directory*
CompuServe	**GO ENT**	*Entrepreneur Magazine*
CompuServe	**GO FORT500**	Fortune 500 Lists
CompuServe	**GO FTCFILES**	Federal Trade Commission
CompuServe	**GO IB**	*Investor's Business Daily*
CompuServe	**GO INC**	Business Incorporation Guide
CompuServe	**GO COINTL**	Company Information
CompuServe	**GO NEIGHBOR**	Neighborhood Demographics
CompuServe	**GO PATENT**	Patent Research Center
CompuServe	**GO SMALLBIZ**	The Entrepreneur's Forum
CompuServe	**GO SUPERSITE**	SUPERSITE Demographics
CompuServe	**GO TRADERC**	TRADEMARKSCAN databases
Internet	**misc.entrepreneurs**	UseNet Newsgroup for entrepreneurs
MSN	Categories, Business and Finance	List of business-related groups, messages, and files
Prodigy	**Jump Business**	Menu of business services
Prodigy	**Jump Nexis**	The Small Business Advisor

I want to learn more about finances and investing

Your stock broker knows one phone number and a little smoke-and-mirrors banter, and you pay a lot of your hard-earned money for that. Check out the online community's financial resources—they'll not only teach you how to manage your finances, but give you the tools to do it all by yourself. Check out table 15.2, which gives you some ideas of places to find financial info.

TIP **Several services include some financial information, but Prodigy really** shines in this area. Their online Investment Center (see fig. 15.2) offers stock quotes, expert advice, and much more.

Fig. 15.2
Check out the Investment Center on Prodigy with **Jump Investment Center**.

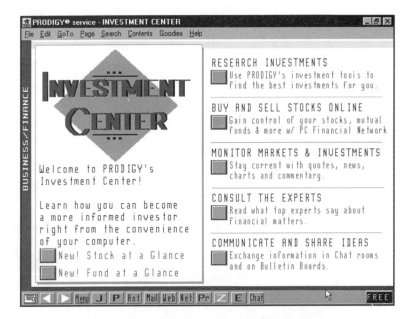

Table 15.2 Sources for financial and investment information

Service	How to get there	Description
AOL	Go To keyword **IBD**	*Investor's Business Daily*
AOL	Go To keyword **STOCKS**	Menu of stock-related services
AOL	Go To keyword **AAII**	American Association of Individual Investors

Service	How to get there	Description
CompuServe	**GO COMBUS**	*Commerce Business Daily*
CompuServe	**GO COMMODITIES**	Commodities information
CompuServe	**GO CPRICE**	Current Commodity Pricing
CompuServe	**GO CSYMBOL**	Commodity Symbol Lookup
CompuServe	**GO EARNINGS**	Financial forecasts
CompuServe	**GO FINANCE**	Menu of several financial services
CompuServe	**GO FINFORUM**	List of financial forums
CompuServe	**GO FUNDWATCH**	FundWatch by *Money Magazine*
CompuServe	**GO LOOKUP**	Ticker/Symbol Lookup
CompuServe	**GO MORTPAY**	Mortgage Calculator
CompuServe	**GO SNAPSHOT**	Current Market Snapshot
CompuServe	**GO SYMBOLS**	Securities Symbols Lookup
Internet	join **misc.invest newsgroup**	Discussions on investing
Internet	join **misc.invest.stocks** newsgroup	Discussions on stocks
Internet	join **misc.invest.funds** newsgroup	Discussions on mutual funds
MSN	Categories, Business and Finance, Investing	Research on companies and a personal investing forum
Prodigy	**Jump Finance**	Menu on several financial services
Prodigy	**Jump Business**	List of business services offered
Prodigy	**Jump Investment Center**	Full range of investment services and suggestions
Prodigy	**Jump Investment Digest**	Business advice column
Prodigy	**Jump PCFN**	PC Financial Network online brokerage service

Consumer beware

The major online presence in the consumer information field, not surprisingly, is Consumer Reports. The company behind *Consumer Reports* magazine and books offers the full text of its profiles on all the Big Three online services. Its shown from AOL in figure 15.3. Table 15.3 tells you how to get to consumer information on other services too.

Fig. 15.3
Don't set foot in that showroom until you know what the car's *really* worth—and what it'll cost in the long run.

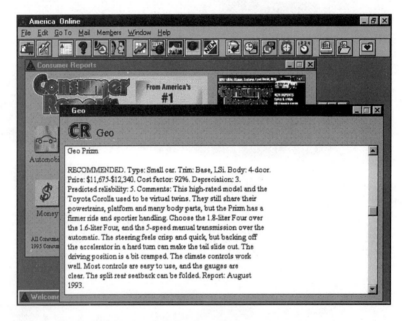

Table 15.3   Sources for consumer information

Service	How to get there	Description
AOL	Go To keyword **CONSUMER REPORTS**	*Consumer Reports*
CompuServe	**GO CONSUMER**	*Consumer Reports*
Internet	join the **misc.consumers** newsgroup	Discussions on consumer information
Internet	join the **misc.consumers.house** newsgroup	Discussions on consumer information on household goods
Internet	join **the misc.kids.consumers** newsgroup	consumer information on products related to kids
MSN	Categories, Public Affairs, Consumer Services and Information	A wide range of consumer information on various product categories
Prodigy	**Jump CR**	*Consumer Reports*

Look it up in an online encyclopedia or dictionary

They're not quite as slick as the gilt-edged ones in the den, but online reference books have quick search functions that get you the right information fast. Don't look for a lot of pictures in online encyclopedias and dictionaries, though—for that, get the CD-ROM. Table 15.4 shows you where to look.

Table 15.4   Sources for online encyclopedias and dictionaries

Service	How to get there	Description
AOL	Go To keyword **COMPUTER**	Computer dictionary terms
AOL	Go To keyword **ENCYCLOPEDIA**	*Compton's Encyclopedia*
CompuServe	**GO DICTIONARY**	*American Heritage Dictionary*
CompuServe	**GO ENCYCLOPEDIA**	*Grolier's Encyclopedia*
CompuServe	**GO GENALMANAC**	*Information Please Almanac*
MSN	Categories, Education & Reference, Reference Microsoft Encarta Encyclopedia	*Microsoft Encarta Encyclopedia*
Prodigy	**Jump Encyclopedia**	*Grolier's Encyclopedia*

Debate fuel: government and political information

What does the Dukes of Hazzard's Cooter have to say about Newt Gingrich? Quite a bit (actor Ben Jones lost an election to Gingrich in 1994 and has since filed an ethics complaint against one of the speaker's non-profit corporations).

Many U.S. government agencies (including the White House and Congress) have embraced the information-sharing nature of the online world, publishing press releases, daily briefings, and transcripts. If you missed it on C-SPAN, check it out online. Check out table 15.5 for some places you can visit online with government and political information.

Table 15.5 Sources for government and political information

Service	How to get there	Description
AOL	Go To keyword **POLITICS**	Current events/information
AOL	Go To keyword **WWIR**	*Washington Week in Review*
CompuServe	**GO DEMOCRATS**	Democratic Forum
CompuServe	**GO EFFSIG**	Electronic Frontier Foundation
CompuServe	**GO CONGRESS**	Members of Congress
CompuServe	**GO FCC**	Federal Communications Commission
CompuServe	**GO GPO**	Government Publications
CompuServe	**GO INFOUSA**	Information USA's Government Giveaways Forum
CompuServe	**GO POLITICS**	Political Debate Forum
CompuServe	**GO REPUBLICAN**	Republican Forum
CompuServe	**GO STATE**	Department of State
CompuServe	**GO WHITEHOUSE**	White House Forum
Internet	join **alt.activism** newsgroup	Discussions on activism
Internet	join **alt.politics.usa.congress** newsgroup	Discussions on U.S. congressional politics
Internet	join **alt.politics.usa.constitution** newsgroup	Discussions on the U.S. constitution
Internet	join **alt.politics.usa.misc** newsgroup	Discussions on U.S. politics
Internet	join **alt.politics.usa.republican** newsgroup	Discussions on the U.S. Republican party
Internet	join **alt.politics.democrat** newsgroup	Discussions on the U.S. Democratic party
MSN	Categories, Public Affairs, Government Agencies & Departments	A huge listing of government agencies
Prodigy	**Jump Political Profile**	Profiles on all current members of congress

Who, what, when: history and statistics

If your research goes beyond the trend-of-the-week, the online world has plenty for you. You can find the full text of almost all historic documents, photographs from The Smithsonian and other major archives, statistics, and blow-by-blow accounts of all the world's wars. Table 15.6 has the scoop.

Table 15.6   *Sources for history information*

Service	How to get there	Description
AOL	Go To keyword **DISCOVERY**	The Discovery Channel
AOL	Go To keyword **ENCYCLOPEDIA**	*Grolier's Encyclopedia*
AOL	Go To keyword **SMITHSONIAN**	The Smithsonian Institution online
AOL	Go To keyword **TLC**	The Learning Channel
CompuServe	**GO BETTMAN**	Bettmann Archive Forum
CompuServe	**GO ENCYCLOPEDIA**	*Grolier's Encyclopedia*
CompuServe	**GO GENALMANAC**	Information Almanac
CompuServe	**GO GUTENBURG**	The Gutenburg Collection
CompuServe	**GO MILFORUM**	Military Forum
CompuServe	**GO ROOTS**	Genealogy Forum
Internet	join **soc.history** newsgroup	Discussions on history

I love books!

You're a reader, right? In the online world, you can find all kinds of information on printed books (reviews, synopses, and publisher and printing information). For instance, Barron's Bookstore on America Online can offer you all kinds of "Cliff Notes" type information about the book that you were supposed to have read for tommorrow's lecture (see fig. 15.4.)

Fig. 15.4
With Barron's Book
Notes on AOL, you
can get background
information and
encapsulations for all
of history's major
literary works.

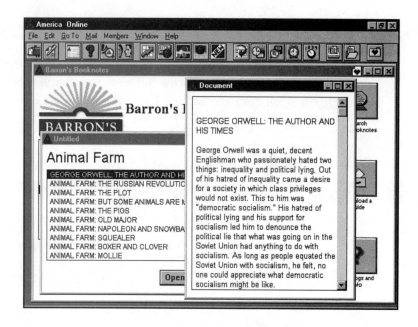

You may also run across the relatively new electronic books (also called **e-books**). These are books that are formatted to be read on your screen, instead of printed out.

To find e-books, try using your online service's file search function with the keyword "e-book" or "e book." Don't expect to find Jurassic Park, but you'll probably run into some fine novels and nonfiction books. Almost all of the classics (Shakespeare, Chaucer, Plato, Sherlock Holmes—anything over 100 years old) are also available in electronic form. (You can also find all the classics available in regular text files, suitable for saving to your hard disk and printing out to read on paper at your leisure.)

Table 15.7 can help you find just the thing to satisfy your literary cravings.

TIP **Book-lovers' tip: Most major online services and some Internet** sites have online bookstores that offer discounts on the same books you'd normally get at the mall stores.

Table 15.7   Sources for Book Information

Service	How to get there	Description
AOL	Go To keyword **BARRONS**	Barron's Booknotes (encapsulations of classics and literature)
AOL	Go To keyword **BOOKS**	Best Seller lists
CompuServe	**GO BOOKS**	Books in Print database and *Book Review Digest.*
CompuServe	**GO EBOOKS**	Electronic Books area and libraries
CompuServe	**GO PREVIEW**	Book Preview Forum
Internet	Join the newsgroup **alt.books.reviews**	Book reviews by other people like yourself
MSN	Categories, Arts & Entertainment, Books & Writing	Discussion and reviews of current books

Celebrities, movies, and music

Keep up with your favorite idol with online glitter magazines and fan forums. You can also read reviews of popular videos before you head out to the video store, like in figure 15.5. Table 15.8 gives a list of some places for the star-struck to find info online.

Fig. 15.5
Get the thumbs up or thumbs down before you plunk down your hard-earned cash for a video rental or an afternoon at the movie theatre.

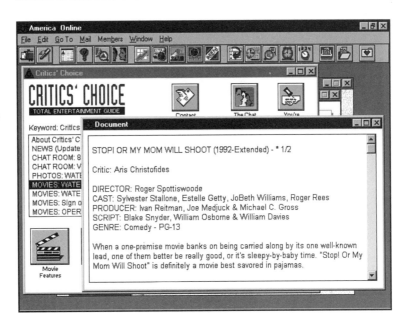

Table 15.8 Sources for celebrity, movie, and music information

Service	How to get there	Description
AOL	Go To keyword CRITICS	Critics Choice reviews
AOL	Go To keyword **ENTERTAINMENT**	Celebrity News
AOL	Go To keyword **MTV**	music and video information from MTV
AOL	Go To keyword **ROCKLINK**	Several sources of music information
CompuServe	**GO ALLMOVIE**	All-Movie guide
CompuServe	**GO ALLMUSIC**	All-Music guide
CompuServe	**GO EBERT**	Roger Ebert's Movie Reviews
CompuServe	**GO FLICKS**	Hollywood Online Forum
CompuServe	**GO GLAMOUR**	Glamour Graphics Forum
CompuServe	**GO HOLLYWOOD**	Hollywood Hotline
CompuServe	**GO MOVIES**	Movie Reviews
CompuServe	**GO PEOPLE**	*People* magazine
CompuServe	**GO STARPIX**	STARPIX Download Area
Internet	**alt.celebrities**	UseNet mailing list for celebrity information
Internet	**alt.binaries.pictures.celebrities**	Photos of celebrities and famous people
Internet	**alt.fan.?????**	Fill in the question marks for your favorite celebrity—there are many fan clubs on the Internet.
MSN	Categories, Arts & Entertainment	Forums and discussion groups, broken down by media (movies, TV, etc.)
Prodigy	**Jump Movie Guide**	Movie Guide

Become a cyberchef: recipes and cooking tips

Looking for a way to get rid of those cans of wax beans, pumpkin pie filling, and saurkraut that've been in your cupboard since 1989? Check out online cooking resources. You can find everything from appetizers to table settings (see fig. 15.6 and table 15.9).

Fig. 15.6
Mmm... Codfish. My favorite.

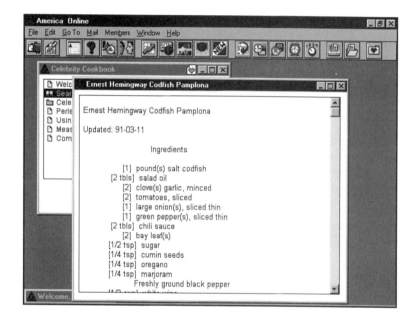

Table 15.9 Sources for recipes and cooking information

Service	How to get there	Description
AOL	Go To keyword **CELEBRITY COOKBOOK**	Your favorite stars' favorite meals
AOL	Go To keyword **COOKING**	Cooking special interest group
CompuServe	**GO AIF**	CompuServe's Adventures in Food
CompuServe	**GO VEGETARIAN**	Vegetarian Forum
CompuServe	**GO WINEFORUM**	Bacchus Wine Forum
Internet	join **rec.food.cooking** newsgroup	Discussions of cooking techniques and recipes

continues

Table 15.9 **Continued**

Service	How to get there	Description
Internet	join **rec.food.recipes** newsgroup	Recipe exchange
Internet	join **rec.food.veg** newsgroup	Vegetarian recipes and cooking
Internet	join **alt.creative-cooking** newsgroup	Discussions of cooking and entertaining techniques
MSN	Categories, Interests, Leisure, & Hobbies, Home Interests, Food, Spirits, and Cooking	Discussion of recipes, wines, and cooking techniques
Prodigy	**Jump FOOD BB**	A bulletin board for food lovers

16

Finding Software Online

● **In this chapter:**

- **What kinds of software can I find online?**

- **Techniques for online software hunting**

- **Software sources on CompuServe, America Online, Prodigy, the Internet, and BBSs**

- **How to tell if a program will work on your computer**

- **What do I do with "compressed" or "archived" files?**

The best bargains in software aren't in the closeout bin at the mall—they're online . . . . ➤

Z ilch. Zip. Nada. I just spent two hours online and I got a word processor, an accounting program, a database program, and some incredible games, and the entire bill was: zero. My only cost was the fee for the time I spent online.

Not all the software you find online is free, but most of it has a free trial period where you check it out for a month or so before you decide whether you like it or not. Do you think the software store at the mall has a deal like that? Nope.

The online world is more than just gobs of information—there is also good-quality (usually low-cost) software available that you can use right away. This chapter shows you how to use your modem to sniff out the best software online.

All about shareware

If you've had your computer for more than a week or so, you've probably paid a visit to a software store, or to the software section of a local department store. The prices per program ranged from around $10 to over $500, right? Well, forget that.

Every kind of software you saw in the store—word processors, spreadsheet programs, database programs, electronic mail programs, utilities, tutorials, games, and more—is available online, often for a fraction of the cost you would pay in the store. The downloadable stuff is a different brand, of course, and may not be as fancy or have as many features as the store-bought version, but in many cases it works just fine for what you need it for.

One big difference is that if you go to the store to buy software, you'll come home with diskettes, printed manuals, a fancy box, and some plastic wrapping to throw away. If you get your software online, the program goes directly to your disk and you have to read the manuals on your computer screen or print them out yourself. Another big difference is how (and how much) you pay for the software.

Traditionally, the programs you could find online used one of these payment plans:

- Shareware

- Public domain (PD)

- Freeware

In other words, they didn't belong in the other category—**commercial** software, which is the kind you find in boxes at the store. Commercial software is usually published by bigger companies. Once you pay for it in the store, it's yours. Shareware, public domain, and freeware, on the other hand, are usually published by individuals, small companies, or universities. There's no charge for freeware or public domain software, and you don't pay for shareware unless you decide to keep using it.

 Plain English, please!

Shareware is a method of distributing software where you can use the programs for free during a trial period before you decide whether you want to buy it.

Public domain means the software's author gives up all claims to it. You can use it, change it, put it on a disk and give it away, or anything else, all without payment to the original author.

Freeware is a method of distributing software where you don't pay anything at all, but the software's author keeps all the rights. You can use it, but you can't change it or sell it.

The shareware concept is pretty simple, but a lot of people have a hard time with it—mostly because it's too good to believe. You don't pay anything when you get it. Really. It's almost like test-driving a car. When you take a new Mercedes for a spin around the block, you don't have to slap $100,000 on the counter first. You take it for free, check how it feels, peek around under the hood, and see whose heads turn at stoplights. You pay for it *after* you've decided whether you like it, just like shareware (but shareware test drives usually last 30 days). With commercial software, you can look at the box in the store, but you can't try it out until you've already paid for it.

You might find some interesting variations on the shareware concept. Some of my favorites are **cardware** (where your registration is considered paid in full if you send the author a tacky post card), **beerware** (registration price = one case of beer), and **charityware** (donate $5 or so to your favorite charity in the author's name and you're registered).

Individual programmers and small software companies distribute their products as shareware because they don't have to pay very much for distribution, and they don't have to print manuals or boxes up front. Their prices reflect this savings, too—shareware programs can cost one-half the price of comparable commercial programs, sometimes even less. If you decide to keep a shareware program, you send the payment to the author, at which point he or she will probably send you a printed manual, and perhaps an upgraded version with more features.

The quality of shareware (especially older shareware) varies widely. This is another good reason you get to try it before you buy it. Some shareware products go on to be international hits, like Netscape and PKZip, and others even become commercial products in later versions, such as PROCOMM.

How do I register shareware?

Every piece of shareware comes with instructions on how to register it. Some of them show the phone number and address right onscreen, nagging you to register. When you register, you're sent a code or a new version that makes the "nag screen" go away. Figure 16.1 shows a nag screen from Moraffware, one of my favorite shareware companies.

Fig. 16.1
Most shareware will continue to nag you until you register.

Other programs include registration information in a separate file, usually called REGISTER.TXT or something like that. This typically includes a registration form you can print out, fill out, and mail in, along with your money.

Can I get commercial software online, too?

It used to be that the only software you could download was either free or shareware—you never saw commercial software available for download. Or, if you did, the person who uploaded it was guilty of copyright violation. That's no longer true, though. Because online software distribution is so cheap and easy, many *commercial* software companies have recently begun using that method. So now you can use your modem to get some programs that were previously only available by mail order or in stores.

Where to find software

Each major online service handles programs differently:

- America Online has a section called Software Center (see fig. 16.2), which is organized by type of software (applications, games, etc.) There are also files available for download in many of the specialized forums.

Where to *avoid* commercial software

If you stumble across a BBS with commercial software in one of its file libraries, avoid the software (and the BBS) like it was a rabid salesperson. For example, if you find a copy of Microsoft Word, PROCOMM PLUS for Windows, Stacker, or any other popular commercial program, especially if there's no extra charge for downloading it, it's 100-percent illegal and can get you in federal-strength trouble. The BBSs that release commercial software are called **pirate boards**, and their sysops are often only

weeks away from serious fines and time in a penitentiary.

In most cases, innocent folks wouldn't be able to tell a pirate board from a regular BBS, because the illegal stuff is in a separate, restricted area. The only way you'd be able to see the illegal files would be if you talked to the sysop and, usually, paid a little extra. They do this to throw FBI types off their track.

For instance, a game manufacturer may have demos of their products available for downloading through their own area, and a special interest group may have an area where members of the group can upload specialized files, like photos of themselves.

Fig. 16.2
America Online's Software Center makes it easy to search for files.

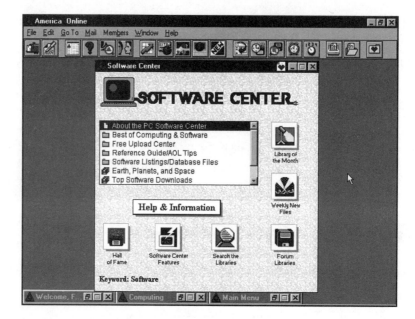

- CompuServe's files are in the library sections of various forums. For example, the DATASTORM forum (GO DSTORM) has files related to communications and DATASTORM products. Two software forums you should keep in mind are PCFUN (GO PCFUN to browse lots of games) and IBMAPP (GO IBMAPP to find most major shareware, freeware, and public domain applications). Check out "How do I search for files and information in a forum," in Chapter 8, for more details.

- Prodigy's files, for the most part, are in the ZiffNet section (Jump ZIFFNET). It costs extra to use ZiffNet, so it may be more economical for you to join a second service, like CompuServe, than it would be to pay the download fees.

- On the Microsoft Network, files are scattered all over the place, according to their subject. For instance, computer games are found in a special computer games section. You have to hunt around to find all the file areas, or do a Find and look for the word "Files" (see "Finding good stuff" in Chapter 11).

- BBS files are almost always in a "Downloads" or "Software" section that is divided into libraries. If the sysop is doing her job, you'll be able to find the section listed on the BBS's main menu.

- The Internet is anybody's guess, with millions of computers offering files. A few sites (called "archive sites") that are known for well-organized file collections are **ftp.cica.indiana.edu**, **oak.oakland.edu**, and **wuarchive.wustl.edu**. You transfer files on the Internet using File Transfer Protocol, or FTP. There's more on this in "FTP" in Chapter 12.

If you know the name of the file you're looking for, you may be able to find it more quickly with an online search than by browsing through lots of files. The following table lists the search functions of some major online services.

 TIP   You like FREE stuff, right? Use your online service's file search program with the keyword "FREE" to see all the freeware and other free files.

File search tools

Online service	How to get to the software search
CompuServe	**GO IBMFF**, choose "Access File Finder"
AOL	Go To keyword **Software Search**
Prodigy	**Jump ZIFFNET**, choose Search by name or Search by category
Microsoft Network	Click the Start button, then select Find, then On the Microsoft Network.
Internet	Use Archie

(For information about each online service's file offerings, check the chapter dedicated to that online service.)

Will the software work on my computer?

When you're looking at a program description or a list of names, it's not always easy to tell if the program will work on your computer. America Online's file descriptions include notes about what kind of computer you need for each file (see fig. 16.3), but most other services leave it up to your best guess as to whether each program will work on your computer.

Fig 16.3
On some services, you can see a description of the file before you download it.

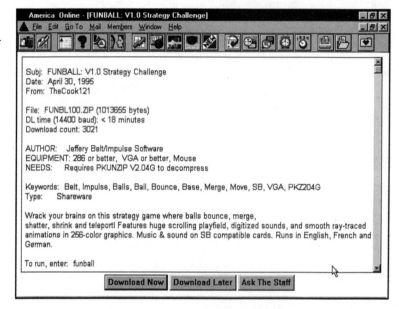

Since most Macs won't run PC software, and vice versa, here are some rules of thumb (although, like all rules, there are some exceptions):

- Look at the file extension. Files with the extensions EXE, COM, ZIP, ARC, ARJ, LZH, LHA, or ZOO work on PC compatibles.

66 *Plain English, please!*

Most files have two parts to their names: the part before the period (usually called the **file name**) and the part after the period (the **file extension**). For example, if you have a file called WOMBAT.ZIP, "WOMBAT" is the file name and "ZIP" is the file extension. Together, they form the complete name. 99

- Files with the extensions SEA, SIT, or CPT work on Macs.

- Though SIT and CPT files are designed for Macintosh computers, you can use *some* of them on your PC. If the SIT or CPT file is not a Macintosh program or an add-in for a Macintosh program, you may be able to use it on your PC. For example, if it's a PageMaker file, you may be able to open it with a Windows version of PageMaker. If it's a BMP, EPS, or PCX file, you'll probably be able to use it in your word processor or desktop publishing program. You'll need a special program to convert the SIT or CPT file to PC-compatible format first (see table 16.1).

- Files with other extensions GIF, BMP, DOC, TXT, and many others) usually require other programs to work—and if you have the right software, you can get them to work on just about any computer. For example, a file with a GIF extension is a graphics file that (with the right software) can be viewed on a Macintosh, PC, Amiga, or anything else. Some word processing programs can open graphics too.

- If you don't know if the program requires special hardware (like a sound card or a joystick), check for a file called README (or READ.ME, README.NOW, README.1ST, README.WRI, README.DOC, or any other variation on the theme). Read that file with a text editor or word processor before you try to run the program you've downloaded. It'll give you any special instructions or warnings you might need.

- Documentation for programs you've downloaded is almost always in a file with the extension DOC, TXT, WRI, RTF, or MAN.

What do I do with compressed files?

Most files you find online are **compressed** or **archived**, which means they've been run through a special encoding program to make them smaller (so they'll take less time to download). Compression also packages all the files needed to run the program in a single archive, so you're guaranteed to have all the files you need. These files have extensions like ZIP, ARC, PAK, ZOO, LHA, LZH, and ARJ, with ZIP being the most common. To get the shrunken files back out to their original stature, you need the same compression program (see table 16.1).

TIP **Before you decompress a file you've downloaded, it's a good idea** to put it in a directory of its own. For example, if you've just downloaded BIGGAME.ZIP, create a directory called BIGGAME on your disk. Move BIGGAME.ZIP to that directory, then run the decompression program (PKUNZIP in the case of ZIP files) on it.

Table 16.1   What to do with compressed files

Extension	Program you need to extract it	Command to extract it
ARC	PKUNPAK by PKWare	PKUNPAK <filename>
ARJ	ARJ by Robert K. Jung	arj -e <filename>
CPT	ExtractorPC by Bill Goodman	extract <filename>
EXE	none	<filename>
LZH or LHA	LHARC by Yoshi	lha -e <filename>
PAK	PKUNPAK by PKWare	PKUNPAK <filename>
SIT	UNSTUFF by Jody P. Nickel and John Kent	unstuff <filename>
ZIP	PKUNZIP by PKWare*	pkunzip <filename>
ZOO	ZOO by Rahul Dhesi	zoo -e <filename>

The ZIP format is by far the most popular online, so if you get only one compression/decompression program, make it PKUNZIP.

There are some multipurpose programs on the market these days, such as WinZip (a shareware program), that will compress and uncompress in several different formats. So instead of downloading all the programs listed in the middle column of table 16.1, you might look for a multipurpose program instead, especially if you need to decompress the less common file types only infrequently. (I can't remember the last time I ran into a ZOO-compressed file.)

Consider putting the compression and decompression programs in your DOS directory, so they'll be available no matter what directory you're using. Programs in your DOS directory are almost always available, while programs in most other directories only work *while you're using that program's directory.* If you're comfortable working with your AUTOEXEC.BAT file, you can take an alternate route. Put your compression and decompression programs in a directory called UTILS or COMPRESS, then add a semicolon and that directory's name to the end of the PATH statement in your AUTOEXEC.BAT file.

17

Finding Like-Minded Users

● In this chapter:

- What kinds of people hang out online?

- Meeting places on CompuServe, America Online, Prodigy, MSN, the Internet, and more

- Tips for online interaction

Not all of the millions of people online are computer geeks. You can meet lots of interesting folks online who share your real-world interests . . . . ❯

When you're chatting with other people down at the local pub, does everybody talk about pubs? Of course not (I hope). They talk about fishing, work, hobbies, current affairs, history, biology, and everything else. So if all pub talk isn't about pubs, why do so many people think all computer talk is about computers? The people you meet online have real lives just like you (well, *most* of them do), and they use their computers to talk about fishing, work, hobbies, and everything else.

The only differences are

- When you talk to others online, you may be talking to people on the other side of the world

- You don't have to argue with anyone about the tip or who ordered the champagne brownie fizz

Somebody online thinks like you do. Promise.

If you're a normal, slightly cynical person, you're probably thinking, "Sure, you can find people online who want to talk about politics and recipes, but I'm sure nobody's talking about (X)." You're wrong. You name a topic that's on your mind, even one you're *sure* nobody else is interested in talking about, and there's somebody online talking about it right now. Really.

There are two main types of online discussions:

- Realtime chats

- E-mail special interest groups

Realtime chats resemble bar conversations more closely than anything else. They're not particularly focused, even though the comments may revolve around a common interest. For example, if you enter a chat room called "Beer Fans," 100 percent of the talk probably won't be about home brewing, beer ratings, or hangover cures. You'll probably see comments on everything from music to travel to taxes mixed in with the beer conversation.

(For specifics on using chat rooms on your online service, see the chapter dedicated to that online service.)

TIP **The name of a chat room will usually tell you in very general terms** if the participants are *talking about* a topic or are just *interested in* that topic. In a room called "Quilt*ing*," for example, the conversation will probably be about making quilts, but in a room called "Quilt*ers*," it's more likely to touch on a broad range of topics that concern people who make quilts.

E-mail or message-based special interest groups (usually called **SIGs**) or forums spring up around just about every issue. They're usually a little more focused than realtime chats, and they're much more stable. For example, if you go online one night wishing specifically to talk about guitar playing, you may not be able to find other guitar players for a realtime chat. You can always participate in an ongoing e-mail or message conversation with guitarists, however, because they don't have to be online at that moment to read your questions and comments.

A typical SIG conversation goes like this:

1 A member of the group **posts** (sends) a public message with a question or comment. Their message's title ("New CD-ROM titles," for example) becomes the "title" for the conversation.

2 Other members reply to that message using the Reply feature in their software. To make sure everyone knows which message they're responding to, their responses' titles are usually the word "Re:" with the original title ("Re: New CD-ROM titles," for example). These responses may quote portions of the original message, as in figure 17.1.

TIP **Sometimes SIG members respond to messages, but use brand new** titles for their responses. In many cases, they'll tack the old title on the end of the new one in parentheses, like this: "Billie Holiday CD-ROM (was New CD-ROM titles)."

Fig. 17.1

This SIG message uses a quote from an earlier message to show readers what the author is responding to.

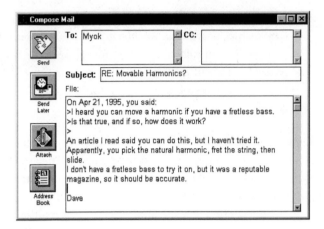

Are all SIG messages public?

Yes. If you use your online service's Reply feature on a SIG message, anyone who is part of the group can see your response. You can, however, send private messages to the e-mail addresses of individual participants—just remember to compose private messages from scratch instead of using the Reply function. And on most online services, if you've signed on at the same time as someone else, you can send them an **instant message**, which is kind of like a "news flash" that interrupts their online work (and is therefore not always appreciated, especially from strangers).

Also, on the Internet, there are **closed mailing lists**. These are special interest groups that meet by e-mail. You send a message to the list, not to an individual, and the list broadcasts your message as a separate e-mail to each of the people on the list. Then you get e-mails containing all the messages other people on the list have written in your own mailbox. Membership is limited to the people in the group, so the number of messages arriving in your inbox daily stays manageable.

Finding special interest groups

Although they're really all the same thing, SIGs have different names depending on the online service you use:

- on CompuServe, they're **forums**
- on AOL, they're **SIGs** or **conference areas or message boards**
- on Prodigy, they're **BBs** or **bulletin boards**
- on MSN, they're found in **Categories**
- on BBSs, they're usually **conferences**, **areas**, or **echoes**
- on the Internet, they're **mailing lists**, **LISTSERVs**, or UseNet **newsgroups**

Finding areas that interest you on an online service is easy—you just click the icons or words that match up with your interests. For example, to find the Vegetarian forum on CompuServe, you'd follow these steps:

1 Pick the Home/Leisure icon.

2 Pick Food/Wine from the list that pops up.

3 Choose the Vegetarian Forum from the new window.

The trick is to figure out which category your interest fits into. But don't rack your brain too much—if an interest could fit into more than one category, it'll most often show up in both menus. On CompuServe, for example, Roger Ebert's Movie Reviews show up in the Fun & Games and Entertainment sections.

 Most online services also have Search or Find features that enable you to find topics that interest you online. You can read about these features in the chapters of this book that deal with each individual online service.

SIGs on the Internet

Hooking up with special interest groups on the Internet isn't as simple as it is on an online service, but it's not overwhelmingly difficult. The two main types of interest groups you'll probably deal with are: UseNet newsgroups and mailing lists.

Let's look at each separately, shall we?

What's a newsgroup?

UseNet newsgroups are topics circulated around the world. If you can imagine a discussion topic, it's got a UseNet newsgroup somewhere. There are about 12,000 topics at this writing, and more are being created every day. Most Internet services (including the major online services) provide a selection of 3000-4000 topics, weeding out the least popular and/or illegal ones.

 CAUTION   **UseNet newsgroups are usually unmoderated and uncensored, so you can expect some profanity and some off-topic messages. UseNet is also inhabited by more experienced users who are less patient with beginners, so be sure you read the FAQ file before you post.**

UseNet is actually not part of the Internet or even a separate network, but a set of rules for managing newsgroups. Most computers supporting UseNet are also on the Internet, but that does not necessarily have to be the case. The opposite holds true as well—not all computers connected to the Internet provide UseNet to their users.

UseNet is one of the terms least understood by many Internet users. Proper understanding of it will portray you as a knowledgeable Internet user rather than a "newbie."

UseNet is a means to broadcast articles (UseNet's term for messages) among a large number of computers. Technically speaking, UseNet newsgroups are propagated using a store and forward procedure. An article is sent to a given host who saves it and then feeds the article to other hosts in the UseNet network. Using store and forward, an article can usually be distributed widely in a matter of moments.

Plain English, please!
UseNet stands for "Users Network." Technically, UseNet is a method for distributing messages, but it's come to mean the group of newsgroups that are distributed using it.

Since no one could hope to read all those groups, the major online services let you subscribe to the ones you'd like to keep up with. You enter the newsgroup-reading program online, browse your subscribed newsgroups, and read any messages that you think might be interesting (based on their subject lines). You can then post a response back to the newsgroup for everyone else to read.

Newsgroup names are a little weird. In a somewhat futile effort to keep them organized, the names all start with meaningful prefixes like "comp" (computer topics), "rec" (recreation), "soc" (social), and "alt" (alternative topics). Though there were only a few prefixes when newsgroups first became popular, there are now hundreds, including individual online services, countries, and organizations. In short, too many to keep track of (so much for trying to keep them organized).

The important part of the name is after the prefix anyway. For example, the members of the **alt.fishing** group presumably don't care if it's alt.fishing, soc.fishing, or rec.fishing. Some newsgroups have several parts to their names, and the parts don't necessarily make sense together (**alt.food.coffee** springs to mind). Check out the following list for a few newsgroups you can try.

 TIP **In spoken conversation, the periods in newsgroup names are** pronounced *dot*, so the **alt.music.classical** group is said *alt-dot-music-dot-classical.*

- alt.books.reviews
- alt.fan.addams.family
- alt.fan.blues-brothers
- alt.fan.douglas-adams
- alt.fan.monty-python
- alt.fan.penn-n-teller
- alt.fishing
- alt.food.coffee
- alt.guitar.tab
- alt.rock-n-roll.classic
- alt.save.the.earth
- rec.arts.books
- rec.arts.comics.misc
- rec.collecting
- rec.crafts.brewing
- rec.food.cooking
- rec.food.drink.beer
- rec.food.drink.coffee
- rec.food.recipes
- rec.food.veg.cooking
- rec.hunting
- rec.music.bluenote (jazz and blues)
- rec.music.classical
- rec.music.makers.percussion
- rec.outdoors.fishing
- rec.outdoors.fishing.fly
- rec.outdoors.fishing.saltwater
- rec.travel.air
- rec.travel.cruises

If you're a music fan, check out one of the several newsgroups in the **alt.music** list (**alt.music.brian-eno**, **alt.music.jethro-tull**, **alt.music.pink-floyd**, and many more). Almost all professional sports teams have newsgroups (**alt.sports.basketball.nba.chicago-bulls**, **alt.sports.football.pro.dallas-cowboys**, etc.). There are even support groups for many difficult situations (**alt.support.asthma**, **alt.support.depression**, **alt.support.divorce**, **alt.support.stop-smoking**, and many more).

To search for and subscribe to newsgroups on AOL:

1 Go To keyword **Newsgroups.**

2 Choose Search All Newsgroups.

3 In the Search Phrase box, type a word that accurately describes the newsgroup you're looking for.

4 Click Search.

5 Select the group you want from the Search Results window (see fig. 17.2) and click the Add button.

Fig. 17.2
Skip the Description button—there are so many newsgroups, none get more than a few words.

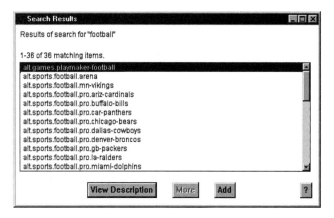

To read your newsgroups on AOL, Go To keyword Newsgroups and select the Read My Newsgroups button.

To search for and subscribe to newsgroups on CompuServe:

1 GO INTERNET.

2 Select the USENET Newsgroups button.

3 Select USENET Newsreader (CIM). You'll have to click OK on a few disclaimers and warnings before you get to the USENET Newsgroups window.

4 Select Subscribe to Newsgroups.

5 On the line under the word Keyword, type in a word that describes the newsgroup you're looking for.

6 Select Search.

7 Click the box beside a group you want to subscribe to, then click Subscribe. CompuServe notifies you that you're subscribed to the group.

In future sessions when you want to read your newsgroup(s), follow steps 1–3, then select Access Your USENET Newsgroups.

Mailing lists

Mailing lists are simpler to deal with than newsgroups, but they can be more of a pain, because all the posts are right there in your face (or at least in your mailbox) and you have to deal with them. With a newsgroup, you can just not look at it if you get bored. When you subscribe to a mailing list, all the posts come directly to you, as if they were important, personal e-mail.

CAUTION **A lot of people don't like mailing lists because they tend to clog** up one's inbox. If you go away for a week, you can come back to 500 new messages and no way of easily weeding through to figure out which ones are legitimate e-mail and which ones are from the mailing list. If you're going to subscribe to a mailing list, make sure your online service has good e-mail handling capabilities, or if you're using the Internet directly, make sure you get a good e-mail program, such as Eudora (for direct Internet connections). Of the online services, Prodigy has one of the best e-mail programs, and America Online has one of the worst; though, as with most everything the online services offer, this could change at any time.

To subscribe to a mailing list from any Internet account (whether it's a commercial online service or a direct access provider), just send a message to the list's host with the word SUBSCRIBE in the subject line and the message area. You'll receive all the messages from that group in your electronic mailbox, and any replies you send out will go to everyone else in the group.

 Plain English, please!

> A **host** is a computer that runs a special interest group mailing list, among its other duties. Mailing lists are also called LISTSERVs, because of a software program called LISTSERV that hosts use to manage mailing lists. (The term LISTSERV is often used generically, like "Kleenex" is used to describe any brand of tissues. MajorDomo is another program that does the same thing as LISTSERV.) **99**

There are not quite as many mailing lists as there are newsgroups, but they cover most major topics. On some online services there's a list of mailing lists, or a feature that lets you search a master list of them. (America Online has this, for instance.)

 CAUTION **Don't join very many mailing lists, at least until you get a good** feel for them. Some lists receive 100 pieces of mail a day, and your online service may charge extra for large quantities of mail or numbers of messages.

SIGs on BBSs

Interest groups on BBSs are a whole different ballgame. Though some offer UsseNet newsgroups, most smaller BBSs can't afford to spend the hundreds or thousands of dollars per month it takes to provide them. Many BBSs, however, use lower-cost global networks to give their subscribers access to worldwide discussions—FidoNet is the big one, but there are many others.

FidoNet's interest groups are called **echoes**. The Rocky Horror Picture Show interest group, for example, is the ROCKY echo. These echoes are picked up by BBSs all over the world, so posting a message to an echo is sort of like posting one on an Internet newsgroup. Table 17.2 shows some cool FidoNet echoes you might want to check out.

Not all BBSs carry all the echoes. Check with your sysop for a current list of the available echoes, and you may be able to request echoes that aren't currently carried on your BBS. Understandably, some sysops will agree to carry a new echo only if you subsidize their additional long distance costs.

Table 17.2 A few interesting FidoNet echoes

Echo name	Description
ASL	American Sign Language echo
AVIATION	International Aviation echo
BB-CARDS	Baseball card echo
BRIT_CAR	British car echo
COMICS	Comics echo
DEADHEAD	Grateful Dead discussions
ECOLOGY	Ecology, problems and potential solutions
EDUCATOR	Teachers
ENTREPRENEUR	Entrepreneur conference
FEMINISM	Feminism and gender issues
FISHING	Fishing discussions of all kinds
GOURMET	Gourmet cooking
GUITAR	Guitar topics
HAM	Amateur Radio topics
HOMEPOWR	Alternative energy systems and homemade power
HOMESCHL	Home schooling support
HOME_COOKING	Home cooking and related topics
HOTROD	Race cars of all types
JAZZ	Jazz music
JFK_ASSN	John F. Kennedy assassination
MEMORIES	Nostalgia
MILHISTORY	Military history
MONTE	Monty Python echo
MOTORCYCLE	Motorcycle echo

Echo name	Description
PARROTS	Tropical birds discussions
PHIL	Philosophy
PHOTO	International photography echo
POLITICS	Political discussions
RECIPES	Recipes
SF	Science fiction and fantasy literature
TREK	Star Trek
UFO	UFO topics

If you're satisfied with local interest groups, look for a selection on the BBS's menu that says something like "Messages," "Conferences," "Discussion Areas," or "Rooms." When you select that option, you should see a list of topics to read. Select a topic (you'll probably have to type its number) and read through the messages. At the end of each message, you'll probably see a prompt that lists your options at that point (reply, read the next message, go back to the main message menu, etc.).

How can I keep my kids out of adult areas?

Most online services offer some kind of parental controls that enable you to limit the newsgroups and areas that your account can access. Prodigy is especially vigilant in this area. The "A" ID (the head of the household) can assign varying access privileges to each member of the family. MSN requires you to specifically request unlimited access to newsgroups and other Internet features—otherwise you can access only a limited, sanitized list of groups. There are also rumblings

afoot of some Internet software to be available shortly that will screen incoming text and block out certain subjects.

But as always, the best way to limit your children's exposure to adult materials is to be an active participant in your kids' online experiences. Don't let your computer become a babysitter. Sit down at the computer with your child and talk about what you're reading and playing and learning.

18

Online Gaming

● **In this chapter:**

- An introduction to online gaming

- What games can I play, and where do I find them?

- You can even play games modem-to-modem *without* online services

The online world is more than numbers, dates, and data—it's also a place for challenge, conquest, and fun . . . . ▶

oss out the warped card table with the coffee rings—you know, the one that only stands still if you put the phone book under that too-short leg. Your gaming partners in the modern world aren't in folding chairs in your living room, they're in desk chairs all over the world. You don't even have to plan the game or know who you're going to play with. If you fancy a game of cribbage, chess, poker, or just about any other game you can think of, just crank up your PC and dial into a virtual game room. You can bet there'll be other people there, waiting for a gaming partner like you to come along.

If you'd rather play alone or against a computer, there are plenty of online games for you as well, from simple adventure games to completely graphical arcade games. Any type of contest you're looking for (except maybe arm wrestling) is online somewhere.

What online games are out there?

There are three main types of games you can play using your modem:

- **Solo games on online services.** These include the same types of games you might play by yourself on your computer, like arcade games, trivia games, and adventure games.

- **Games with other people on online services.** Instead of playing "beat the clock" or outwitting a computer, you square off against real live opponents all over the world. Play board games, interactive adventures, and simple arcade games.

- **Games with one or more people outside of an online service.** In specially-designed games (called *modem aware* or *modem-to-modem* games), the game can use your modem to call another player's modem. The other player controls a character on your screen and vice versa.

Of the major online services, Prodigy is by far the most game-oriented, but they all pale in comparison to BBSs, The ImagiNation Network (a graphical, games-only online service), and the Internet.

The big guys: Who's got what?

CompuServe and America Online both offer a lot of games to download and play on your own PC, as you learned in Chapter 16, Finding Software Online. But both are rather weak when it comes to games you can actually play while you're online. (The ImagiNation Network, of course, is different, as I'll explain momentarily.) Here, in approximate order of best-to-worst, are the offerings of each online service.

The ImagiNation Network

If games are your number one interest, do yourself this favor: don't waste time hunting down the few games available on the other online services until you've tried the ImagiNation Network (INN), shown in figure 18.1.

Fig. 18.1
The ImagiNation Network is the premier online service for game fanatics.

INN is multiplayer games only. Period. (Well, there's also e-mail, but you get the feeling that the only reasons people use it are to set up games to play.) But there are lots of games, and it's a lighthearted, fun atmosphere.

Before you sign on, you use INN's software to create a cartoon character of yourself (they call them **toons**). Don't worry if you don't know how to draw—you just choose different face shapes, hair styles and colors, eye shapes and colors, and so on until your toon looks like you. When you're playing with somebody else, you see their toon on your screen and they see yours.

The games themselves are slick and fun. There are card and board games like Hearts, Spades, Cribbage, Backgammon, Euchre, and Go; graphical fantasy role playing games; moneyless gambling in the casino; games for kids; and phenomenal arcade games.

What more do you need? Other online services have their strengths, but games aren't high on the list.

Prodigy

Prodigy's long-standing graphical nature gives it an advantage over its recently-turned-graphical competitors, as does its family focus. After all, you *should* find games in an online family room, right?

Jump Games for a menu of games like AJ Dakota (much like Windows' Minesweeper), Where in the World is Carmen Sandiego? (see fig. 18.2), and many others.

Fig. 18.2
Most of Prodigy's games (like this adaptation of Where in the World is Carmen Sandiego?) are highly graphical and fast.

Prodigy also offers several extra-cost games as Custom Choices. You sign up, pay an extra fee (about $30), and then you get the privilege of playing for a set period of time (such as twelve weeks or so). The most popular of the custom choice games are the fantasy sports team games, like Fantasy Baseball. In it, you construct your own team based on real players in the Major League, and then play your dream-team against other people's. Hardcore sports fans say these games are worth the extra cost!

America Online

Surprisingly, America Online's gaming selection doesn't match its excellence in most other areas. **Go To** keyword **Gaming** for a list of game-related forums, but unless you're into word games or fantasy role-playing, don't expect much. Even the Kids Only area lacks good arcade or graphical games.

Fantasy role-playing is the one area where America Online scores over the other services, with a role-playing coliseum, Advanced Dungeons and Dragons (Neverwinter Nights), and several other role-playing forums.

AOL offers a casino, called RabbitJack's Casino, where you can play blackjack, bingo, and several other casino games, but you have to download special software in order to use this feature, and this software has a tendency to be a bit cranky. (Plus, the software is DOS-based, so Windows users have to run it in a DOS window, which can be troublesome.)

CompuServe

CompuServe offers lots of games, but they're mostly pretty weak. They're almost all text-based and rather dated. However, for nostalgia fans, CompuServe does offer the original Adventure game, the text game that started the adventure gaming craze over a decade ago. The computer gives you a description of your surroundings, and you type in commands to move around. (It's kind of like Multi-User Dungeons, or MUDs (discussed in "Internet MUD, MOOs, and other virtual worlds," later in the chapter), on the Internet, except only one player plays at a time.) As a long-time Infocom junkie (that's the company that made all those great text adventures in the 80s), I found Adventure to be a nice trip down memory lane.

Gamers do have one big advantage on CIS: other gamers. You can talk with thousands of other game fans on CIS to find out about new games and local gaming clubs (where, presumably, you play in the *real* world). **GO GAMES** to see the Fun & Games menu. It'll take you to a menu of games (like the trivia game in fig. 18.3) and game-related forums. There are hints and cheats for regular computer games (like Doom, Myst, Sim City, etc.), patches and updates you can download, and so on.

Fig. 18.3

CompuServe *is not* a haven for gamers, but you can get caught up in some adequate time–wasters.

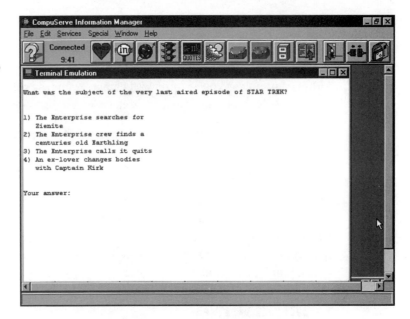

The Microsoft Network

The Microsoft Network does not have many online games, and the games do have cost extra to play, so enthusiastic gamesters may want to look for a different service. However, as I've said before, MSN is new, and by the time you read this, there may be much more to choose from.

To access the games area, select Categories, Interests, Leisure & Hobbies, Games & Gaming. The day I visited, there was an Online Fantasy & Strategy Games, etc. folder, where I found the following games to play:

- **Diplomacy.** This is a board game, but you can play with other MSN members by sending your moves via e-mail. (You have to go out and buy the board game, and set it up at your home, then plug in all the moves as they arrive via e-mail.) It's a $20 extra charge to play this game.

- **Online Sports Games.** For $25 each, you can sign up to play Fantasy Football, Fantasy Hockey, Fantasy Basketball, and Fantasy Baseball. With these games, you assemble your "dream team," then pit them against other people's teams.

BBS door games

BBSs have almost always had games for their users, and in fact, game players represent the heaviest traffic on most BBSs. The games are typically called *doors* or *door games*, because in order to play them, the caller "leaves" the main BBS management program and enters a sub-program that runs the game, almost as if he or she were going through a doorway.

Early door games were like the text adventure games you've probably seen. (Like the Adventure game I was telling you about in the CompuServe discussion earlier!) You'd see some text like this:

```
You're standing at the door to a small barn. There is a path
leading to the left and right.
```

Then you'd type F to go forward, R to go right, and so on. You can still find adventure games like this, and some new ones spring up from time to time. But faster modems have paved the way for the new generation of door games, which use more graphics and animation. As you may know from other chapters, it takes a lot more data to draw graphics on your screen than it does to draw text. Now that modems are faster, it's not totally maddening waiting for the modem to transfer enough data to draw the image on your screen.

When you play door games on a BBS, you don't usually play against other people in realtime, but (confusingly enough) you may have real people as opponents. Multiplayer door games are usually set up so that you can only take one "turn" per day. For example, if you log on to your BBS at 7 a.m. to take your turn, you won't be able to have another turn until the next day (maybe just after midnight that night). Other players won't be able to see what you've done until the next day, because these games update their "playing fields" only one time per day (again, usually in the middle of the night). All the moves from all the players are stored up throughout the day, then when it's time to update the playing field, the computer figures out how each player's moves have affected all the other players.

> 66 *Plain English, please!*
>
> **Realtime**, in relation to gaming, means you and your opponent are logged on and playing at the same time. 99

Some BBS door games don't use the "one turn per day" rule. If you're playing against only one or two other people, you may be able to take another turn as soon as everyone else has had a turn. For example, if you're playing against one other person and each of you logs on several times a day, you may be able to take any number of turns throughout the day as long as neither gets two turns in a row.

Sometimes "online" is actually "offline"

A similar type of game you'll run into on BBSs is the *offline game*. In offline games, you spend as little time as possible online (which makes them great for long-distance BBSers), but you usually have to make two calls per day. You make all your moves with a separate program on your computer's disk (*not* on the BBS) while you're not connected to the BBS. The playing cycle goes like this:

1 You call the BBS and download the game's daily file. This file tells your program what other players did the previous day.

2 You hang up on the BBS and exit out of your terminal software.

3 You run your game program and open the daily file. You'll see what happened with the previous day's moves from you and your opponents.

4 You use the game program to make new moves, and it creates a file of these moves.

5 You call the BBS again and upload the game's file.

Offline games are very popular, since you spend very little time online. That's handy even on local calls, not only because many BBSs limit the amount of time you can spend online per day, but also because you don't have to tie up the modem's telephone line for very long (and if you're like most people, that phone line is the only one in the house).

Some BBSs are now completely graphical and their games are usually very fancy (see fig. 18.4). In most of them, you can use your mouse to control the action, taking you much closer to the action than games where you have to type commands or remember which keys to push.

Fig. 18.4
Door games are a natural for the new graphical BBSs. This one is Escape from Languor.

Internet MUDs, MOOs, and other virtual worlds

One of the weirdest places to meet people online is in an Internet virtual world, usually called a **MUD** (**Multi-User Dimension**, or **Multi-User Dungeon**). MUDs are a lot like the chat rooms you may have read about in other chapters, but instead of just chatting with other people like you're all in a pit group somewhere, you interact with a whole online environment. It's rather like a combination of a text-only adventure game and a chat room.

For example, in a chat room, you might strike up a conversation about flower pressing and talk that over until someone changed the subject. In a MUD, you might start the exact same conversation, only to have a homicidal troll jump in a few moments later and start stabbing at you with a spear. (You'll get a message saying A troll jumps from behind a bush and stabs you. You lose 10 energy points. Or something to that effect.) I hardly need to say that MUDs are rarely boring.

❝ *Plain English, please!*

You'll see MUDs with other names, like MUSH, MOO, and MUCK. They're all variations on the same theme, and you can usually get away with using the general term "MUD." Each individual one has its own rules, capabilities, and culture. Some are virtual classrooms, with real scheduled classes and meetings. In general, MUSHes and MOOs are friendly, non-competitive places, whereas MUDs are more traditional gamelike environments. ❞

In some MUDs, you can design your own room (usually without intruding monsters) with whatever kind of trappings you want. These private rooms are great for talking with friends from the Net, because you can make the environment fit any mood. If you're reminiscing, your room may be the one you had in college, or maybe the interior of that rust-heap you used to take on road trips.

They operate along the same lines as text-based adventure games. You type **GO UP** when you get to the bottom of a ladder, **SWIM** when you fall in the river, and **DRINK TEA** when you're sure the person offering you tea isn't trying to turn you into a newt. When you want to chat with another player, you would start your command with that character's name—something like **THOR, HOW ABOUT THAT DRAGON FIGHT LAST WEEK, EH?**

There are several MUDs on the Internet, each with its own commands, membership restrictions, and other rules. You can usually count on one thing, though: if you type HELP as soon as you show up, you'll see very simple instructions for joining and using the MUD.

Finding MUDs isn't easy, since most appear and disappear quickly. Your best bet is the current FAQ of the **alt.mud** or **rec.games.mud** UseNet newsgroup. If you use Gopher, you'll usually find them in the **/Fun and Games/** directories of major public sites (like the main Gopher at the University of Minnesota). You may also want to look for directories called **/MUD/** or **/MOO/** with Veronica. For information on using Gopher and Veronica, and finding FAQs, see Chapter 12, "Calling the Internet."

Private modem-to-modem gaming

Some games you can buy include modem support, so you can play the game via modem against another person rather than against the computer. With such modem-aware software, you can play everything from chess to shoot-em-ups against a friend across town (or, if you can afford the long-distance phone bills, anywhere else). Games that adapt well to modem play include:

- Action games such as Doom and Doom II (see fig. 18.5), where your opponent becomes another character on your screen. If you're cooperating, you can join forces to blast through waves of baddies, but a lot of people prefer the Death Match mode, where the opponent is just another target.

- Military-style simulation games, especially aerial combat games.

- Sports simulations, especially games such as golf.

- Fantasy role-playing games, where the characters really come to life on your screen.

- Board and parlor games such as chess, backgammon, checkers, Othello, Go, and others.

Setting up modem-aware games to use your modem is usually not too tricky—especially with newer games. If you dig up a vintage modem-to-modem game, however, you may as well resign yourself to an evening of setup before you can make the first move. The same rules and terms apply to installing modem-aware games as to installing other modem software (see Chapter 3, "Installing Your software").

Fig. 18.5
The next best thing to paintball—splatter your opponent's innards with a shotgun in Doom 2.

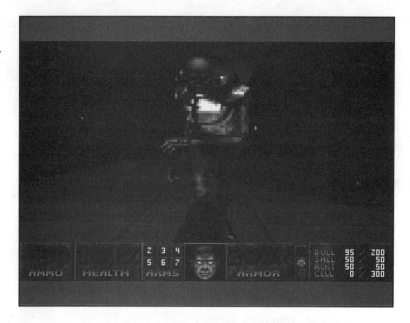

19

Getting the News and Weather

● **In this chapter:**

- What's the news across the nation? You can get the information!

- You mean I can find my favorite syndicated columns, too?

- Keeping up with sports

- What's the weather going to be like in Detroit tomorrow?

- And funnies, too!

You can get up-to-the-minute news, weather, and sports from the comfort of your own computer. With service like this, who needs a TV?. . . . . ⮞

Two centuries ago, a fellow by the name of Paul Revere galloped his horse through the streets of Boston to warn his fellow citizens that the British were coming. This single act became one of the most famous feats of heroism in American history.

If Paul were alive today, he'd probably just post a message online and be done with it.

How much news do you want?

You can find literally hundreds of sources for online news. Want to know what the weather is like in Dallas, Texas this afternoon? How about the Bulls vs. Pacers score at halftime? Or maybe you need to learn about the latest developments in the search for a cure for cancer.

It doesn't matter which online service you use—chances are you'll find what you're looking for...and then some. You can dial up for electronic news from the Associated Press, CNN, Reuters News Service, even the *Jerusalem Post*. Like in your favorite daily newspaper, you can find current events, box scores, political commentary, comic strips, and classifieds online. Even Miss Manners has a column.

Reading the freshest news

What your local newspaper can't provide is continuous, immediate coverage of everything. By the time the morning paper hits your front porch, most of the front-page stories you'll find are old news compared to the up-to-the-minute information available online.

TIP **The sites and services listed in this chapter are just a small** sampling of what's available online. More are being added all the time. These are enough to get you started, but you'll quickly find more sources to explore once you're online. Check the "What's New" section of your service periodically to learn about the most recent offerings.

Also keep in mind that sometimes the keywords you use to get to an area change from time to time. If you typed **GO NEWS** yesterday just fine, but today got unexpected results, try hunting down what you want using the service's search tool.

Where do I find news on CompuServe?

If you're a CompuServe subscriber, the quickest route is **GO NEWS**. As soon as the News window opens, you'll see an extensive list of sources.

 CAUTION

Remember that anything listed under Basic News Services is free if you're in the Basic Services Plan, but items under Extended News Services may involve a connect-time fee or premium surcharge, or both.

- To learn what's happened in the last 60 minutes, choose Associated Press Online (**GO APO**), click Proceed to acknowledge the disclaimer, then double-click Latest News-Updated Hourly, as shown in figure 19.1.

Fig. 19.1
Online news services provide 24-hour-a-day access to the latest news stories.

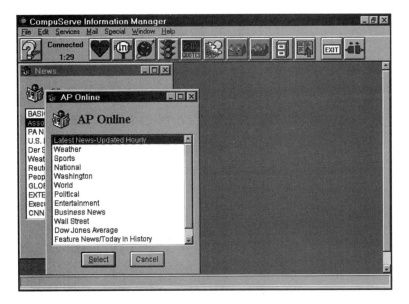

- AP Online offers a variety of other features, too. If you're a trivia buff, you might want to check out Feature News/Today in History for a quick rundown of what was happening and who was born on this day in years past. It even includes a closing "Thought for the Day," which you may or may not find inspiring.

- CNN Online (**GO CNN**) sponsors a lively collection of news clips, photos, and hot topics all wrapped up in a colorful push-button interface (see fig. 19.2).

Fig. 19.2
You get easy click-of-
a-button access to
news and headlines
through CNN Online.

- *US News and World Report*'s forum (**GO EUN**) is similar to CNN's. In addition, it includes an extensive library of archived articles, photos, conference transcripts, and other information. This is great for research.

- Online Today (**GO OLT**) is a daily service devoted to tracking what's happening in cyberspace and other things technical.

- The Executive News Service (**GO ENS**) is like your own clipping service. You can designate what particular topics you want to read about, and the service will search its database for those stories each time you visit. You don't have to hunt through lists of headlines manually (but you can). ENS is handy for folks who don't have a lot of time to keep current.

- Other popular news areas include People Weekly Online (**GO PEOPLE**) and Reuter/Variety Entertainment News (**GO RTVARIETY**).

 TIP **GO NEWSPAPERS for a list of some other sources you might want** to peruse.

AOL has news too

America Online knows you want to stay on top of current events. In fact, the AOL Welcome screen offers to tell you the hottest story of the moment as soon as you connect.

- Click the Top News Story button on the Welcome screen to scan the current headlines (see fig. 19.3). From there you can click any headline for the whole scoop.

Fig. 19.3
You can read the latest headlines on AOL over breakfast and still have one hand free to hold your coffee cup.

- The US & World button (keyword **US News**) provides access to more stories on what's happening. Click the drop-down list shown in figure 19.4 for specific categories.

Fig. 19.4
Like sections in your newspaper, headlines are conveniently organized by topic—but you don't have to turn umpteen pages to get to them.

TIP **Save yourself some money: Don't read the stories while you're** logged on to your service. In most cases, you can download the story to a file and read it later.

- US & World also features *The New York Times Online* area (which is similar to CompuServe's CNN forum), as well as services provided by *Time* magazine and ABC News.

Dear Mr. Cronkite:

How many times have you been watching the tube and wishing you could give the network a piece of your mind about one thing or another? The presence of the media on online services provides you with unique opportunities to do just that.

AOL's ABCNEWS On Demand features an e-mail "hotline" to each of its major news programs, such as "DayOne," "Nightline," and "20/20."

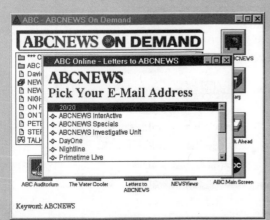

Keyword: ABCNEWS

Keep an eye out for these as you're watching your favorite shows, too. These days it seems every

program flashes its e-mail or Internet address across the screen, inviting you to drop them a line or check out their little corner of cyberspace.

By sending feedback and questions to the networks, newspapers, and shows that reside online, you can let them know that yes, you're out there, and no, you don't want to hear any more about Topic X. On the other hand, if you particularly enjoyed a program or story, you can tell them that, too, and encourage more coverage in the future.

So, if you really liked Barbara Walters' interview with Elton John or Peter Jennings' special undercover exposé of telephone solicitors out to rip you off, zap them an e-mail and let them know. It's not unheard of to get a personal response thanking you for your comments, or answering whatever question you might have asked.

Of course, this is all assuming you do shut down your computer and actually turn on the television from time to time.

Finding news on Prodigy

As you've probably noticed by now, the online services offer about the same things in the way of news and information, and Prodigy is no exception. And one nice thing about Prodigy is that it gives you a button to click to see a news photo—it doesn't automatically assume you want to see the photo. Transferring photos slows down America Online, for example, which can be annoying at times (not to mention expensive).

- **Jump News** to get to the Prodigy Headlines and all the features it contains (see fig 19.5).

Fig. 19.5

Like AOL and CompuServe, you can access late-breaking stories from across the globe, news photos, and other interesting journalistic items.

- **Jump Magazines** to get Prodigy's list of online magazines. In addition to being interesting reading, these can come in handy. For example, if you're looking to buy a new minivan but want to make sure it's sturdy enough to haul your family safely, check out *Consumer Reports* (see fig. 19.6). In fact, if you jump **CR Index**, you can even see a list of the different topics and services available from Consumer Reports.

Fig. 19.6
To buy or not to buy.
Consumer Reports can
help you decide.

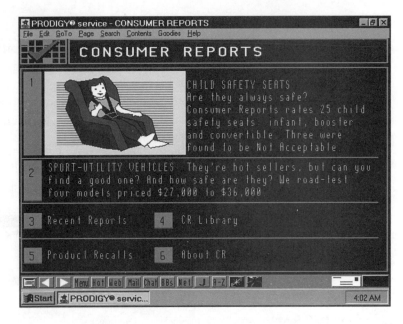

- CompuServe has *US News and World Report,* AOL has *Time* magazine,
so it's no surprise to find *Newsweek Interactive* on Prodigy. **Jump
Newsweek** for a view of the latest issue, like the one shown in figure
19.7.

Fig. 19.7
Prodigy offers a weekly
update of *Newsweek.*

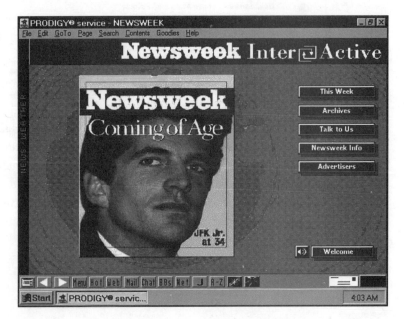

TIP   **Need to check those Powerball lottery tickets to see if you finally hit the jackpot? Jump Powerball** for the most recent numbers as well as an archive of past winning numbers.

Prodigy offers the same thing for state lotteries, arranged by region.

The latest news on the Microsoft Network

The first place to look for the top stories is on the MSN Today page. You'll sometimes find direct links to hot stories here (for instance, as I was writing this book, I could usually find something about the O.J. Simpson trial on MSN Today.)

The main source of news on MSN is the News & Weather category. You can reach it directly by selecting Edit, Go To, then typing **NEWS**; or clicking Categories, then News & Weather. As you can see in figure 19.8, MSN's news offerings come from some powerful hitters: USA Today, Time Warner, and NBC. The USA Today online offerings include a nearly complete online version of the printed paper—so you can cancel your subscription! And NBC Supernet provides all the same information that watching the newscast on TV would bring, except you get to choose which stories you're interested in. (Fig. 19.9 shows the NBC News screen.)

Fig. 19.8
Get to MSN's News & Weather by using the Go To word "News."

Fig. 19.9
The NBC Supernet offers up all the same news as the daily NBC newscast, except *you* control the action.

Don't forget the Internet!

For every newspaper, magazine, and TV network you find on the commercial online services, you'll find a dozen or more on the Internet.

Here's a few of your choices (some are free, others you can preview but must buy a subscription):

- ClariNet e.News claims to be "the first and largest" electronic news service on the Internet. It features AP and Reuters news, sports updates, stock information, technical and computer industry news, and more (visit **http://www.clarinet.com**).

- NewsPage from Individual, Inc. As its home page states, NewsPage has a comprehensive collection of news categories, from insurance to environmental science to pharmaceutical news (see fig. 19.10). To check it out, visit Web site **http://www.newspage.com**.

- Go to **http://www.trib.com** to get online with the Casper, Wyoming *Star-Tribune* newspaper. It features news from United Press International and Canadian Press, as well as MarketWatch, a special feature that updates Dow Jones and Standard & Poor's indexes every three minutes. And of course, plenty of information about the great state of Wyoming.

Fig. 19.10
NewsPage is full of comprehensive information similar to this page on Eli Lilly.

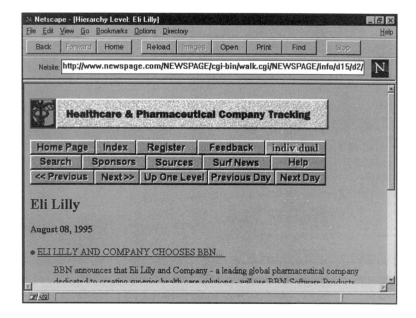

- Want to read your *Wall Street Journal* every morning, but don't want to kill the trees? Ensemble Information Systems, Inc., offers what they call Personal Digital Newspapers (PDNs). The program was still under development at press time, but you can check out a sample edition at **http://www.ensemble.com** along with subscription information (no, the real thing is not free).

When minutes don't count, but content does

If you're more interested in specific topics than headlines, there are a number of electronic magazines just waiting for you. Go to **gopher:// gopher.enews.com:70/11/magazines/** for one great collection.

You might also want to check out *Hotwired* (published by *Wired* magazine) one of the most popular electronic magazines on the Internet (**http://www.hotwired.com/**). *Hotwired* covers a lot of territory, but focuses on the wild, wild world of the Internet.

Political activists will be happy to know that the beloved *Mother Jones* magazine is available on the Net, too, at **http://www.mojones.com**.

More than just the facts: Online opinions and insights

Of course, all that news is fine, but what does it all really mean? Thousands of syndicated columnists, comedians, and analysts across the world are happy to tell you their spin on things.

You can find a wide variety of syndicated columns and opinion-oriented magazines online, from political satire to advice on social behavior.

On CompuServe

- **GO COLUMNS** for daily or weekly editions of Joel Makower's *The Green Consumer* (environmental concerns), *Ailing House* by Henri de Marne (home improvement), *Susan Bondy on Money* (financial advise), *Roger Ebert's Movie Reviews* (this column includes a lot more than just movie reviews!), *Joyce Jillson's Horoscope* (weekly updates), *Miss Manners* (ethics and social behavior), and opinion columns from an impressive list of contributors including Mikhail Gorbachev, Jack Anderson, Richard Sullivan (see fig. 19.11), and Alan Dershowitz.

Fig. 19.11
Everyone's entitled to their own opinions...and you'll find lots of them online.

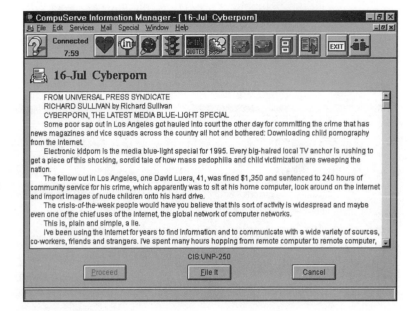

- **GO MAGAZINES** for forums sponsored by *FORTUNE* magazine, *People* magazine, *IndustryWeek Interactive*, Macmillan Computer Publishing, and more.

- Magazine Database Plus (**GO MAGDB**) is a searchable archive of articles (some as far back as 1986) from over 200 publications including *Time, Forbes, The Atlantic, Kiplinger's Personal Finance, Cosmopolitan* and many others.

On AOL

- Soundbites Online is a political humor forum that features downloadable audio files. If you're into satire, this is the place to get it (keyword **Soundbites**).

- The Atlantic Monthly forum is always a good source for commentary on politics and the social scene (keyword **Atlantic**).

- Keyword **Columnists** gives you a whole slew of offerings to satisfy your appetite for political commentary. You'll find regular postings here from Hodding Carter, Ben Wattenberg, and Sara Eckel, to name but a few. You also might want to keep an eye on "Smart Money," a column by long-time talk radio host Bruce Williams.

On Prodigy

- Jump **Columns** for a listing of the available columns on Prodigy. (There were about two dozen on the day I looked, including Ask Beth (a teen advice column), Horoscopes, and Block on Taxes.

On the Microsoft Network

There's no central location for advice columns on MSN at this writing. But you can get a listing of the current columns easily enough. Just select <u>T</u>ools, <u>F</u>ind, on the <u>M</u>icrosoft Network. Search for the word "column." Here are the ones that my search pulled up, but there will probably be more by the time you read this:

- Her Health (women's health issues)

- Pregnancy Q&A

- Cyberspace Business

- Future Smart (articles about the future of business online)

- GameWIZ Weekly (information about online gaming on MSN)

On the Internet

- There's *way* too much out there to even attempt a sampling. The best way to find what you're looking for is to use your Web browser's search tool and enter words like "column" or "advice." You'll find everything from scientific newsletters to advice for the lovelorn. (I'm particularly fond of **http://www.hyperweb.com/loquita/loquita.html**, or Ms. Loquita's Advice Column on Love.)

Online sources for sports fan

When you're finished reading the news, the next logical progression for many is to turn to the sports section. Whether it's box scores, photos of your favorite superstar in action, or the latest odds on the upcoming boxing match, you won't be disappointed.

Where do I find it on my service?

Where *won't* you find it? Here's a quick list of the highlights:

- On CompuServe, *Sports Illustrated Online* is the best area for sporting news, scores, statistics, and some interesting sidelines activities (see fig. 19.12). **GO SPORTS** to enter the area. For up-to-date information on trading, scores, and other news, click News, Scores & Stats.

- America Online subscribers will find the ABC Sports forum equally satisfying. It offers most of the same services and features as *Sports Illustrated Online*. Keyword **ABC SPORTS** to go straight there, or just type **SPORTS** for a more general collection of sports topics.

- Prodigy's sports guru is ESPN (**Jump Sports**). ESPNET is full of interesting tidbits, and everything is easy to get to, as figure 19.13 illustrates.

Fig. 19.12
What? No swimsuit issue?

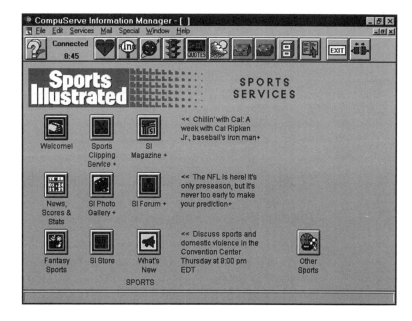

Fig. 19.13
Just click the button next to the headline that grabs your attention for more sporting news.

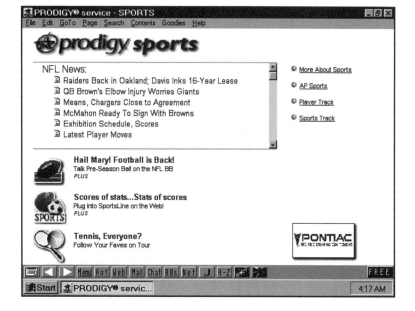

- On the Microsoft Network, check out the Sports and Recreation category. The content is still changing, but you may find folders there for everything from sports psychology and sports medicine to the discussions about motor sports and the Olympics.

- Both The World Wide Web of Sports at **http://www.tns.lcs.mit.edu/ cgi-bin/sports** and The Sports Server from *The News & Observer* of Raleigh, North Carolina (**http://www2.nando.net/SportServer/**) give global coverage of sporting news on the Internet.

CAUTION **The first address in the preceding bullet takes forever to appear,** even with a 14.4 bps modem—but if you can stand the wait, it's got some really nice graphics.

- Starwave's ESPNET SportsZone is a sister of the Prodigy site, with many of the same features. Surf over to **http://espnet.sportszone.com**.

Q&A ***My neighbors' son plays professional badminton. I like to follow his tournament progress, but I usually can't find it in the paper, and TV sportscasters sure don't spend any time on it. Will I have better luck online?***

Sure! Information on football, baseball, and basketball are always easy to find. Even if you follow something less dominant, like bowling or handball, you won't be left out. Remember, "something for everyone" is the cyberspace pledge. ABC Sports' "Other Sports" coverage includes news on everything from Auto Racing to Yachting, for example (see fig 19.14).

Fig. 19.14
Someone, somewhere will appreciate having this information available.

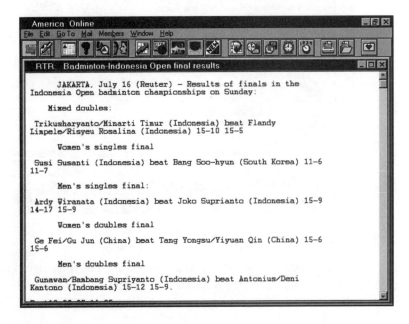

There's lots of other neat things to do on ESPNET

Even if you'd rather get the results of last night's game from a more traditional source, any sports fan will want to explore the other areas of the ESPNET SportsZone. You can get logo merchandise, sign up for an on-going Fantasy Sports tournament, or use the Sports Clipping Service to get automatic updates on only your favorite teams.

If you're into statistics, try out Prodigy's Player Track, which you find on the ESPNET main window. During baseball season, Player Track helps you monitor the batting and pitching statistics of your favorite players on any team, week by week or cumulative for the season. The best part is that you can download the stats as a text file and use the records in other places, such as a database program. In the fall, of course, there's Fantasy Football.

Other sporting areas to check

In addition to the biggies like Sports Illustrated and ABC Sports, there are a fair amount of individual sports forums online as well.

Case in point: I've recently developed an interest in sailing, and during the last America's Cup series, I was closely following the story of the all-woman crew of Mighty Mary. Imagine my delight to find a whole area on Prodigy devoted to this very topic! In addition to data about the ship, the crew, and the history of the America's Cup race, there's even a glossary of sailing terms to help me bone up on my new-found hobby (see fig 19.15).

 TIP **Like flannel shirts and bathing suits, some areas are seasonal or** temporary, and are only around as long as it's pertinent. In other words, don't expect to find as much information about a particular sport or event if it's not happening right now. (But that doesn't mean you won't find *any* information.)

- To find other sports-related topics on CompuServe, click Find and enter **sports** or the name of the specific sport you want to look for. CompuServe will search its database and present you with all the forums you can visit (including a sailing forum!).

Fig. 19.15
OK, so what the heck's a "sloop?"

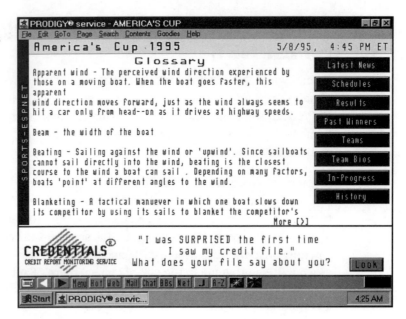

- If you want to see what other sports stuff is on AOL, do a keyword search for **sports**.

- Check the Sports A-Z index for a comprehensive list of everything Prodigy has to offer to sports fans.

- Most of the online newspapers feature sports reports, too, so don't forget them! They are especially good sources for coverage on their home teams.

- If you're a Web surfer, try using your browser's search utility to locate specific information. Try keywords like **sports** or **baseball**. Of course, if you search for **surfing**, you might get more info about the world's best Web sites than you do about the world's best beaches.

TIP **Virtually every sports team in the nation has its own Web site or** home page. For everything you've always wanted to know about where to find sports coverage on the Internet, check out *Sports on the Net*, also from Que.

It's a Family Tradition

In keeping with its family-oriented content, Prodigy offers *Sports Illustrated for Kids*. This cool area will keep the kids busy for hours. (Actually, some adults enjoy *SIK* as much or more than their kids!)

Each month, *SI for Kids* features "Ask the Athlete," where children can send questions via e-mail to

the guest of the month. They can also participate in contests, express their opinions in debates, and make new friends on the *SIK* bulletin board.

To check it out, **Jump SI FOR KIDS** (or just **SIK** for the BB).

What about the weather?

If you travel frequently (or even if you don't), you will appreciate knowing that the latest weather information is right at your fingertips. CompuServe, Prodigy, and AOL all offer comprehensive weather services to subscribers, and with a few internal differences, the services all work very similarly. It's just like having Willard Scott make a personal appearance right there in your home.

Generally, you'll find the following information on your service:

- Satellite images: snapshots of the Earth's atmospheric conditions can sometimes be viewed from various perspectives, like "northeastern USA."

- Surface maps: these look just like the weather maps you see on TV, without that guy or gal standing in the way telling bad jokes (see fig. 19.16).

Fig. 19.16
Raining in Indiana again? Gee, what a surprise.

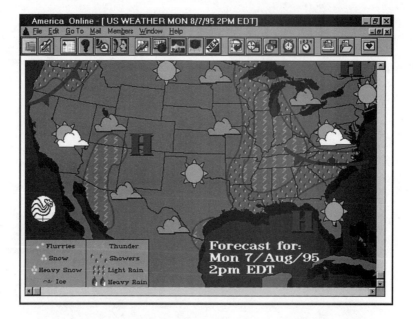

- Short-term forecasts for your region or state: usually in text form, these give the no-frills data on what to expect in your area. Figure 19.17 shows information for Indianapolis.

Fig. 19.17
Actually, I think they just post the same forecast for Indianapolis every day between February and May.

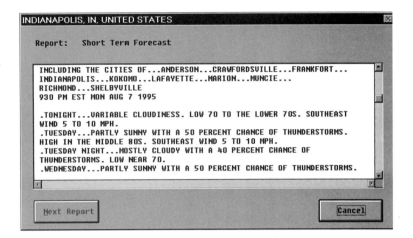

```
INDIANAPOLIS, IN, UNITED STATES                                [x]

Report:   Short Term Forecast

INCLUDING THE CITIES OF...ANDERSON...CRAWFORDSVILLE...FRANKFORT...
INDIANAPOLIS...KOKOMO...LAFAYETTE...MARION...MUNCIE...
RICHMOND...SHELBYVILLE
930 PM EST MON AUG 7 1995

.TONIGHT...VARIABLE CLOUDINESS. LOW 70 TO THE LOWER 70S. SOUTHEAST
WIND 5 TO 10 MPH.
.TUESDAY...PARTLY SUNNY WITH A 50 PERCENT CHANCE OF THUNDERSTORMS.
HIGH IN THE MIDDLE 80S. SOUTHEAST WIND 5 TO 10 MPH.
.TUESDAY NIGHT...MOSTLY CLOUDY WITH A 40 PERCENT CHANCE OF
THUNDERSTORMS. LOW NEAR 70.
.WEDNESDAY...PARTLY SUNNY WITH A 50 PERCENT CHANCE OF THUNDERSTORMS.


   [Next Report]                                    [Cancel]
```

Q&A *Where do I go to find the weather information on my online service?*

This is an easy one:

- CompuServe: **GO WEATHER**

- AOL: Keyword **WEATHER**

- Prodigy: **Jump Weather** (noticing a pattern here?)

- MSN: Categories, News & Weather

- or search for "weather" on any of them

Activities for a rainy day

Some people like to study meteorology as a hobby, for good reason—its a fascinating science. So along with current conditions and forecasts, you will find an assortment of weather-related topics on each of the services.

CompuServe, for example, features a forum sponsored by The Weather Channel. The Weather Channel, if you don't already know, is a 24-hour cable channel whose only programming is, you guessed it—the weather. TWC's forum (**GO TWCFOR**) gives you access to libraries stuffed with downloadable weather, climate, and geological information. For the truly committed TWC fan, you also can get GIF files of TWC's anchorpersons (see fig. 19.18).

Fig. 19.18
Maybe not a house-
hold name—but then
neither was David
Letterman when he
was a weatherman on
the local Indianapolis
news.

AOL also has a number of discussion groups and posting areas related to
weather and meteorology. To get there, Keyword **Weather** and click Weather
Talk. One of the most interesting ones I've visited is the Storm Chasers forum
(see fig. 19.19). People from all over the world tell their "war stories" about
chasing tornadoes and other natural disasters they've witnessed.

Fig. 19.19
You chase 'em, dude.
I'll be headed for
cover.

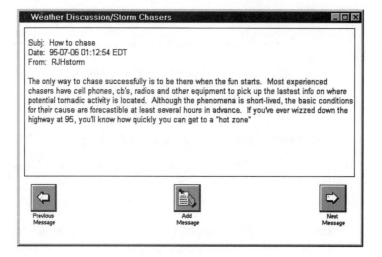

If you subscribe to Prodigy, you get easy access to not just the weather in
North America, but worldwide. From Acapulco to Zurich, a click on
Internat'l Weather will give you the next three days' highlights (or lowlights,
as the case may be.)

Does the Internet have weather information?

Of course it does. Although local conditions and forecasts are sometimes tricky to find, there are several Net sites that specialize in the same type of satellite and surface maps you see on the commercial services. Here are a few to get you started:

- **http://thunder.atms.purdue.edu**: As the domain suggests, the WXP Weather Processor is maintained by Purdue University's Department of Earth and Atmospheric Sciences. It also includes a lengthy list of other WWW Weather Servers across North America.

- **http://www.atmos.uiuc.edu/wxworld/html/top.html**: Weather World is a sister site of Purdue's, maintained by the University of Illinois.

- **http://www.resortsportsnet.com/biz/rsn/cam.html**: In addition to US weather maps, the Resort Sports Network's RESORT WEATHER CAM features current conditions and extended forecasts for popular ski resorts such as Lake Tahoe, California and Copper Mountain, Colorado.

TIP **The fastest way to find a variety of sources for any topic of** interest is to do a search for key words. For example, to find more comics in CompuServe, click Find, enter **comic** or **cartoon** and click OK. CompuServe returns with a list of places you can go to find what you're looking for. Check the member services section of your online service or the Frequently Asked Questions (FAQ) file maintained by your Internet access provider for specific search instructions.

The lighter side of the news

No morning paper is complete without cartoons!

By using your modem and doing a little exploring, you can find electronic versions of your favorite comic strips and political cartoons along with some brand new ones that are exclusive to cyberspace. You can even download entire issues of some well-known comic books.

One of the most popular strips—especially on the Internet—is *Dilbert* (created by Scott Adams), that bizarre collection of misfits who work together in an oh--so-typical Corporate America office. I found nine sites featuring *Dilbert* in a simple "dilbert" search; I'm sure that's just the tip of the iceberg. The official Dilbert Zone home page, however, is located at:

http://www.unitedmedia.com/comics/dilbert/

Dr. Fun is another favorite among Internet cybernauts. Check out the daily version at:

http://sunsite.unc.edu/Dave/Dr-Fun/ latest.jpg

Prodigy's NewsToons is a daily collection of political and editorial cartoons that is certainly worth checking out on a regular basis. **Jump Newstoons**.

On CompuServe, you'll find the Comics Publishers Forum, the Comics/Animation Forum, Generation X Comics Download, and other forums stuffed with everything from Marvel Comics cover art to some more obscure strips.

AOL is home to TOON Online, a forum sponsored by cable TV's The Cartoon Network. You can download all kinds of GIF files here, from old familiar favorites like Quickdraw McGraw to art submitted by AOL subscribers. Go To keyword **TOONS.**

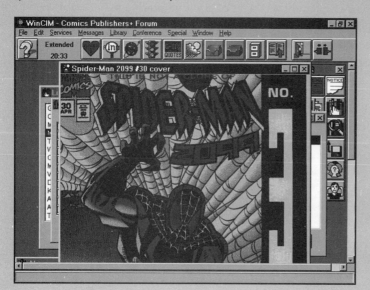

20

Shopping!

● **In this chapter:**

- **What kinds of shopping can you do online?**

- **Visiting online stores**

- **Finding used merchandise in online want ads**

- **Shopping tips for your online mall crawl**

Have you ever spent a day at the mall—dressed only in your bathrobe? With your modem, you can have the world's largest shopping center delivered right to your desk . . . . . ▶

Home shopping now means more than just staring at a rotating cubic zirconia ring on TV for ten minutes. Retailers have now created electronic catalogs and "virtual stores" where you can pick up everything you can get at the local mall. Sure, you'll miss out on the junior clerks spritzing cologne on you when you're not looking, but you can probably get one of your neighbors to do that.

What can I buy?

You can use your modem (with the aid of your credit card) to buy almost anything—not just computer products. New or used, luxury items to essentials, somebody's selling what you want online:

- Send flowers, gifts, and greeting cards anywhere in the country—and sometimes all over the world; FTD, 1-800-FLOWERS, and many other flower and gift companies have online stores.

- Buy name-brand clothes, usually with a free-return-if-they-don't-fit policy

- In some areas, you can order meals (like pizza!) and groceries to be delivered to your home or office

- Check out nifty gadgets from specialty retailers like The Nature Company, Hammacher Schlemmer, and many others

- Get free travel brochures for any destination in the world, and order your tickets online

- Buy tools, housewares, and other everyday items from Sears (one of the partners in the Prodigy service), JCPenney, and most other major department store chains

- Books, music, videos, and magazines are all heavily represented online

- Get clothing, stuffed toys, videos, and other merchandise from every major TV network and movie studio (see fig. 20.1)

 TIP **Most major auto makers are represented online, but most don't** sell cars that way. You will, however, find pricing, specs, reviews, and the addresses of local dealers.

Fig. 20.1
The Big Guys like
Disney, Warner
Brothers, Paramount,
and the major
networks aren't the
only ones with online
stores.

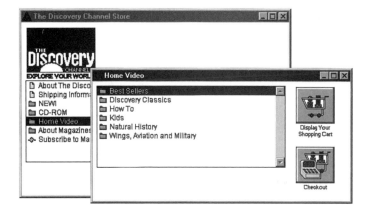

- Computers, software, accessories, and computer services are a natural for online shopping, so you'll find plenty of everything—and mostly at low mail-order prices

 **CAUTION** **When buying computer equipment, no matter where you buy it** from, make sure that a) it's what you really want, and b) that you can return it if you don't like it.

- Every online service has a want ads area for individuals and small companies to sell their wares

As long as you've got a major credit card and a street address, you're shopping. (Checks and C.O.Ds are frowned upon, and most delivery services won't deliver to a post office box.)

Online stores

Each of the major online services has several "stores," mostly run by companies *other* than the online service itself. The first time people visit an "online mall," some are slightly disappointed that you can't take a visual tour of a real store (especially if they've seen what we can do with games like Myst and Doom). Sorry—online shopping technology hasn't caught up with gaming technology. Instead, online stores look a lot like all the other areas you visit on your online service.

Online shopping is almost always very easy, and with good reason: who'd bother to shop online if you had to jump through all kinds of hoops to do it?

Time you spend in online stores is also usually free of connection charges, for the same reason.

Online stores usually try to act like regular stores. On AOL, for example, you have a "shopping cart" where, when you see an item you like, you click the Add Product to Cart button, and when you're ready to leave the store, you choose the Checkout button (see fig. 20.2). Some other services have an Order item button on each product description or individual ordering methods in each store. Rest assured, however, you'll never wonder what you have to do to order a product—that'll always be *very* clear.

Fig. 20.2
AOL's online stores have you put products in a virtual shopping cart while you're shopping.

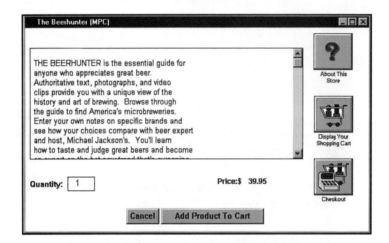

In many cases, you can see photographs or drawings of the products before you buy them (see figures 20.3 and 20.4).

Fig. 20.3
While you won't find a lot of photos of tires or software packages, unique items like these shorts usually include photos with their descriptions.

Fig. 20.4
At Lands' End on Prodigy, you can see the items you're buying.

The FREE sign means your online time is free while you're in the store.

Some people worry that the companies *behind* the online stores are all little mail order companies run out of somebody's garage, but nothing could be further from the truth. Some of the biggest companies in retail are also the biggest online. Sears, for example, is part of the joint venture that presents Prodigy. JCPenney, Hammacher Schlemmer (see fig. 20.5), FTD, and the Home Shopping Network are just some of the other household names with online stores.

Each online service has a substantial area devoted to shopping—which is not surprising, since the online services get payments and kickbacks from the vendors. The following table tells where to go on "the big three" services when you're ready to shop.

Online service	How to find its stores
Prodigy	**Jump Shopping**
AOL	Go To keyword **Marketplace**
CompuServe	**Go Mall**

Fig. 20.5
Hammacher
Schlemmer is just one
of the major "real
world" names in
online retailing.

 TIP   **On the Microsoft Network, use the Tools, Find, On The Microsoft**
Network command to search for the word "shopping." This will bring up a
list of all the shopping areas on MSN.

The Internet is also filled with shopping opportunities. For instance, The
Home Shopping Network's online branch is the Internet Shopping Network,
available through the Worldwide Web at **http://shop.internet.net**. And you
can order computer books like this one from Macmillan Computer Publishing
at **http://www.mcp.com** (see fig. 20.6).

Fig. 20.6
Buy computer books, and get free information, at the Macmillan SuperLibrary site.

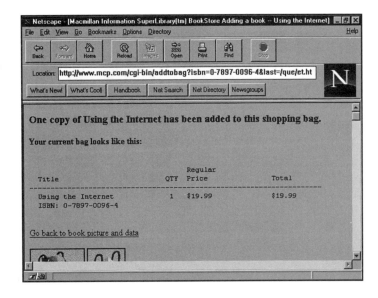

Want ads

If you want to buy or sell anything, you'll get quick results with online want ads.

Every online service has a respectable want ads section (see table 20.1), but the big gun in want ads is Traders' Connection (T-CON), as shown in figure 20.7. Through the Internet, you can read or place classified ads in dozens of major newspapers. T-CON also has a remarkable search feature where you can specify the item, price range, or location you're interested in, and see all the ads that match your needs. You'll probably end up using the search feature, unless you want to browse through more than half a million individual ads. As a T-CON representative told me, "We've got more late-model Mustangs in our database than other places have cars."

Table 20.1 Where to Find Want Ads

Online Service	What to do
CIS	**GO CLASSIFIEDS**
AOL	Go To keyword **Classifieds**
Prodigy	**JUMP MARKETPLACE BB**
Internet Telnet	**TRADER.COM**

continues

Table 20.1 Continued

Online Service	What to do
Internet newsgroups	**misc.forsale**
	misc.forsale.computers.monitors
	misc.forsale.computers.modems
	misc.forsale.computers.other.misc
	misc.forsale.computers.pc-clone
	misc.forsale.computers.printers
	misc.forsale.computers.storage
Internet newsgroups	**misc.forsale.pc-specific.audio**
	misc.forsale.pc-specific.cards.video
	misc.forsale.pc-specific.misc
	misc.forsale.pc-specific.portables
	misc.forsale.pc-specific.software
	misc.forsale.non-computer
	rec.music.marketplace

To connect with T-CON through the Internet, telnet to **TRADER.COM** or use the World Wide Web (**http://www.trader.com**). You can also make a toll-free **modem** call (not voice) to 1-800-FUN-T-CON to get a local direct access number in most areas.

Other online services also have classified ads (see fig. 20.8), which are set up like normal forums.

Fig. 20.7
Trader's Connection links you with classified ads from many major newspapers as well as its own enormous ad database.

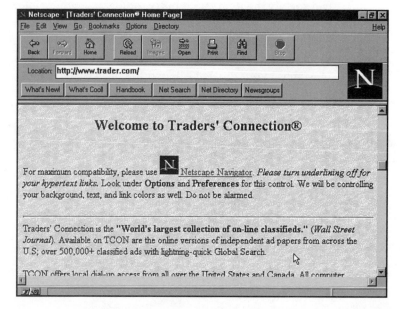

Fig. 20.8
Prodigy's MARKET-
PLACE BB is a typical
online want ad forum,
with individual
categories for each
interest.

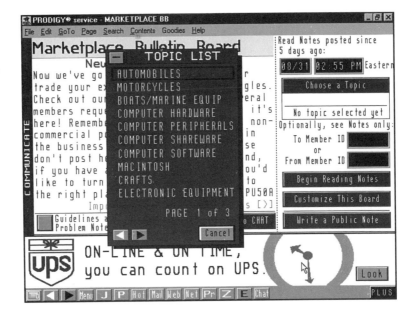

Be a smart consumer

The big thing to remember is that the regular shopping rules don't change
when you shop online. Use common sense, the same as you would when
visiting a physical store. These tips should help:

- Above all, keep your credit card information private unless you're
  absolutely sure you're dealing with a reputable company. Just as you
  wouldn't give your credit card number to a street vendor selling $30
  Rolexes, you shouldn't give it to anyone you meet online, especially in a
  chat room. Reputable companies do not do business that way. And
  don't be afraid to call the Better Business Bureau to request a report on
  the company.

- You don't have the benefit of a dressing room, so make sure you can
  return any clothing that doesn't fit. Believe it or not, not all stores that
  sell clothing online offer a liberal return policy.

- Be wary of used products that are easily damaged: CDs, video and audio
  cassettes, electronics, etc. If you're considering buying several used
  CDs, for example, tell the seller your intentions, then buy only one to
  make sure the quality is acceptable before you buy the rest.

- Make sure all damageable shipments are insured. Large companies do this as a matter of course; smaller vendors might not.

Also, to stay on top of consumer ratings and product information, check out Consumer Reports' forum on CompuServe, AOL, or Prodigy.

21

Pictures and Movies

● **In this chapter:**

- **Are all those nasty rumors about online pictures true?**

- **What kinds of pictures and movies can I find online?**

- **Where to look for them**

- **How to see them on your computer**

What good is that expensive color monitor if you don't give it a workout once in a while?. . . . . ➤

You need a picture of Abe Lincoln for a report? How about a detailed map or a few news photos for some extra visual punch to your article? Maybe you'd like to throw some professional animation into a business presentation, or just catch a preview of the new Brad Pitt film before it comes out. With the new popularity of multimedia, pictures and movies are all over the online world (like in fig. 21.1), waiting for you to snap them up.

Fig. 21.1
The Bettman Archives on CompuServe is a great source of pictures from the historical to the hysterical.

©1994 Bettmann

Online services used to shy away from pictures (especially moving pictures) because picture files are big (sometimes a megabyte or more), and movies are infinitely bigger (often multiple megabytes). At 1,200 or 2,400 bps, they took forever and a week to download. But now that most folks have 9,600 bps, 14,400 bps, and faster modems, pictures and movies cost only a few minutes of online time. Consequently, today's online world is very, very visual, with museums, libraries, and zoos showing off their collections, Hollywood studios releasing trailer clips of upcoming movies, and lots of amateur and professional photographers and visual artists sharing their work.

Plain English, please!

A **megabyte** (**M**) is a measurement of storage capacity equal to 1 million bytes (1,048,576 bytes to be exact—but who's counting?). 99

Kinds of pictures and movies you can find (no, it's not *all* smut)

If you've heard anything about online pictures and movies, it's probably this: "Ewwwwww! It's all nasty pictures from perverts in Amsterdam." The truth is if you really want to find Dutch pornography (or indeed pornography of any kind) online, you can, but almost all of the pictures and movies online are family-friendly. The online world is often compared to a library, and that analogy works in this respect, too: most of the pictures in library books are for general viewing, but you can find adults-only material if you really want to.

Pictures and movies on online services run the spectrum of visual art (like the picture in fig. 21.2), including:

- current and historic events

- celebrities

- art (including everything from cave paintings to Da Vinci to computer-generated pictures)

- cartoons

- diagrams and technical illustrations

- TV and movie clips

Fig. 21.2
Check out online magazines for the newest pictures (this one's from *People* magazine on CompuServe).

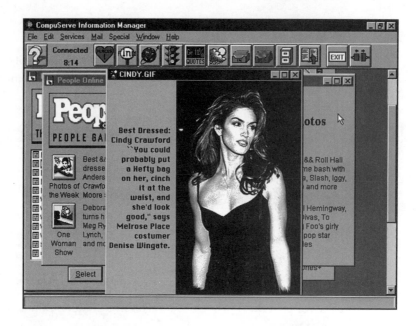

Good places to look for pictures and movies

If pictures and movies are your main interest in the online world, sign up for CompuServe. The **GO GRAPHICS** libraries on CIS are positively the mother lode of online pictures, with the Bettman Archives (historic and current events photos), EFORUM (popular entertainment), and several special interest graphics forums. CompuServe also has a graphics-only file search program (**GO GRAPHFF**—see fig. 21.3).

TIP If you use a file search program on an online service, make sure you have an idea what you're looking for. If you just look for all the GIF files or JPG files, you'll end up with several thousand listings to sort through.

AOL's graphics libraries (Go To keyword **Graphics**) are fairly respectable, and getting better all the time. The daily news and online magazines also include photos. Some of the real gems on AOL, however, are special areas like the Smithsonian Online (Go To keyword **Smithsonian**).

Fig. 21.3
GO GRAPHFF on
CompuServe to
search for graphics by
keyword. When you're
reading a description,
you can choose the
View button to
download the picture
immediately.

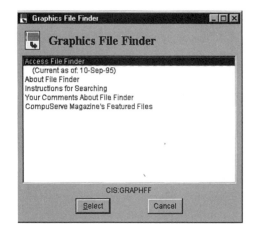

Ironically, while Prodigy is pretty much a wasteland if you want to *download* graphics, it's probably the most graphical online service of the Big Three. Many of Prodigy's graphics show up in news stories (see fig. 21.4)—look for a See Photo button or stories with an asterisk beside the title. There is also a quaint graphics section (**Jump Gallery**) with original art and photographs.

Fig. 21.4
Many of Prodigy's news
stories and features
include photographs.

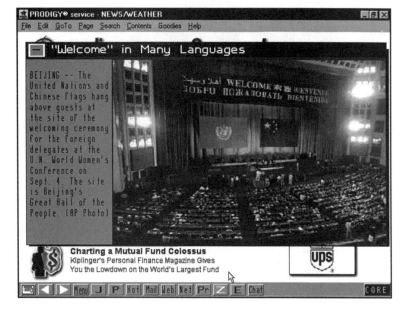

If you're more interested in motion pictures than stills, the online world has much to offer. AOL's Graphics and Animation section (Go To keyword **Animation**) has video captures and computer animation, and CompuServe's EFORUM and EMOVIES forums offer an incredible selection of movie clips. Some of the special interest and education forums (like CompuServe's Dinosaurs forum—see fig. 21.5) also have Animation or Motion libraries.

66 *Plain English, please!*

Video captures are movie clips (usually short) you can watch on your computer. They're "captured" from videotapes or TV programs with special computerized video equipment, then transformed into a form you can watch without any special equipment. 99

Fig. 21.5

The multimedia revolution has brought many classic textbook pictures (like this skeleton drawing from CompuServe's Dinosaurs forum) to life through animation.

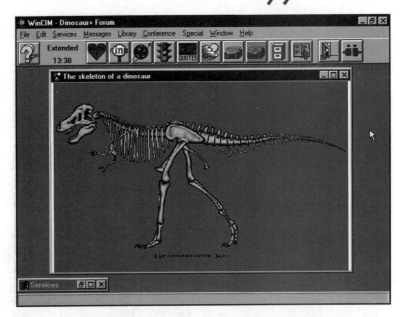

The Internet is another great source for pictures. The two main places to look are in UseNet newsgroups and on the World Wide Web. (See Chapter 12 for more UseNet details.)

In UseNet, look in groups that begin with **alt.binaries** (for instance, **alt.binaries.pictures**). These files will be encoded, so you'll need a decoder such as UUDecode to convert them to viewable format, unless you're lucky enough to have a newsgroup-reading program that will decode for you (WinVN does this, for instance). You can find these utility programs available for download on most online services and FTP sites, and some may be built into your newsgroup reader.

CAUTION If you're trying to avoid smut, stay away from the alt.binaries groups with suspicious-sounding names, like **alt.binaries.bestiality.hamster.duct-tape**. (Yes, that's a real group—unfortunately.)

On the World Wide Web, you'll see lots of graphics as you visit various sites. Depending on your browser program, you may be able to save the graphics you see onscreen to disk. (Check with the help information that came with the browser. Some browsers, like Prodigy's, don't let you do this.)

You can also find graphics available for FTP transfer. It's good if you know exactly what you're looking for, including the file name, but don't count on being able to preview a picture before you invest the time in downloading it. The larger FTP sites like **wuarchive.wustl.edu** have their graphics *almost* sorted by category, but you may find a picture of a cockatoo in the **/cars/** directory. Chapter 12 has all the info you need about using FTP.

TIP The **/graphics/** directory on most FTP sites contains software programs that make or view pictures—not the pictures themselves. The real pictures will probably be in a **/gif/**, **/pictures/**, or **/jpg/** directory.

If you can't afford to hook up with one of the bigger services, you may be able to find an inexpensive local BBS with a good graphics selection. Pictures and movies are very popular on BBSs, and many local BBSs have entire CD-ROMs of pictures and/or movies available.

How to see pictures and movies on your computer

When you've got your pictures and movies on your disk, you need a software program called a *viewer* (sometimes an *editor*) to see them. Online pictures and movies come in several different formats:

- popular picture formats include GIF (pronounced *"jif "*), JPG, BMP, PCX, WMF, WPG, and TGA

- animations are usually AVI, DL, FLC, FLI, GL, MOV, or MPG

Your viewer program has to be able to understand the format you want to view. It's like the ancient conflict between VHS and Betamax videotape formats—if you had a player that worked with one format and a movie made in the other format, you were sunk. The following table can help you find a program that can view the picture or video that you want to see.

Type of picture	Programs you can use to see it
BMP	Windows Paintbrush (Windows 3.x) or Paint (Windows 95), VidVue, PaintShop
GIF	VidVue, PaintShop, WinCIM, WinGIF, any other GIF viewer
JIF	VidVue, PaintShop, WinPEG, any other JPEG/JIF/JFIF viewer
JPG	VidVue, PaintShop, WinPEG, any other JPEG/JIF/JFIF viewer
PCX	VidVue, PaintShop, Windows Paintbrush, any other PCX viewer
TGA	VidVue, PaintShop, any other TGA (Targa) viewer
WMF	VidVue, most word processors
WPG	WordPerfect, VidVue

Type of movie	Program you need to watch it
AVI	VidVue, or any other Video for Windows player, including Media Player (Windows 3.x and Windows 95)
DL	DLVIEW
EXE	None, just run it like any other program
FLC	AAPlay, VidVue, or any other FLI/FLC player
FLI	AAPlay, VidVue, or any other FLI/FLC player
GL	GRASPRT
MOV	VidVue, or any other QuickTime player
MPG	MPEGPLAY

Thankfully, many multimedia viewers handle several different picture and movie formats. VidVue for Windows is a good shareware option, supporting every major graphics and animation format. For still pictures (not movies), PaintShop is another good shareware choice.

Q&A *Where do I get these programs that show videos and graphics?*

You can download them from almost all online services and many Internet FTP sites. See Chapter 12 for info about FTP, and see the chapters in this book that pertain to each individual online service for details on where each one keeps its files.

TIP **If you use GIF or JPG pictures (the vast majority of still pictures fall into these two categories) and WinCIM or America Online, you don't need a separate viewer. Just choose File, Open (AOL) or File, View (WinCIM) and you'll be able to look at any GIF or JPG pictures on your disk.**

Q&A *Is one graphics format better than another?*

It's hard to say, because there aren't all that many differences between the formats. Some tend to be a little smaller (JPG files, for example, are usually smaller than other graphics files), which makes them quicker to download, but you won't see a lot of difference between them once you get them on your disk. Some people in the online community rabidly support various favorite formats over the others, but in the end, all that matters is that you can see the picture.

Pictures' descriptions will not only tell you what format they're in, but usually what resolution as well. Along with the width and height of the picture in pixels, the resolution often includes the number of colors or gray levels that are used in the picture. For example, you might see a picture labeled $300 \times 470 \times 256$. This means it's 300 pixels wide, 470 pixels high, and has 256 colors. Sometimes you'll see a "c" or "g" after the last number, telling you the picture is color or **grayscaled** (a fancy word for different shades of black-and-white).

 Plain English, please!

Computerized pictures are usually just rows and rows of colored or gray dots, called **pixels**. The dots are so small, you can't see them (just like you don't see the individual threads in cloth) unless you look very closely. **Resolution** is the number of dots in each row and the number of rows, so "640 by 480 resolution" means the picture has 640 dots in each row and 480 rows.

Another thing you'll probably notice when you start looking for graphics online is that a healthy majority of them are made on Macintosh computers. Don't panic if you have a PC with Windows—you'll still be able to see the Mac-born pictures. Graphics and movies are sometimes described as cross-platform, because in most cases you can use them on a PC with Windows, a Macintosh, or just about anything else. With the right kind of software on your computer, you can look at pictures and movies made on any number of different types of computers.

Plain English, please!

Cross-platform means software that works on multiple kinds of computers: PC-compatibles, Macintoshes, and others. Most software is **single platform**, meaning it only works on one kind of computer.

 I tried to look at a picture, and it's all a muddy mess of (black, red, yellow, whatever). What's going on?

Not only does the picture use a certain number of colors, but your computer's monitor does as well. The monitor *must* use at least as many colors as the picture. If the picture uses more colors than your monitor is willing to use, it may look wrong. For example, if you get a picture that uses 16 million colors (yes, they're out there) and your monitor is only using 256 colors, the picture may look like a big, muddy mess unless the software you're using can compensate for it. It's like trying to put a large bouquet of flowers in a baby food jar—you can try it, but if it works at all, it'll look pretty screwy. With many monitors (especially newer ones), you can increase the number of colors it uses by installing different software or a more powerful video card. Check with your dealer or the documentation that came with your computer to find out what options you have.

Part IV: Troubleshooting: Should the Modem be Smoking?

Chapter 22: **Spotting and Fixing
Common Problems**

22

Spotting and Fixing Common Problems

● **In this chapter:**

● I can't connect! Help!

● Testing for problems

● I see a bunch of garbage on my screen!

● My communications session doesn't work right

● I keep losing my connection. What I can do to finish transferring this darn file?

If you're lucky, you'll plug your modem in and it'll work. If you're not, reach for the Alka Seltzer. Then, use this chapter to work through the most common problems . . . . ●▶

Computers can be pretty frustrating sometimes. In fact, I know one guy who got so annoyed at his computer one night that he threw it out of a second story balcony onto his driveway. That'll teach it!

Murphy's Law is alive and well in the world of modems. As the old saying goes, "If something can go wrong, it will," and communications problems can be among the most difficult to detect and correct.

Still, you can put on your "Computer Doctor" stethoscope and work through most problems with a little trial and error, and perhaps the help of your computer dealer or the maker of your modem and communications software (or even a knowledgeable ten-year old!). In this chapter, you'll learn about the most common problems you might see and get some suggestions for correcting them.

Is it a hardware problem or a software problem?

Many problems may appear to be hardware-related, but are in reality software problems. And many problems that you might think are software-related are really due to hardware. There's no clear-cut way to tell the difference, except in a few cases. Mostly, you just need to work through the problem, looking at both hardware and software as possible sources of the difficulty.

Troubleshooting problems

There are many different symptoms that can indicate communications problems. Use table 22.1 to find the symptom you're experiencing, and the possible solutions. Each solution is discussed afterward, in alphabetical order.

Table 22.1 Common communications problem symptoms

Symptom	Possible causes
Message says Can't initialize Modem	COM port conflict Wrong modem cable External modem not plugged in to power source Internal modem not seated completely Modem needs to be configured or reconfigured
No dial tone when trying to connect	COM port conflict Wrong modem cable Telephone line not connected correctly
Modem won't dial	COM port conflict Wrong modem cable Telephone line not connected correctly
Garbled data	COM port conflict Static on phone line Wrong terminal type Incorrect communications parameters Change port settings
Dials, but won't connect	Static on phone line Problem on remote system Change port settings
Speaker too loud or quiet	Speaker volume needs adjustment
Connects fine, but keeps losing the connection after some time	Static on phone line Problem on remote system
Modem won't connect	Timeout too short
I type, but nothing appears	Echo setting wrong
Everything I type appears twice	Echo setting wrong
The modem works too slowly	Unable to negotiate speed
My file downloads keep dying	Use recovery protocol Change timeout
I can't cancel a download!	Common communications keys
The information is scrolling faster than I can read it!	Common communications keys

COM port conflict

The most common modem problems arise from an incorrect COM port setting. Here are the four sources for this problem, and what to do to correct them:

- **The modem itself is using an incorrect COM port.** Review Chapter 2, "Installing Your Modem," and change the COM port assignment on the modem itself, or plug it into a different serial port connector on the back of your computer if it's an external modem.

- **Something else in the computer is interfering with the COM port that the modem is using.** Review Chapter 2, "Installing Your Modem," for the rules on COM port assignments in your computer and interrupt conflicts. Either move the modem to a different COM port, or move the interfering device to a different COM port (it's probably a mouse or printer).

- **The software is trying to use the wrong COM port.** Make sure that your software is set to use the same COM port as the modem. Both the modem and the software you use have to be set to the same COM port.

- **Missing COM port**. It's possible to have two COM ports built into a computer, and then to set an internal modem to use COM4. Or, to have one COM port in the system and the modem's set to COM3 or COM4. The problem is that your computer can't have any "missing" COM ports. If you have a device set to COM3, there has to be a COM1 and COM2. If you have a device set to COM4, there has to be a COM1, COM2, and COM3. And so forth. Resolve the setting of your internal modem so that there are no "empty" COM ports.

Common communications keys

There are a number of keystrokes that almost all remote systems can respond to, at least in certain circumstances. These keystrokes let you cancel whatever is happening, or pause and resume a lengthy display of data. Table 22.2 lists these common keys and tells you what they do.

Table 22.2 Common communications keys

Keystroke	What it does
Ctrl+A	Resume (after pausing)
Ctrl+C	Cancel operation
Ctrl+S	Pause
Ctrl+X	Cancel download

Echo setting wrong

Both your modem and the software you use can **echo**, or repeat, the characters you type. When you type into your communications program, what you see displayed is actually either the software or the modem repeating your characters back so you can see them.

An incorrect echo setting in your software can be a common source of trouble if the software and modem are both echoing characters. In this case, you'll see two letters for every one you type. Type **Hello** and you'll see HHeelllloo. To solve this, find the echo setting in your software program and turn it off.

The opposite problem often happens, too, where you type but nothing appears on your screen. Fixing this is as easy as turning on the echo feature in your software.

Internal modem not seated properly

If you've just installed a new internal modem, and it's not functioning, one possibility is that it's not completely seated into the circuit board slot. You should try turning the power off to the unit, disconnecting the power cord, removing the cover, and firmly pressing down on the modem board. If the modem board is installed correctly, the metal tab into which you insert the screw will be flush with the computer case without needing any pressure from the screw itself.

Modem needs to be configured or reconfigured

Windows 95 now manages modems more closely than previous versions of Windows did. Under Windows 3.1, for instance, it was up to you to tell your communications software what kind of modem you had, and it had to contain all the possible settings for different modems. With Windows 95, you only have to set up your modem with Windows 95 itself, and then your Windows 95-based communications programs automatically use those settings.

When you install a new modem, you need to configure Windows 95 to work with it. You do this with the Add New Hardware icon in the Control Panel. When it starts, you see the Add New Hardware Wizard start, as shown in figure 22.1.

Fig. 22.1
Use the Add New Hardware Wizard to set up a new modem.

Go ahead and start the wizard by clicking the Next button. You then see the screen shown in figure 22.2.

If Windows 95 can't correctly determine what kind of modem you have, you may have to choose it manually. To do this, choose No on the screen shown in figure 22.2 and then click the Next button. You now tell Windows 95 what kind of device you need to configure, shown in figure 22.3.

Fig. 22.2

Choose whether to define new hardware yourself (choose No) or let Windows 95 search your computer for new hardware automatically (choose Yes).

Fig. 22.3

After choosing No in the previous wizard screen, you have to tell Windows 95 what kind of device you're setting up. Select Modem and click the Next button.

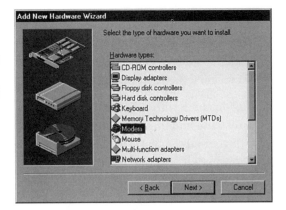

Next, the Add New Hardware Wizard wants to know if you want Windows 95 to try and identify your modem automatically. Typically, this works well and you can simply click the Next button to proceed. Sometimes, however, you have to manually select your modem from a list. To do this, make sure that the Don't Detect My Modem; I Will Select from a List checkbox is selected before clicking the Next button. With that checkbox selected, you then see the screen shown in figure 22.4.

Fig. 22.4
Here you see a list of modem manufacturers and their modem models.

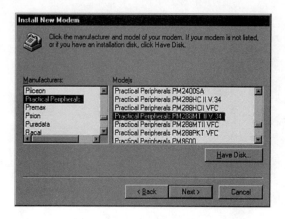

In the screen shown in figure 22.4, there are many possible things you can do:

- Choose your modem manufacturer on the left list, and then the specific type of modem you have in the right list. In figure 22.4, I've chosen my modem. Then click the Next button to proceed.

- If your modem came with a diskette that contains a Windows 95 driver, insert the diskette and then click the Save Disk button. This causes Windows 95 to read the diskette, find out about your modem from the diskette information, and then set the modem up correctly for use on your computer.

- If your modem isn't on the list, and you don't have a diskette that came with your modem that's expressly for Windows 95, then you can still use one of the standard settings. Figure 22.5 shows you these selections. Scroll the left-hand list to the top, to the entry marked Standard Modems, and select that entry. Then, select the appropriate modem speed in the list to the right. Click the Next button to proceed.

After choosing the correct modem from the list, you need to tell Windows 95 what COM port you've connected the modem to (for external modems), or that you've set it to use (for internal modems). Figure 22.6 shows you this screen.

Fig. 22.5
Sometimes you have to use the Standard Modem settings. Choose the speed that best matches your modem on the list to the right.

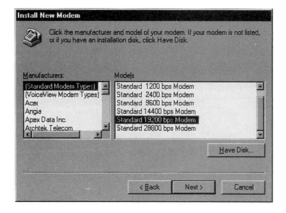

Fig. 22.6
Select the port (one of the COM ports) that corresponds to the port that you've installed the modem to use, and then click the Next button.

Finally, Windows 95 sets up your modem. Assuming that your modem is working properly and isn't broken, you're rewarded with the screen shown in figure 22.7.

Fig. 22.7
Success! Your new modem is now set up to work with Windows 95.

If installing your modem for Windows 95 doesn't solve the problem, you might have a problem in how Windows 95 is set to use your existing modem. These problems are solved by using the Modem icon in the Control Panel. When you open the Modem icon, you see the screen shown in figure 22.8.

Fig. 22.8
Use the Modem Control Panel in Windows 95 to change the settings for your modem.

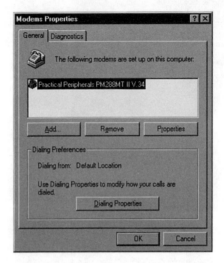

The first tab of the Modem Control Panel lists all the modems that are installed in your computer. There are lots of settings available through this Control Panel. The following sections discuss each page of choices.

Modem Diagnostics

The second page of the Modem Control Panel is called Diagnostics. Clicking the tab reveals the page shown in figure 22.9.

The window lists the serial ports on your system and any modems connected to them. You should see your modem on the list. There are three buttons below the list of ports, which do the following:

- **Driver** shows you the version number of the communications driver software that Windows 95 is using. Technical support may ask you for this information to determine which version of the driver is in use.

Fig. 22.9
The Diagnostics page of the Modem Control Panel lets you carry out tests on your modem

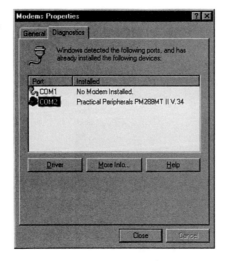

- **More info** communicates with your modem and displays some technical status information about it, shown in figure 22.10. If you're talking to a technical support person, they may need some information from this display.

- **Help** starts the Windows 95 Modem Troubleshooter, shown in figure 22.11. This is a special help file that assists you in tracking down and solving some modem problems.

Fig. 22.10
The More Info page displays a wealth of information about your modem. Note that seeing the word Error listed in the display does not mean your modem is broken, just that it doesn't support a particular mode.

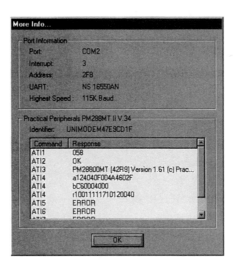

Fig. 22.11
The Windows 95
Modem Trouble-
shooter can help you
diagnose and solve
simple modem
problems. Follow the
screen prompts to work
through your problem.

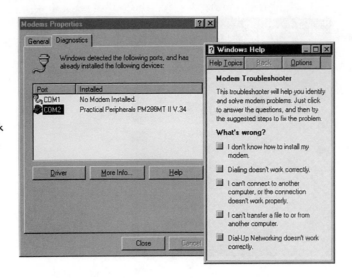

Modem Properties

From the main screen of the Modem Control Panel (refer to fig. 22.8) you can
access the properties for your modem with the Properties button. Clicking
this button displays a new notebook, shown in figure 22.12.

Fig. 22.12
The Properties pages of
the Modem Control
Panel let you control
how your modem is
configured.

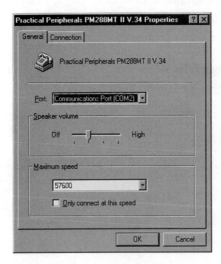

On the first page you can control what port Windows 95 expects to find your
modem set to, the speaker volume that Windows 95 will set your modem to
use (when using Windows 95-specific software) and the default speed for
your modem. In most cases, you do NOT want to select the checkbox marked

Only Connect at This Speed, because you want your modem to be able to connect at whatever speed it can manage with a remote system.

The second properties page, Connection, is shown in figure 22.13 and contains a wealth of settings about your modem. All of these settings are detailed in table 22.3.

Fig. 22.13
Use the Connection page to access many of your modem's detailed settings.

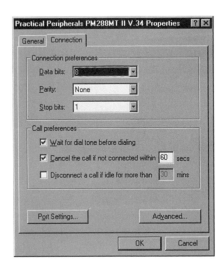

Table 22.3   Connection Page

Setting	What it means
Data bits	The number of data bits to use when communicating. Generally, this should always be set to 8.
Parity	The parity setting. Parity is used to ensure accuracy in transmissions. Set this to None.
Stop bits	The number of stop bits has to match on both sides of a connection (as with the previous two settings). Set this to 1.
Wait for dial tone before dialing	When selected, Windows 95 will ensure that your modem senses a dial tone before it starts to dial the number. Selecting this helps make sure that you don't accidentally dial with your modem when someone else is using the same phone line.
Cancel the call if not connected within xx secs	This setting lets you set a maximum amount of time that Windows 95 will wait for a connection until it cancels the call. 60 seconds is fine for most uses, although you might need to increase the setting if a particular call takes a long time to complete.
Disconnect a call if idle for more than xx mins	Here is where you set the timeout value that causes Windows 95 to hang up a call if you don't type anything for the number of minutes indicated. For most uses, set this in the ten to twenty minute range to ensure that you don't accidentally run up too many charges with your online service.

Change port settings

Windows 95 tries to buffer data being transmitted as much as possible. This is a software mechanism that improves the performance you see when using communications software. However, some computers or modems may not be able to handle the maximum amount of buffering that Windows 95 can offer. If you're having problems with lost characters, garbled displays, or slow downloads, changing these settings may help.

To access the port settings, click the Port Settings button found on the Connection Page. This brings up the Port Settings dialog box shown in figure 22.14.

Fig. 22.14
If you're having trouble with uncompleted connections, lost characters or garbage on the screen, try reducing the buffer settings on this page.

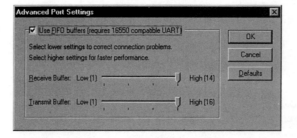

Problem on remote system

There's not much you can do to fix these problems, but you can test to find out if this is the source of your difficulty, and then inform the remote system operator that there appears to be a problem in their system.

To find out whether it's the remote system or your system that's having trouble, simply try to connect to a different system that you know works. You can use a local BBS, for instance, to try this. If you can connect OK to another service or BBS, then there's probably a problem with the original service you've been having trouble with. Give them a call on their voice number and tell them! If you can't connect to any number you try, then the problem's on your end of things, or possibly in your phone lines (see the following section, "Static on phone line," for help with line problems).

Static on phone line

This problem often results in symptoms such as lost connections, garbled data, or even the inability to connect. Sources for this problem, and what you should do about them, include:

- **A bad telephone line leading from your modem into the wall.** Try connecting a telephone to that cable and listen to the quality of the dial tone. If it's clear, then the cable's not the problem. If the dial tone sounds like it has static, try replacing the cable with another one from elsewhere in your home or office.

- **A bad wall connection.** Get another telephone line and telephone from elsewhere in the house or office and connect it to the wall jack. Does the dial tone still have static? Then it's possibly the wall connector, or even the phone wiring in the house. Unless you're used to working with wiring, call your phone company to get the problem cleared up.

CAUTION **Onsite service calls from your phone company are probably very expensive.** Be sure to exhaust all other possibilities before asking them for help.

- **A problem in the phone system.** With a normal telephone, you can dial the modem number you're trying to connect to and listen for static. If you hear static only when the remote phone number starts ringing, it's a problem in the phone system. Call either your local phone company or, if you're calling a long distance number, your long distance carrier for help.

 TIP **The sound you hear from a normal modem connection sounds a lot like static.** When your modem is working well, listen and become accustomed to how a modem link-up sounds. Then, if you get additional static on the line, you'll be able to hear the difference.

- **A problem on the remote end.** If static suddenly becomes apparent when the remote system answers (normally, you hear the squealing of their modem, but you can also hear static on top of it) call the operator of the remote system. They could be having one of these problems themselves!

Speaker volume needs adjustment

While this problem won't keep you from using your modem, it can be annoying. Depending on the modem you own, there are two possible ways to adjust its speaker volume: through hardware and through software.

Some modems have volume control knobs on them. If this is the case with your modem, then it's can be as easy as turning some knobs, adjusting the modem's speaker volume. Many modems, however, do not have volume control knobs. Instead, you have to adjust the modem's programming to choose the volume level you want.

You can send commands to the modem using your terminal communications software, such as HyperTerminal, PROCOMM PLUS for Windows, Crosstalk, QModem, or even the Windows 3.1 Terminal program. To do this, follow these steps:

1 Start your communications software and enter its terminal mode.

2 Make sure the modem can reply to your commands. To check this, type **ATZ** and press Enter. You should see an onscreen reply from your modem that says OK. In some cases, the number 0 may appear instead, which is also a normal response. If you don't see either of these things, find the setting in your software that controls the Local Echo; if this setting is turned OFF, turn it ON. Also, make sure your communications software is set to use the right COM port and modem speed and matches those settings for your modem.

3 Now you can send a command to the modem that changes its volume level. There are three levels you can choose, from low to high. Type the command **ATL1** to select low volume. **ATL2** chooses medium volume, while **ATL3** chooses high volume. After entering the command you want, press Enter. You should see an OK response from the modem.

TIP   **If you don't want to hear the modem sound at all, you can use the** modem command **ATM0** to turn OFF the speaker. You usually type this into your communications software in a field marked Modem Initialization String or something similar. You can usually recognize this because this setting will contain a lot of weird letters and numbers, but always starting with the letters **AT**.

Plain English, please!

All modem configuration commands are preceded with the letters **AT**, which stands for Attention. As in, "Pay attention, Modem, here's a command!"

4 Store the new setting into the modem's permanent configuration by typing **AT&W** and pressing Enter. The modem should respond OK.

5 Reset the modem. Type the command **ATZ** and press Enter. Again, you should see the OK response.

Q&A *I'm typing the commands you're telling me, but I keep getting an error message from the modem.*

Different modems use different commands, although the commands just seen are commonly used for most modems. Check the manual that came with your modem to see if it lists volume-level control commands, and what the exact settings are for your modem.

Telephone line not connected correctly

It's important that the telephone wire coming out of the wall be plugged into the jack on your modem labeled "Line" and not the one labeled "Phone." If it's not connected to the right one, you'll have all sorts of bizarre problems; you won't be able to connect, or if you do, things won't work properly at all. Check the manual for your modem to find out which of the two jacks should be used for the line leading to the wall (LINE), or to a telephone set connected to the modem (PHONE).

Timeout too short

When your modem connects to a remote modem, they both keep trying different speeds and settings until they find the best one that they can both handle. This is why you can connect to a 9,600 bps modem on the remote end, even when you're using a 14,400 bps modem; they negotiate a 9,600 bps speed and both end up running at that rate.

Your communications program has a timer that controls how long it will wait for a connection to be established before giving up and disconnecting. If the amount of time the modems spend negotiating a speed exceeds this timer, your software will hang up on the remote system, even when everything's really working just fine. To solve this problem, increase the timeout setting in your software.

TIP **Some services will automatically disconnect you if you don't type** anything for a period of time, and some software programs also include this feature. It's intended to keep you from running up too high of a bill if you get distracted by some emergency and have to leave your computer. If you have this feature available, be sure to enable it with a reasonable time limit, such as ten minutes.

Unable to negotiate speed

As mentioned in the last section, your modem and the remote modem negotiate the fastest speed they can both achieve. The highest speed they negotiate is heavily dependent on the quality of the telephone line. If it has static, the modems will end up running more slowly than they're capable of. To solve this, see "Static on phone line," earlier in this chapter.

Another possibility is just that the remote system is bogged down for some reason. You can wait and try to use it again at a different time to see if things speed up. Other than that, there's not much you can do about a slowdown on the part of the service, except write a letter of complaint to the customer service department.

Use recovery protocol

If you're trying to download a large file, and keep getting disconnected before you can finish the download (intermittent static can cause this, as can someone in your house picking up another telephone on the same line!), you might not be able to fix the underlying problem, but you can save time and aggravation by transferring the file with a file transfer protocol that supports recovery.

A **recoverable file transfer protocol** has the capability to resume interrupted downloads or uploads from wherever it was when the connection was lost. This way, you don't have to start all over again if you lose your connection after transferring most of the file.

The best recoverable file transfer protocol is Zmodem. It also happens to be the most efficient in most circumstances. You should always choose the

Zmodem protocol if it's available in both your communications software and on the remote system.

Keep in mind, however, that some communications programs don't include the recovery feature of Zmodem. Generally, this is true with shareware programs; they leave this feature out unless you register the software. Commercial programs, such as PROCOMM PLUS for Windows, almost always include this important feature.

TIP If you're using CompuServe, the CompuServe B+ protocol is also recoverable.

If you're using a recovery protocol such as Zmodem or CompuServe B+ protocol, and your download is canceled, when you go to redownload the file you'll be asked if you want to overwrite the file on the disk or continue downloading (see fig. 22.15).

Fig. 22.15
If you're offered the choice to resume a lost download, take it to pick up the download from where you left off.

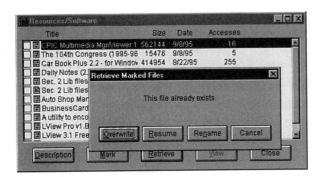

In order to minimize the amount of time you stay online with your service provider, you should always choose to resume an aborted download if you're offered the choice. With a recovery protocol, you should always be offered this choice, and you should take it.

Wrong modem cable

If you just hooked up a new external modem and you can't get it to work, maybe you have the wrong cable. Not all cables that can plug into both your modem and your computer are wired correctly for that use. You need to use a cable designated for a PC-to-modem connection, and not one that has a label on the package that says something like "Null-Modem" or "Modem eliminator." Also, some cables are made as inexpensively as possible, and you might have one that's broken; try to borrow a friend's cable or one from a computer and modem that you know works to test out this possibility.

Wrong terminal type

When you connect to a remote system such as a BBS, the remote system may interpret keystrokes and display characters differently than your computer does. To solve this problem, all communications programs support different terminal types for use with different remote systems. If you're using the wrong terminal type for communicating with the remote system, you'll experience one or more of the following symptoms:

- Garbage (meaningless characters) will display on your screen

- Your Enter key won't work right

- The Backspace key won't work right

- Arrow keys won't work right

Solving this problem is easy, but you do have to know what terminal type the remote system uses. You should have learned it when you got the phone number for the system, or there may even be an option on the remote system that lets you choose what terminal type it will use. Simply set your software to use the same terminal type and all will be well.

 TIP   **The most common terminal type for BBSs is ANSI, also called** ANSI-BBS. If that doesn't work right, you can also try VT100 and VT220, two other popular terminal types.

Part V: Appendix

What's on the CD?

What's on the CD?

● **In this appendix:**

- **How do I install these programs?**

- **Reference Materials (stuff that wouldn't fit in the book)**

- **Commercial services: AOL & Prodigy**

- **For the rest of the world: Internet startup kits**

- **If you're BBS inclined...**

- **Handy tools and utilities for working online**

- **Extra toys we've provided out of the kindness of our hearts**

Done your homework and read up on all the places you want to explore online, but don't have the means to get there? Use this book's CD to merge onto the Information Superhighway . . . . >

This CD-ROM contains a variety of software that you can use with your modem, including software for both commercial online services and Internet service providers, communications programs, utilities, and some extra programs you'll enjoy.

Accessing the software

Windows 95 automatically runs the installer on the CD-ROM when you insert it into your CD drive. The installer creates a program group called *Using Your Modem CD* on your Start-Up Menu (see fig. D.1); the group contains icons that you'll use to install the software on the CD-ROM. To install any of the programs, click the appropriate Install icon in the *Using Your Modem CD* program group and continue through the installation process as directed for each program.

Fig. D.1
Here's what you'll see when the install program kicks in.

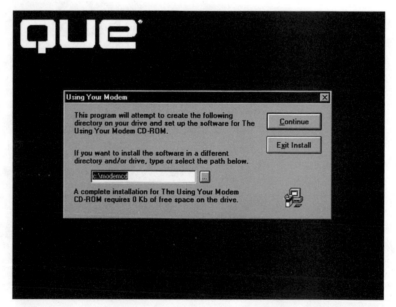

 TIP **To run the install program manually, double-click the CD-ROM** drive icon in Explorer and double-click the Install icon in the file list.

Most of the programs on this CD-ROM also work under Windows 3.1. To create the *Using Your Modem CD* program group in Windows 3.1, choose File, Run in the Program Manager. Type **d:\install.exe** (assuming d is the letter of your CD drive) and click OK. In the *Using Your Modem CD* program group, double-click the Install icon for the program you want to install and continue through the installation process as directed for each program.

After you've installed a program, simply choose the program from the Start-Up Menu in Windows 95 or from its program group in Windows 3.1.

Reference materials (stuff that wouldn't fit in the book)

We've packed a lot of great information in the book, but we had so much more that we had to put some of it on the CD. There are three reference appendixes you can open up and read right from the disc (they look just the chapters in the book), or you can print them out and keep them at hand for quick reference:

- **Places.pdf** includes dozens of interesting places to visit and write to online: Web sites and e-mail addresses, all arranged by topic. If you see a site you want to visit, you can just highlight the address, copy it, and paste it into your Web browser. Cool, eh?

- **Smileys.pdf**. If you're flabbergasted by all those funny looking symbols people use online, here's a listing of many of the common—and some of the bizarre—**emoticons** you're likely to run across.

- **Glossary.pdf**. This just might be the most valuable part of this entire book: we've included plain English definitions and descriptions of more than 300 words, symbols, abbreviations, and acronyms related to the online world, from "access number" to "ZIP file." If you need to know what it means, you'll find it here.

In addition, you'll find the file ISDN.pdf. This bonus book chapter gives you the full scoop on the up-and-coming technology, ISDN, which promises to revolutionize online communications within the next decade. If you need that information, or if you're just curious what ISDN is all about, be sure to read this chapter.

To use these files, you'll first need to install the Adobe Acrobat Reader, discussed later in this appendix. When you have the Reader running, choose File, Open and select the file name you want to view. For example, to look up something in the glossary, you'd use **d:\appndx\glossary.pdf** (if your CD-ROM drive uses a letter other than d, substitute whatever is appropriate).

The big guns: commercial online services

America Online and Prodigy are two of the large commercial online services that give subscribers access to news, business information, entertainment and a lot more.

America Online

After you install and start the America Online software, your modem will dial into a toll-free number where you'll choose the primary and secondary local access numbers. Next, your modem will dial the primary local access number and you'll open your account. Have the certificate number and certificate password from the last page of this book handy, along with a credit card or the number of your checking account. You'll need all these things to open an account. To contact America Online, call (800) 827-6364.

Prodigy

To open a new account with Prodigy, install the software, then start it up. Your modem will connect to Prodigy's Local Access Number directory by using a toll-free number. Choose the primary and secondary local access numbers that you'll use to connect to Prodigy. Next, allow the software to call the local access number so you can open your account. You'll need a major credit card to complete the process and you'll get ten free hours. To contact Prodigy, call (800) PRODIGY (776-3449).

Infobahn made easy: Internet software

The majority of the Internet software on this CD-ROM is provided by specific Internet Access Providers (translation: if you use the provider's software, you'll be buying an account through that company). Except for NetShark, each of them allows access to a number of Internet features, including the World Wide Web, e-mail, newsgroups and more. You can find more information about each of the products or the companies by checking out their World Wide Web pages at the addresses given.

Automatic Internet Chameleon Websampler

This software supports FTP transfer, Telnet, e-mail, World Wide Web access, and more. You must register the software before you can use it, either through the NetManage server or one of the supported access providers. After you install the software and start it, select the tab for the service provider you want and click Signup. Enter the requested information in the dialog box and press Send.

Provided by:

> NetManage
> 10725 N. DeAnza Blvd.
> Cupertino, CA 95014
> (408) 973-7171.
>
> WWW: **http://www.netmanage.com**

 TIP **This is one of the suites that does let you use your own existing** Internet account. If you're unsure of the settings you need to enter for your current account, check with your service provider.

You will need a credit card to register the software or sign up for a demonstration account.

NetCruiser

NetCruiser is the client-server interface for NetCom, a large Internet service provider. You can access the World Wide Web, Gopher, FTP, e-mail, and more all from the one client. After you install and start NetCruiser, you'll need to open an account with them. The software is set up to dial an 800 number so you can register. Have your credit card ready!

Provided by:

> NetCom
> (800) 983-5970
>
> WWW: **http://www.netcom.com/faq/**

NetShark

NetShark isn't an all-in-one provider package, but it is an interesting Web browser/e-mail combination that you can use if you already have TCP/IP software set up. Information on Web pages displays quickly and inline viewing of JPEG, GIF, QuickTime and other similar files is supported. The e-mail part of the program lets you select a font as well as assign a size and style to the text. The lite version is free; you can upgrade to the retail version for $39.95. You can register either version of the program online through InterCon's Web site. InterCon provides free customer support for both the lite version and the retail version by telephone or e-mail.

Provided by:

> InterCon Systems Corporation
> 950 Herndon Parkway
> Herndon, VA 22070
> (703) 709-5500
>
> WWW: **http://netshark.inter.net**

Pipeline USA

The Pipeline gives you access to e-mail, the World Wide Web, Internet Relay Chat, newsgroups, and more. It provides unlimited Internet access for residential users for a flat fee. You will need a credit card to open an account with Pipeline.

Provided by:

> PSINet
> 510 Herndon Park Drive
> Herndon VA, 22070
> (703) 904-4100
>
> WWW: **http://www.usa.pipeline.com**

WinNet

WinNet Communications provides nationwide toll-free access to the Internet, as well as toll-free technical support 9 a.m. to 9 p.m., Monday through Friday. Their software supports offline e-mail and news reading, so you don't have to be connected during these tasks. Have a credit card ready when setting up your account.

Provided by:

WinNet Communications
330F Distillery Commons
Louisville, KY 40206
(502) 589-6800

WWW: **http://www.win.net**

Use these to check out BBSs

These communications clients can be used like the Windows HyperTerminal
or Terminal. They're both good for connecting with local Bulletin Board
Systems.

Qmodem Pro for Windows (lite version for Windows 3.1)

Qmodem Pro allows group dialing so you can dial several numbers continuously until you are connected. You can drag and drop files from the File
Manager to the File Transfer area, and assign WAV files to Qmodem events.
The software also contains a fax printer driver that allows you to send faxes
from within Windows applications. This program is for Windows 3.1, but
works just fine under Windows 95 as well.

Provided by:

Mustang Software
6200 Lake Ming Road
Bakersfield, CA 93306
telephone: (805) 873-2500
BBS: (805) 873-2400

WWW: **http://www.mustang.com**

WinComm Lite

You can use WinComm Lite to connect to commercial online services such as
CompuServe, as well as to BBSs. It supports Xmodem, Ymodem, Zmodem,
and CompuServe B+ protocols. Visit Delrina's Web site on the Internet (if you
have access to the World Wide Web) for a special upgrade offer to either
WinComm PRO or the Communications Suite, which contains WinFax PRO
and WinComm PRO.

Provided by:

Delrina
(416) 441-3676

WWW: **http://www.delrina.com**

These utilities will come in handy, too

Once you've spent some time online, downloaded a million files, and racked up some big phone bills, you'll appreciate having these nifty programs.

Adobe Acrobat Reader 2.1 for Windows

If you're downloading anything that says it's in "pdf" or "Acrobat" format, you'll need this program to view it. Acrobat takes files from sophisticated programs like PageMaker and converts them into something you can view, print, or copy from even if you don't *have* that sophisticated program. Here's a good example: during tax season, you can download almost all of the various IRS income tax forms in Adobe format. Just open 'em, print 'em out, and fill 'em in. It saves you all those extra trips to the public library each time you discover you need yet *another* form you don't have.

 TIP **Use the Acrobat Reader to view the appendixes and bonus** chapter included on the *Using Your Modem CD* (see "Reference materials" earlier in this appendix).

Provided by:

Adobe Systems, Inc.
1585 Charleston Road
PO Box 7900
Mountain View, CA 94039-7900

WWW: **http://www.adobe.com**JASC Media Center

The Media Center keeps your various multimedia files organized and can play or view the files too. It supports 37 file formats including GIF, JPEG, MIDI, WAV, and AVI.

Provided by:

JASC Inc.
P.O. Box 4497
Eden Prairie, MN 55344
(612) 930-9171

Log Tick for Windows

If you worry about the charges you're running up while you're online, Log Tick is the utility for you. Start it when you connect, and the display will show you how long you've been on line. You can also calculate your charges. This is shareware and requires a $25 registration fee to the author after a 30-day trial period. See the REGISTER.WRI file for more information.

Provided by:

Ton Martens

tmartens@xs4all.nl

VuePrint (16bit)

This graphics editor and utility can be upgraded to the 32 bit version once you have the 16 bit version installed. A good place to find the 32 bit version is at **http://cswapps.texas.net**.

Provided by:

Ed Hamrick

71470.3236@compuserve.com

WinZip 5.6 and WinZip 95

Most files you'll find online will come to you compressed, and the vast majority of them can be puffed back up using WinZip. Both versions support drag-and-drop zipping and unzipping. Use the WinZip 5.6 version for Windows 3.1 and WinZip 95 for Windows 95. This is shareware and well worth the $29 registration fee.

Provided by:

Niko Mak Computing, Inc.
115 James P. Casey Rd.
Bristol, CT 06010

Extras: just because

With a few exceptions, these programs have little to do with being or getting online, but they're excellent examples of the types of things you can *find* online (that's where I found them). The following software is either shareware or freeware. Please make sure to register the software if you plan to use it.

Checkers

This checkers game is used through your modem—call your friend and play a game over the telephone line! Be sure to give your friend the software as well!

Registration information: Checkers is freeware, so there is no registration fee. However, if you enjoy the software, please let the author know it.

Provided by:

Brooke Hedrick

brookeh6@aol.com

Doom

Doom is the immensely popular 3D adventure game. This demonstration version will give you an idea why. Not only is this a playable first level of the game, but you can play with or against other people by using your modem or network. This is a DOS game, so be sure to run it from DOS if you're using Windows 3.1. In Windows 95, you can run it in a DOS Window. The latest version of the shareware can be downloaded from **http:\\www.idsoftware.com** on the World Wide Web. You must buy the full version of the game to play higher levels.

Provided by:

Id Software

(800) IDGAMES (434-2637)

First International Backgammon Server Software (FIBS)

This software lets you connect to the First International Backgammon Server by using terminal emulation (a straight dial-up) to connect to the Internet or going through your TCP/IP. You can then play backgammon with other people connected to the server. Try it before you buy it; then the registration fee is $40.00.

Provided by:

Robin Davies

rdavies@fox.nstn.ns.ca

Home Accountant for Windows

The Home Accountant provides no services online, but it's a nice program for managing your home finances. You can keep separate accounts (checking, savings, etc.), set up a budget, and many more specialized tasks. If you like it, register the software through CompuServe's Shareware Registration Service for $15.00.

Provided by:

Brad Winslow

Touch Type Tutor for Windows

Do people refuse to chat with you because they can't understand a word you're typing, or because it takes f-o-r-e-v-e-r for you to type your parts of the conversation? If your typing skills leave something to be desired, why not brush up before going online? This easy-to-use program tells you how many words per minute you type, as well as your errors. There's also a game to play to increase your familiarity with the keyboard. The registration fee is $20.00.

Provided by:

David Gray

73607.2105@compuserve.com

When you're done installing

After you've installed all the software you want from the CD, you can remove the Using Your Modem CD program group from Windows. To remove the group from Windows 95, open the **c:\windows\start** menu directory in Explorer and delete the Using Your Modem CD file folder.

To remove the program group in Windows 3.1, click once on each of the icons to select it and press the delete key. After you've deleted all of the icons, click the title bar of the Using Your Modem CD group window and press delete.

Index

Que's *USING* Series

For the fastest access to the one best way to get things done, check out other *Using* books from Que! These user-friendly references give you just what you need to know to be productive—plus no-nonsense tips and shortcuts in plain English. Whatever the topic, there's a *Using* book to ensure computer confidence!

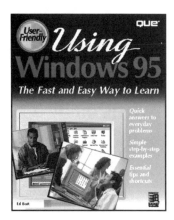

User Identification Level

New   Casual   Accomplished   Expert

Que's *SPECIAL EDITION USING* Series

For accomplished users who desire in-depth coverage, *Special Edition Using* books are the most comprehensive references. These books contain professional tips and advice—as well as valuable tools and software—to optimize results with all major hardware and software topics.

User Identification Level

New   Casual   Accomplished   Expert

*Look for **Using** books and **Special Edition Using** books at your favorite bookstore!*

 QUe®

Go Online With America's Most Popular Online Service...FREE!

Explore the benefits of being online for 10 hours—free!
Everything you need to try America Online
is on the enclosed
CD-ROM.

IT'S EASY TO GET ONLINE!

1. Insert the CD-ROM into your CD-ROM drive.

2. Click on the **File Menu** of your **Windows Program Manager**, then select **Run**. Type **D:\AOL\SETUP** (or whichever letter corresponds to your CD-ROM drive) then press **Enter**.

3. When installation is complete, click on **OK**. Then double-click on the America Online icon, and follow the online instructions.

4. Use the temporary registration number and password below when prompted.

20-6486-1904

GISMO-CLONE

® AMERICA Online

If you need another type of disk, or have questions about connecting, call us toll-free at 1-800-827-6364

20796

Complete and Return this Card
for a *FREE* Computer Book Catalog

Thank you for purchasing this book! You have purchased a superior computer book written expressly for your needs. To continue to provide the kind of up-to-date, pertinent coverage you've come to expect from us, we need to hear from you. Please take a minute to complete and return this self-addressed, postage-paid form. In return, we'll send you a free catalog of all our computer books on topics ranging from word processing to programming and the internet.

Mr. ☐   Mrs. ☐   Ms. ☐   Dr. ☐

Name (first) ☐☐☐☐☐☐☐☐☐☐☐ (M.I.) ☐ (last) ☐☐☐☐☐☐☐☐☐☐☐☐

Address ☐☐☐☐☐☐☐☐☐☐☐☐☐☐☐☐☐☐☐☐☐☐☐☐☐☐☐☐☐☐

☐☐☐☐☐☐☐☐☐☐☐☐☐☐☐☐☐☐☐☐☐☐☐☐☐☐☐☐☐☐

City ☐☐☐☐☐☐☐☐☐☐☐ State ☐☐ Zip ☐☐☐☐☐ ☐☐☐☐

Phone ☐☐☐ ☐☐☐ ☐☐☐☐ Fax ☐☐☐ ☐☐☐ ☐☐☐☐

Company Name ☐☐☐☐☐☐☐☐☐☐☐☐☐☐☐☐☐☐☐☐☐☐☐☐☐☐☐☐

E-mail address ☐☐☐☐☐☐☐☐☐☐☐☐☐☐☐☐☐☐☐☐☐☐☐☐☐☐☐☐

1. Please check at least (3) influencing factors for purchasing this book.

Front or back cover information on book .... ☐
Special approach to the content .... ☐
Completeness of content .... ☐
Author's reputation .... ☐
Publisher's reputation .... ☐
Book cover design or layout .... ☐
Index or table of contents of book .... ☐
Price of book .... ☐
Special effects, graphics, illustrations .... ☐
Other (Please specify): _____ ☐

2. How did you first learn about this book?

Saw in Macmillan Computer Publishing catalog .... ☐
Recommended by store personnel .... ☐
Saw the book on bookshelf at store .... ☐
Recommended by a friend .... ☐
Received advertisement in the mail .... ☐
Saw an advertisement in: _____ ☐
Read book review in: _____ ☐
Other (Please specify): _____ ☐

3. How many computer books have you purchased in the last six months?

This book only .... ☐   3 to 5 books .... ☐
2 books .... ☐   More than 5 .... ☐

4. Where did you purchase this book?

Bookstore .... ☐
Computer Store .... ☐
Consumer Electronics Store .... ☐
Department Store .... ☐
Office Club .... ☐
Warehouse Club .... ☐
Mail Order .... ☐
Direct from Publisher .... ☐
Internet site .... ☐
Other (Please specify): _____ ☐

5. How long have you been using a computer?

☐ Less than 6 months   ☐ 6 months to a year
☐ 1 to 3 years   ☐ More than 3 years

6. What is your level of experience with personal computers and with the subject of this book?

	With PCs	With subject of book
New	☐	☐
Casual	☐	☐
Accomplished	☐	☐
Expert	☐	☐

Source Code ISBN: 0-7897-0270-3

7. Which of the following best describes your job title?

Administrative Assistant .... ☐
Coordinator .... ☐
Manager/Supervisor .... ☐
Director .... ☐
Vice President .... ☐
President/CEO/COO .... ☐
Lawyer/Doctor/Medical Professional .... ☐
Teacher/Educator/Trainer .... ☐
Engineer/Technician .... ☐
Consultant .... ☐
Not employed/Student/Retired .... ☐
Other (Please specify): _____ ☐

8. Which of the following best describes the area of the company your job title falls under?

Accounting .... ☐
Engineering .... ☐
Manufacturing .... ☐
Operations .... ☐
Marketing .... ☐
Sales .... ☐
Other (Please specify): _____ ☐

9. What is your age?

Under 20 .... ☐
21-29 .... ☐
30-39 .... ☐
40-49 .... ☐
50-59 .... ☐
60-over .... ☐

10. Are you:

Male .... ☐
Female .... ☐

11. Which computer publications do you read regularly? (Please list)

_____
_____
_____
_____
_____
_____
_____
_____
_____
_____

Comments: _____

Fold here and scotch-tape to mail